EXPLORATIONS IN LANGUAGE AND MEANING

For those who have shown me
what it is to be a human being

EXPLORATIONS IN LANGUAGE AND MEANING

Towards a Semantic Anthropology

Malcolm Crick

Malaby Press   London

BP45

First published in 1976
by Malaby Press Limited
Aldine House, 26 Albemarle Street, London W1X 4QY
© 1976, Malcolm Crick

This book is set in 10 on 11pt Times New Roman

Typeset in Great Britain by
Computacomp (U.K.) Ltd., Fort William
Printed in Great Britain by
Biddles Ltd., Guilford, Surrey
and bound at
The Aldine Press, Letchworth, Herts.

ISBN 0 460 14012 4

6/3/04

Contents

Contents

Acknowledgements

An anthropologist of all people ought to be conscious of the extent to which his intellectual life is a product of his interaction with other minds. This book has developed out of a Doctoral thesis submitted to the University of Oxford in 1974, and, as will be evident from every page, during the course of my research I acquired a good many debts. Here I wish to express special thanks to my supervisor Edwin Ardener. From an exchange of ideas over four years I learned a language and developed an outlook without which this work could not have been written. For encouragement and much helpful criticism I am grateful to Rom Harré, Dr J. E. A. Tonkin, and Diana Burfield. I am also much in the debt of fellow students at the Institute of Social Anthropology in Oxford. Many of the ideas contained in this book have been previously published in articles and reviews in the *Journal of the Anthropological Society of Oxford,* and my interests have been sustained by the knowledge that they were shared by many other young Oxford anthropologists. I am grateful to them for taking the trouble to read my work and for giving me the benefit of their advice.

I acknowledge with thanks financial support from the Social Science Research Council, and Exeter College, Oxford where I held the Alan Coltart Scholarship in Anthropology.

M.C.
May 1975, Oxford.

1   Introduction

British social anthropology has lost that level of consensus which characterized it in the previous stage of its development. Work in such fields as kinship, symbolism and classification over the last fifteen years has seen an increasing stress on the concern of the discipline with questions of meaning, to such an extent that we are justified in saying that there has been an 'epistemological break' (Ardener 1971a:450). We have left behind the certainty that the old functionalist position conferred, but without as yet securing any new definite identity. Certainly a newer style of anthropology exists, but it does so only in fragmentary form. Thus we can characterize the present state of the discipline in relative terms by describing it as being in a post-functional and post-structural phase; but, as social anthropology has not yet been radically rethought or extensively reshaped, we cannot give the stage in which it finds itself a positive definition. Currently there is little agreement as to what the academic locus of social anthropology is or should be, or even on what the major concerns of the discipline are. Those developments which have brought about this disunity have not yet been incorporated into our textbooks and have not been accorded the place they deserve in the available intellectual histories of British anthropology. There are also many who remain untroubled by the older identity, failing to perceive the import of these semantic trends; so we have a situation where some define their work as post-structural while many of their colleagues still write in a pre-Lévi-Straussian structural-functional style.

The present state of social anthropology in Britain cannot be briefly described. While the older style of writing no longer seems to have much to offer, the recent pioneering work, largely through its inadequacy, has merely highlighted our uncertain and transitional condition. Doubts have even been raised (Needham 1970) as to whether the very discipline has a future. Furthermore, Lévi-Strauss, whose work made so much of our recent progress possible, is now so loudly repudiated that, although the newer anthropology cannot be equated with structuralism, our recent intellectual history is being harmfully disguised. This socio-

1

intellectual scene is worthy of extensive survey in its own right, although I shall not here consider further any questions concerning the structure and future of British social anthropology as an institutionalized discipline. The label 'semantic anthropology' therefore must not be interpreted as the name of a new 'school' or as the announcement of a new subdiscipline. It refers only to an awareness that anthropology is necessarily a semantic inquiry. Indeed, since the word 'anthropology' is legitimately used to describe any reflection by human beings on themselves, it would be far more appropriate to regard 'semantic anthropology' as a style of investigation based upon a certain conception of what it is to be a human being than as the name of a phase of growth in any specific academic discipline. But we can take our present institutional position of disunity and uncertainty as a given, and by accepting its very complexity as a challenge try to react to it creatively and positively. Clearly no single volume could hope to deal with all aspects of those recent developments that have presented us with a problem of identity. In this book I concentrate on that central feature of our recent growth which can be economically expressed as a shift from function to meaning.

The semantic explorations in this volume are offered as ways to take this basic development further. It was Evans-Pritchard who crucially stimulated this trend (Pocock 1971:72), but it is the misfortune of our discipline that his manner of expressing it prevented his offering a more vigorous statement of the fact that what was involved in his dissent was a fundamental disagreement over the nature of anthropology. True, he did occasionally explicitly challenge the assumption that there could be a Radcliffe-Brownian 'natural science' of society (1950). But even then, for lack of an adequate language, Evans-Pritchard was unable to state clearly the issues involved, so that the question of two identities became blurred in such distinctions as law/pattern, or necessary relations/coherence.

Evans-Pritchard's basic contention was that anthropology was not a natural science studying physical systems, but one of the humanities investigating moral systems. Our experiences in British social anthropology since the early 1960's have now provided us with better conceptual resources for stating the contrasts at which Evans-Pritchard hinted, and we are now also far more adequately equipped to see what the opposition involves. If we state the gulf as that between a positivistic functional social science and a semantic style of investigation, we can see that the notion of a mere 'shift' in emphasis cannot properly express the difference between the two identities. Semantic anthropology is not an anthropology which simply emphasizes meaning more and function less. It is an anthropology rooted in the conception of human beings as meaning-makers. Thus our newer style of anthropology is not a development of the old — not a new dialect of an old language — but represents a break which requires semantic anthropology to grow in a new epistemological space. This anthropology is separated both methodologically and ontologically from the old functionalist paradigm, because semantic powers make human beings members of a self-defining species. This necessarily has profound implications for the characteristics which any scientific study of people must possess.

The conception of a human being as a fundamentally semantic creature inevitably highlights the fact that human beings are language-users. This explains why a book written by an anthropologist should be entitled 'explorations in language and meaning'. It also reveals why our past image of social anthropology as one of the social sciences has been responsible for so many of our analytical deficiencies. It is not my purpose here to explore at any length the modern history of British social anthropology, but clearly if we are to appreciate the difficulties we face in building a semantic anthropology we must turn back briefly in order to see how our old identity brought us to our present condition. In particular we must know how our self-image as a functional social science affected our handling of semantic issues, and what kinds of links between anthropology and language subsisted under the old functionalist paradigm.

When we speak of British social anthropology, we are concerned with a discipline which grew out of the functionalism of Malinowski and the structural-functionalism of Radcliffe-Brown. It was their view of anthropology which substantially defined the interests of an academic community for two generations. Perhaps the idea of a general anthropology would not long have survived into the twentieth century in this country in any case, no matter who had become intellectually dominant; but with the advent of a specifically sociological identity the scope of British anthropology contracted severely. No one will deny the value of Malinowski's ethnographic monographs, but in retrospect it is difficult to account for the evident attractiveness of his general functional theory of culture (1944) concerning the fulfilment of the biological and derived needs of human beings. Certainly Radcliffe-Brown played a vital role in institutionally establishing our discipline, but it now seems remarkable that his organicism and rather ill-formed idea of a 'natural science' of society (1957) should have been so intellectually stimulating.

Yet the ideas of these two figures commanded great loyalty. Obviously the old style of anthropology did not remain for two generations in exactly the classical form its founders had given it, but most British social anthropologists were content with the broad framework — satisfied with the kinds of problems it generated, and happy merely to

3

elaborate the general way in which it tackled them. Even when diminishing returns had so clearly set in there was little sense that a fundamental challenge to this basic identity might be productive of significant intellectual advance. Indeed, Fortes was happy to see anthropology defined as an empirical science concerned 'once and for all' with mechanism and function (1953:19,24).

While such satisfaction existed in this country, foreign critics were protesting that British social anthropology excluded so much and had so narrow a range of interests that it hardly deserved the name anthropology at all (Murdock 1951)— a charge whose force we now appreciate, though it was confidently rebuffed a generation ago (Firth 1951). Certainly there was operative in British anthropology a conventional wisdom which specifically promoted the avoidance of intellectual relations with other fields of scholarship. This so-called 'naivety thesis' (Gluckman 1964 ed.) involved a narrow definition of what the problems of social anthropology were, combined with the assumption that it was sufficient to work with extremely simplified notions about the concerns of other disciplines. This attitude has not surprisingly taken a heavy toll. Undoubtedly the ideology itself in large part prolonged the life of the old identity by tabooing those links which could so easily have been a profitable source of diversity and change. Certainly the long-term effect of the naivety thesis has been so to impoverish social anthropology that we now find ourselves lacking in the skills required to tackle confidently the intellectual difficulties which confront us. This is why I stress below not only that we must go beyond our discipline for ideas to help us in our semantic development, but also that it may be wise to locate anthropology in a new and broader academic context altogether.

Of course, all theories are selective, and I certainly do not want to suggest that the functionalist period did not produce work of value. Half a century ago our subject was in real need of a definite theoretical structure to guide its researches, and functionalism served this end very well. The old position is not criticized below for those shortcomings which follow inevitably from selectivity. We have long known that the functionalists had difficulty with topics like social change, and so on. When the expression 'paradigm shift' is employed we are drawing attention to more general defects — in our case the fact that the image of anthropology as a social science gave little guidance as to the profound semantic difficulties that must be faced in the study of human action. Sociology (certainly of the mainstream British variety) has not shown any great interest in language, nor could it highlight for us the basic conceptual difficulties involved in understanding other cultures. There are, by contrast, many disciplines (normally referred to as 'humanities') which share far more of our semantic concerns than do the social

4

sciences. More than this, however, when we speak of an epistemological break separating semantic anthropology and functionalism, we are alleging that the old paradigm left out of consideration the most basic characteristics of the human beings it studied. Functionalism in this light can be regarded as the particular form which positivism took in the history of our discipline; it is a sub-species of a general scientism which has affected all the other subjects concerned with human action. Thus, we object to functionalism here because it was a conceptual structure which, by disfiguring the nature of its objects of study, disguised the nature of anthropological inquiry. These two facts are closely related. This is why I stress that semantic anthropology is not only concerned with meaning, but is based upon the notion of human beings as meaning-makers.

When one looks back at the way in which functional anthropology in this country dealt with issues of meaning, it is evident that these basic powers of human beings were not adequately handled. Indeed, whatever the unacceptable features of the ideological structure in which Victorian ethnology grew, the evolutionists were considerably more interested in systems of beliefs than were the functionalists. For Malinowski, culture was a fundamentally instrumental reality, so it is scarcely surprising that semantic issues were not of primary concern. Thus, myth for Malinowski was not a topic requiring symbolic analysis; his main interest was its functional role as a justificatory charter for established patterns of behaviour (1925). Similarly, for Radcliffe-Brown meaning was a 'sort of social physiology' (1964:230). His main emphasis when discussing ideas was on their role in generating those social sentiments upon which the social structure depended (ibid:264). So much did he stress the primacy of behaviour over ideas that in the field of religion he claimed that one's main interest should be in the social effects of ritual (1945:177). He interpreted Durkheim in such a narrow way as to derive only the most crude of theories about the functional role of religion in society. It was left for Evans-Pritchard to realize the semantic value of the *Année sociologique* school and to establish the really fertile links.

Evans-Pritchard's monographs on Zande witchcraft and Nuer religion (1937, 1956) are landmarks in the growth of British social anthropology, but with a few exceptions they stand out starkly against a general background of the writings of his colleagues, who were mostly content with the way of dealing with conceptual systems that the functionalist position demanded. Beattie's statement about developments in the mid 1950's no doubt accurately conveyed the feelings of most British social anthropologists. Anthropology was concerned essentially with institutionalized social relationships, not with the whole of culture. So, where the anthropologists dealt with religion or language it was not for the interest of these phenomena in themselves but for the light they could throw on social institutions (1955:2). Beattie did note a growing interest in ideas for their own sake, but suggested that this might lead to the development of a specialism besides the more sociological pursuits. Certainly the main monographs on religion in that decade were thoroughly functional. Middleton, for example, spoke of Lugbara religion as a competition for political authority (1960). Likewise, Fortes claimed that Tallensi religion was the ritualization of filial piety: they had an ancestor cult because their social structure demanded it (1959:66,30) — a clear instance of that simple psychologism which ran through so much of the structural-functional writings.

It was an integral part of the positivism of British functional anthropology that subjects like religion should be explained by the needs of society or reduced to duplications of the social structure. This would always be the leading orientation while the old framework went unchallenged. Unfortunately, some explicit challenges to the identity of anthropology were so inexpertly made that they were more easily shrugged aside than they deserved to be. Jarvie's dissent (1964) is notable here, especially since it did not argue for an advance to a semantic identity but as good as returned us to a nineteenth-century intellectualism. Over the past decade there has been a great increase in the number of publications on semantic topics, but it is evident that the ideology that shaped so much of British anthropology in the past fifty years is still strong. For Firth, anthropology is still essentially observationalist and functionalist, and he expresses some dismay that recent developments should be so insistent upon the priority of the 'non-empirical' (1973:165). For him, symbols facilitate social interaction (ibid:90), and the anthropologist's main interest in them is the part they play in this social process. It would require a profound shift in perspective to see the limitations of this view — to grasp that one cannot reduce meaning to social structure, because the conceptual nature of human action means that the social structure *is* a conceptual structure. No extensive collection of ethnographic facts will make acceptable the sort of crude sociological correlationism which Lewis employs in his writings on ecstatic religion (1971). A study of so inherently a semantic topic could not possibly be scientific all the while it so easily ignores conceptual distinctions, cultural categories and linguistic complexities.

This comparative lack of attention to language was typical of the work done during the structural-functional period. Naturally, one learned a language in order to do fieldwork, but language seemed to be just another subject one could afford to be naive about. A surprising attitude, since anthropology at all stages — from the collection of ethnographic data onwards — involves language, and the social life of human beings is thoroughly linguistic. Unfortunately, the functionalists did not see, for all their concern with institutionalized social relationships, that language is the most social of all institutions — at least they did not imaginatively draw out its implications. But then, the social sciences in general similarly failed to perceive this central importance of language.

Exactly as with ideas and beliefs, so with language, the old functionalist paradigm saw a contraction of the involvement of Victorian ethnology with other disciplines. Of course, a great many of the ways in which the early ethnologists used language are no longer acceptable, but they did see the importance of establishing links with comparative philology. By contrast, as Henson has recently documented (1974), in the twentieth century to chart the growth of social anthropology and language one is forced to write the histories of two virtually separate developments. In Radcliffe-Brown's schema, language had no real place. Whilst linguistics made major advances between the wars, British anthropologists came to realize their scientific import only belatedly and indirectly through the work of Lévi-Strauss. Not even the major Chomskyan revolution has excited the interest of British anthropology. Thus, in 1961 not a single British member listed in the A.S.A. directory had claimed his major interest to be in language (Ardener & Ardener 1965: 306). Today, British anthropology can boast hardly anyone with linguistic qualifications, although over the last decade our increasingly semantic focus has meant a greater attention to language. This is what constitutes the truth of Ardener's claim that contrasting attitudes to language are a good index of the difference of outlook between the new and the old style of anthropology (1971b: ix).

Our glimpse at the scantiness of the links which anthropology maintained with language during the functionalist period contains so far a major omission, for Malinowski himself stressed the great importance of linguistics in a science of culture (1923: 326). Indeed, J. R. Firth named him as one of the founders of linguistics in this country (1957: 138). But a close look at Malinowski's linguistic work (Henson 1974: 40ff.) clearly reveals how far, from an anthropological point of view, he still was from a fertile relationship with language. All his practical linguistic skills did not really sensitize him to the problems of translation or classification. Thus, he collected a great many Trobriand magical texts (1966), only to propose the general thesis that ritual discourse was meaningless but that magic did provide confidence in situations of uncertainty. His command of linguistic materials did not produce the kind of semantic analyses of Trobriand discourse which have subsequently been carried out (Tambiah 1968). Moreover, that same dogmatism and pragmatism which pervaded his other work influenced his attitude towards language. Speech was an instrument of behaviour in practical action (1923:312); meaning was the 'effect of sound in context' (1966:232). Certainly no one will deny that language has a performative aspect, and it is right to stress the importance of context in semantic issues; but Malinowski's 'context of situation' approach is quite inadequate as a general semantic theory, especially since he construed 'context' in such a behaviourist manner.

Malinowski's linguistic work was not fruitful in a quite literal sense, for none of his prominent pupils was greatly interested in linguistics and so he left no linguistic tradition in British social anthropology. So we have the situation where Evans-Pritchard (who made no special linguistic contribution) inspired the modern semantic trends through his general sensitivity to language and translation, whereas Malinowski (the only British anthropologist to have actively contributed to linguistics) neither produced nor encouraged a shift from function to meaning. This might appear to be awkward for a book which hopes by an exploration of language to help anthropology towards a semantic identity, but the irony is not real. There are many different types of relationships which anthropology can establish with language, and this book is partly concerned with searching out those kinds of bond which are the most helpful in regard to the semantic problems we have to face. It will soon emerge that there is a striking gulf between linguistic anthropology and semantic anthropology. The latter is language-based, not linguistics-based; that is, it builds on broad and flexible links with language and is not grounded in technical aspects of linguistics.

It would be a double misfortune were a book on meaning to be misunderstood, so it is important here to state the form which my search among different links with language takes, and to make it clear at the outset what the volume does not cover.

The book falls into two parts. The first half consists of critical studies of three different ways in which anthropology and language have been related by other scholars. Two of these chapters concern contemporary anthropological traditions, but the section begins with a revaluation of the work of the Victorian Orientalist Max Müller. It might seem somewhat curious that a work concerned with future developments should begin by returning to the previous century, and to a figure who was not even an anthropologist. But just as an academic community sees itself — like any other social group — in opposition to others, it also defines itself in terms of an image of its past. Naivety as regards other disciplines has thus not unexpectedly duplicated itself in a lack of interest in our intellectual history. Many of the kinds of problems we now confront have been discussed before, but it may be helpful if that larger intellectual context in which the newer anthropology will need to grow includes an enlarged view of our history. The conventional pre-history of anthropology, through the Enlightenment and the positivists and evolutionists of the nineteenth century, is well known. But this standard intellectual lineage excludes many writers who paid close attention to language, the anthropological value of whose writings has not yet been widely appreciated in this country. There is Vico, for instance, whose anti-Cartesianism and stress on the fact that to understand a culture was like understanding a language, because ways of human life are embedded in ways of speaking, really make him a founder of semantic anthropology. Similarly, there is Kant whose 'Copernican revolution' in philosophy produced in his critical trilogy a decidedly anthropological system (van der Pitte 1971). There are a good many other figures whose work could well do with anthropological attention now; but I have chosen Müller since he already has a marginal position in our intellectual history, albeit mainly as a critic of Victorian ethnology. It is instructive to look at his work from our modern viewpoint, and to see how it is very much more relevant to our concerns than is the work of some of those who enjoy the status of founding fathers.

The two other chapters in the first half of the book concern the structuralism of Lévi-Strauss, and recent developments in American linguistic anthropology. The American work is little known in this country, since our naivety has not only cut us off from other *disciplines* but also largely insulated us from other traditions within anthropology. When it comes to Lévi-Strauss, however, British social anthropologists have not been able to ignore his output. Nevertheless, extensive critical treatment here is not superfluous because, despite a familiarity in one sense, the very nature of the reactions of many British anthropologists quite clearly indicates that the structuralist conceptual system and the part which language and meaning play in it has not been properly understood — a rather sad state of affairs in a discipline whose major task is precisely the understanding of conceptual systems.

Each of these studies, of Müller, Lévi-Strauss and the American linguistic anthropologists, has some value in its own right; but in this book they form a strong unit together. If we are to explore language in the interests of the shift from function to meaning, it is obviously useful to examine the potential value of links with language already tried. In this way our critical studies are cases to be used. From the experiences and writings of others we can learn some lessons about which kinds of links have proved suggestive, which have distracted from semantic concerns, and which uses of language are misleading in a more general way. Many of the ways in which Müller tried to use philological evidence are unacceptable, but there are ideas he gained from a close attention to language which are still of interest to us. In the case of Lévi-Strauss, while his effort has made possible a major advance in anthropology, the

9

basic tendency of structuralism is anti-semantic. The American work, for all its employment of such terms as 'ethnographic semantics', is based upon such a narrow conception of a link with linguistics as to be of very limited value.

The first half of the book, then, provides us with specific cases to reflect on in our search for the relationships with language that we want in trying to build a semantic anthropology. The second part of the book comprises a series of semantic explorations based upon a broad and largely non-technical link with language. These four chapters deal successively with the general topics of human action, effecting semantic revisions in anthropology, the understanding of conceptual systems, and the translation of cultures. Each chapter is concerned both with semantic systems and the problem of anthropological comprehension. These discussions aim to suggest the nature of the newer style of investigation; they do not define semantic anthropology in the sense of providing confident textbook coverage. This second section is precisely an *exploration*, which seeks to show with concrete examples the sort of analytical insights we may derive from close attention to language. It is no more an inventory of all the conceivable links between anthropology and language than was the first section a history of their relations. There is no doubt much in contemporary linguistic theory, linguistic philosophy, to say nothing of the work of literary scholars and others, which will be of value in our search and which I have not included in the discussion.

It must also be emphasized that while the subject of language acts as a focus for our semantic explorations it also constitutes a limit on our scope. Not all our recent developments in British anthropology can be accurately subsumed under the general shift from function to meaning, and equally certainly not all aspects of even that trend can be satisfactorily handled by attention to language. As important as language is in the construction of the human semantic world, the realms of language and meaning are not coextensive. Human beings possess far more ways of being creative and articulate than simply that of moving their vocal chords. Man's following of linguistic rules is only one example of his more general capacity to operate sign systems; so, although we have restricted our explorations to the relations of language and meaning, this should not be thought to imply a devaluation of a wider semiological approach.

We have seen some of the deleterious consequences of our past lack of interest in language; but it is surely astonishing, as Ardener has pointed out (1971b:xxxff.), that the functionalist generations should have overlooked the suggestive idea of Saussure that there could be a general science of signs (1949:33). With a few exceptions (Humphrey 1971), there is today virtually no semiological work by British anthropologists, and the reason is not far to seek. If a lack of familiarity with language makes difficult our semantic growth at this point, we are even less equipped to develop a semiological framework since our narrow social anthropological tradition showed no great interest in subjects like material culture, dance, art, and a whole host of other facets of culture. Clearly, if language is only one sign system among many, we should be unwise to overstress language to the extent of diverting our attention from a broader framework. Unfortunately, in semiology itself this very linguistic dominance has been established by Barthes on the grounds that in our sort of society there are no autonomous sign systems *apart* from language (1967:9–11). It is to be hoped that, in the future, anthropological work may make it plain that the original Saussurian vision is the more fruitful.

Lastly, I wish to stress that, while this book is to a large extent the result of a situation brought about by the naivety thesis in association with the old paradigm, it is not a bare disquisition on the benefits that accrue from cultivating inter-disciplinary relations. It is a search for insights which might help us to establish some features of a semantic identity; it is *not* about the relations of anthropology with the disciplines of linguistics or philosophy. We have to go beyond anthropology because functionalism so contracted our discipline that we hardly possess sufficient resources to remove ourselves effectively from our present position. But no mere going beyond established boundaries will of itself solve our difficulties. Looking at what linguistics and linguistic philosophy have said about language is no more than the provision of an opportunity for us to think through some of the problems that confront us. We still have to sort out for ourselves what in these other fields of scholarship will be of value to us in promoting our semantic growth.

It is the more necessary to emphasize this fact because patently neither linguistics nor philosophy has any ready-made solutions to give us. For instance, it is well known that linguistics has attained its present scientific status largely by avoiding questions of meaning. Chomsky himself said that meaning was a catch-all term for those aspects of language which linguists knew very little about (1957:103n10). And post-Chomskyan developments will not have convinced anthropologists that there is a theory of meaning which we can simply transplant from the one discipline to the other. Part of the difficulty with semantic issues has always been, of course, a lack of certainty over what the contributions of various disciplines — linguistics, philosophy, psychology, logic, and so on — ought to be. Certainly from the philosophical writings on language that we shall be exploring there is no satisfactory account of meaning to be taken over. Indeed, philosophy has always provided a multiplicity of very divergent semantic theories.

This is not a state of affairs which should discourage the attempt to build a semantic anthropology, for it seems reasonable to insist that an adequate notion of meaning must take account of the extraordinary shiftiness of the word 'meaning' itself (Black 1968 : 163). If meaning is an odd-job word as Wittgenstein contended (1972 : 43), we need not expect to find one thing which all uses of the term have in common, and thus we should be mistaken to think that meaning was the sort of subject-matter for which a general semantic theory is desirable. The semantic powers of human beings manifest themselves in a diversity of ways, and semantic anthropology has a complex of overlapping kinds of problems to deal with, not just a simple unified field. Thus it is no real impediment that we have to explore a host of different and even competing accounts of the nature of meaning. We can derive insights from all; and indeed this very diversity is itself a significant fact for semantic anthropology.

Having given a brief background to the sort of topics we shall cover, and having set out the structure of the book, we can now begin our explorations in anthropology, language and meaning.

I Critical Studies of Three Conceptions of the Relations between Anthropology and Language

2 The Philological Anthropology of Friedrich Max Müller

The work of Max Müller has a special value in an inquiry into the diverse ways in which anthropology and language have been linked, since he was a contemporary critic of those we commonly regard as the founding fathers of our discipline. Müller was not an ethnologist, but he regarded his writings on Oriental literature, the 'science of language', comparative religion, mythology, and philosophy, as contributions to anthropology in the widest and truest sense of the word (1901a: 19). As we shall see, our present difficulties and endeavours confer on the work of this extraordinary man a relevance which is greater than that of those individuals who have always been honoured by a place in the history of the subject.

It is not my intention here to cover all of Müller's work; but it is worth remembering that at one time he was regarded as an authority over a vast range of scholarship. He became one of the internationally most honoured academic figures of the Victorian era, and as a man of immense dedication and learning he was able to propagate several new areas of scholarship in this country. But he was inflexible, poetic, and capable of very superficial work. Consequently he was overtaken and criticized by younger men, who in some cases owed to his inspiration their initial attraction to a field of study. His reputation had waned seriously even before his death in 1900.

However, neither this fact, nor our lack of concern with intellectual history, adequately accounts for his almost total demise as far as anthropology is concerned. To understand this we must see Müller, who based so much of his anthropology on the evidence supplied by comparative philology, as a victim of a more general loss of interest in language. Language had attained a position of import for anthropology in the nineteenth century — partly as a result of Romantic orientalism — and its centrality was axiomatic for Müller. Addressing the anthropological section of the British Association, for instance, he argued that if anthropology were to retain its position as a science its alliance with linguistic studies could not be too close (1891b: 253). In fact, the Victorian ethnologists took little note of his work, and British anthropology grew after his death with even fewer relationships with language than existed during his lifetime.

Below I shall discuss some of the suggestive ways in which Müller conceived this alliance. In doing so I shall not try to write part of the history of anthropology, but rather shall hold a dialogue with a dead scholar whose work has been seriously undervalued and which supplied a link with a field of ideas of central relevance to the subject. There has been a renewed biographical interest in Müller of late, but his ideas remain to be explored, especially from a modern anthropological standpoint. Evans-Pritchard has described him as an unjustly neglected scholar (1965 : 21-5), but he fails to indicate his value to us now. Some of the ways in which Müller used language are certainly worthless. Others have not lost their value. Indeed, though defeated by the literalism of the ethnologists, we can now look back and realize how close to our modern semantic concerns is the position for which he argued in that controversy, namely the richly symbolic nature of human reality.

Unfortunately, Müller's relations with the Victorian ethnologists have been widely misunderstood. The clash with Lang made the differences between them seem greater than they really were. It would be quite quite wrong, for example, to think that Müller was uncompromisingly hostile to the new discipline, as some have asserted. He and Tylor reviewed each other's early works in favourable terms, and Müller spoke of ethnology as likely to become the most popular science of the day (*Saturday Review*, 24 April 1865). Indeed, he regarded ethnologists as fellow labourers, and on several occasions expressed the hope that the new field would not fall below the achievements of Prichard, von Humboldt, Waitz, and Tylor to become an anecdotic province for mere dilettanti (1897 : 175). It is no doubt true that Müller was far less familiar than he might have been with the materials that the ethnologists used, but he accorded little value to evidence gathered by people unable to converse with those about whose customs and ideas they wrote. For him, command of the language of another society was the *sine qua non* of real anthropological work (1891b : 242), and he gave great encouragement to the efforts of such often forgotten Victorian fieldworkers as Codrington, Callaway, Gill, and Bleek (1884a : 13). He tried to secure the cooperation of colonial administrations in collecting cultural and linguistic information, even proposing a new ethnological journal for storing it, which for lack of finance never became a reality (1892b : 504).

Lang (1900) suggested on the death of Müller that with a few more years Müller and the ethnologists might have buried their differences. In view of the very real gulf between them, and the inability of both parties to respond constructively to criticism, this seems unlikely. Yet it is a matter of regret that this did not happen, for Müller's sense of the relevance of language to anthropological inquiry, which has for so long been lost to our view, could have greatly enriched our past and so made us fitter for that rethinking now in progress.

COMPARATIVE PHILOLOGY AND PROBLEMS OF RACE, HISTORY, AND PHILOSOPHY

Müller's lectures on the 'science of language' did much to introduce a new subject to English intellectual life. On the other hand, he contributed virtually nothing to that detailed technical work which so largely constituted the progress of comparative philology in the nineteenth century. Histories of linguistics tend either to omit him altogether, or else to castigate him for his lack of caution. In his own lifetime there were many critics who regarded his reputation as quite baseless. Müller had been taught by the first generation of comparative philologists, and had the misfortune to live well into the Neogrammarian age to which his linguistic metaphysics was anathema.

However, despite the fact that he held the chair of comparative philology in Oxford from 1868 until his death, we should radically misunderstand the nature of Müller's writings if we regarded him as basically a philologist. After all, it was a failure to gain the chair of Sanskrit which led to his taking this post. If his general work was based on philological evidence, essentially he *used* language in something like the manner of those giant scholars of Romantic Germany — Wilhelm von Humboldt and Friedrich von Schlegel — whom a later and sterner age also found difficult to appreciate. For Müller, comparative philology was really a strict apprenticeship to be served before tackling larger issues (1888a:4). Language was the embodiment of the history of the human mind, and Müller always emphasized when he was lecturing on language that he was dealing with issues of vital significance for philosophers, historians, and theologians. Indeed, one of the initial attractions of Oriental literature was precisely that it gave him access to new areas of speculation concerning perennial philosophical problems.

The context in which Müller's name is most commonly remembered today — the growth of racialist ideologies — is an obvious starting point in considering how he used philological evidence. In this connection we must remember that the discovery of the Indo-European language family suggested an entirely new grouping of peoples. By constituting the basis of a new historical consciousness, philology was able to supply 'race' with a new prominence. In Germany, especially, language was strongly felt as the link with an ancient and noble heritage. Müller by no means invented the idea of a spreading, civilizing Aryan race, but it was

17

'Max's proud Aryans' who reached a wide audience owing to his authority and popular style.

Müller seems to have been held captive all his life by a simple image of Aryan history. Certainly his work is full of poetic and unguarded outbursts. Curiously, however, his general statements on the relation of philology to ethnology always correctly argue for the separation of the two disciplines (1853b: 349-53; 1891b: 230ff.). The classification of languages and the classification of races were two distinct problems, and should be carried out in complete independence: only mischief could result from their confusion. He spoke of an 'unholy alliance' between physiology and philology (1891b: 242), and asserted frequently that 'Aryan' referred only to language, that there was no more an Aryan race than there was a dolichocephalic grammar (1888b: 245).

The Aryan question was part of that wider historical aspect of philology in the nineteenth century called 'linguistic palaeontology' — the effort to use the reconstructed Indo-European *Ursprache* to outline the civilization of its speakers prior to dispersal, and to locate their homeland. Müller made some contribution to these researches. In fact, his was one of the more influential names associated with the idea of an 'Asian cradle' of the Aryans. In retrospect we can only conclude that the whole enterprise reveals what a misleading guide language on its own may be. Linguistic models cannot in fact generate historical time (Ardener 1971c), so the comparative philologists — without the help of archaeology or physical anthropology – constructed a virtually baseless picture of the pre-history of Europe. Such a naivety as this displayed was staggering; yet we should not forget that the contemporary efforts by the ethnologists to construct grand schemes of the evolution of institutions and beliefs were, if anything, more so, simply by virtue of the greater scale on which they were attempted.

The essentially historical orientation of comparative philology, and the ominous association of language and 'national spirit', were two important links between language and anthropology in Müller's work. Such features have long ceased to be a part of linguistics, and there is nothing positive we can take from this area of his writing. Likewise, some of the larger philosophical issues to which he thought linguistic evidence relevant are no longer raised. But his work here strangely overlaps with questions which decidedly are of modern concern. For Müller, the possession of language was central to human nature, and comparative philology therefore yielded evidence as to the place of man in nature. He argued that linguistic facts, with all they presupposed, represented an impassable barrier between man and beast, and therefore made untenable Darwin's view of the descent of man. Müller had little knowledge of the natural sciences, and we would obviously not accept today this use of language to prove such matters. Certainly, too, Müller's objections were not all of a scientific kind. Unquestionably, however, he was right to insist that in such issues the fact of language should not be overlooked, as it tended to be in the materialist environment of evolutionism. Darwin knew himself to be ill-informed about language, and actually admitted the power of some of Müller's objections (in Müller 1902, vol.1 : 452,468). At the same time, Müller claimed himself an evolutionist before Darwin, looking upon the latter's achievement as a confirmation, in a limited sphere, of the general principles of development and diversification which he did accept, and which comparative philology had already established (1884 : ix). But he was fundamentally opposed to that intellectual climate of Victorian England which obscured many important issues concerning human thought and language. For him it was a return to a form of physiological psychology which the philosophy of Kant showed to be illegitimate. In a country so little acquainted with such views, however, critics often suggested that Müller was using philosophy to block the progress of a science which conflicted with his faith.

It was the Darwinian view that language was not a barrier between man and beast, since the intellects of man and the higher animals were not different in kind. The one could therefore have developed from the other. For Müller, however, language was not just a means of communication, but an essentially conceptual organization. Therefore the problem of the origin of language was the same as that of the origin of reason (1878b). He believed that only man possessed reason, and that only he could give articulate expression to conceptual thought. Animals could certainly communicate, but that did not entitle one to conclude that they possessed a language. Some animals undeniably had the physical apparatus necessary for speech, but none possessed that mental characteristic — the faculty of abstraction — necessary for language. Müller regarded human consciousness and language as inseparable: language created a conceptual realm in which man alone dwelt. He was dubious as to what we could know of the mental life of animals, and regretted that reopening of the 'floodgates of animal anthropomorphism' (1873b: 661) which occurred during his lifetime. In particular he refused to accept as valid that parallel which had been drawn between the absence of speech in animals and in human infants, because a child was a 'virtual' speaker (in the Aristotelian sense) having a capacity, still to be matured, which no animal possesses. It was for reasons like these that he so strenuously opposed those mimetic and interjectional theories of the origin of language which tried essentially to derive language directly from natural noises.

Some have remarked that Müller's writings on such questions were too unclear to have been of any great significance. Certainly many of the 'facts' yielded by the 'science of language' were little more than theoretical deposits of a passing phase of comparative philology. And unfortunately, he never made it clear what he meant by his basic contention that language and thought were identical (1888a: appendix; 1889). No doubt his outlook was a part of that general shift from the Enlightenment view that language was merely a means to communicate thought, to the Romantic dogma that language and thought were inseparable. Müller wished to stress the interdependence of human reason and language — the fact that conceptual thought required an articulate system of signs. Language was not just a clothing for thought but its very embodiment.[1] The Greeks had expressed this truth by using the one word *logos* for both thought and language as the inner and outer manifestations of the one rational faculty.

Malinowski protested that aphorisms like that of the identity of language and thought left linguistic studies in the air (1937). But the ways in which Müller used them were interesting, and indeed have a certain resemblance to the modern tradition of linguistic philosophy. For instance, Müller regarded myths as the shadows cast by language on thought, and Waismann in almost the same words claimed that philosophers were 'trying to catch the shadows cast by the opacities of speech' (1968:6). Müller indeed believed that the dependence of thought on language constituted a charter for future philosophy: it provided a new basis for the subject (1887:515). He spoke of the history of philosophy as a battle against mythology (1871:355), as an uninterrupted struggle between language and thought (1878b:478), and he looked to the analysis of language as a solution to philosophical problems. Philosophy was the examination and correction of language (1887:573). He well expressed the unity in his life's work in his translator's preface to Kant's *Critique of Pure Reason*, when he claimed that his plan was to seek in language and literature for an explanation of why it was that man — in religion, mythology, and philosophy — thought he could know so much more than Kant had shown to be possible (1881:xxxiv). Müller felt like some early critics of Kant that after a critique of reason should come a critique of language, and that this should be the essential task of philosophy.

Müller's diverse uses of philological evidence not only relate him to a long tradition of linguistic philosophy, but also earn him a place in that lineage of linguistic relativists — distinguished as much for its suggestiveness as for its unclarity — which can be traced back to von Humboldt. Müller wrote of language as an inherited channel of thinking, and of language as determining the general features of any intellectual structure erected on it (1893:65). Thus, he disputed the contention that the

Semites were 'instinctively' monotheistic, arguing that the difference between the Semitic and Aryan traditions could be adequately accounted for when one took into consideration the differences between the two language families. Semitic tongues possessed a transparent grammatical structure, whereas the inflectional nature of Aryan languages destroyed the etymological consciousness of their speakers, thus allowing a rich growth of mythology (1860).[2]

MAX MÜLLER AND THE ETHNOLOGISTS ON LANGUAGE

Willingness to engage in this kind of conjecture is just one manifestation of the striking differences in attitude to language which distinguished Müller from the ethnologists, although on some issues they were close.[3] The very universalism of the ethnological tradition — that stress on the psychic unity of mankind — militated against the use of 'race' in a central explanatory role. At the same time, anthropology had its extreme racists. While Müller claimed that the origin of races and the origin of languages were separate problems, so that linguistic evidence could provide no definitive evidence either way on the monogenesis/polygenesis issue (1851:16), at mid-century many leading figures in what was then commonly known as 'linguistic ethnology' based their classifications of races on linguistic criteria. Indeed, later in the century linguistic models had a role which is often forgotten today. Morgan, for instance, based his kinship families on philological classifications, and Maine confined himself to societies defined by a language family hoping by means of this 'limited' comparative method to attain the same standard of results as comparative philology itself.

On the other hand, the general picture is one of ethnologists unskilled in their handling of language. Despite the fact that many came from a background in the classics, only Tylor had a really wide interest in the subject. He frequently lectured on philological topics at Oxford, maintained an admirable caution on some of the larger issues in which language was involved, and was fascinated by the more general subject of sign systems — although he was nowhere near a semiological viewpoint. But even for Tylor, language did not, indeed without the relevant intellectual background *could* not, possess the significance that it did for Müller.

Perhaps this general point can be made with reference to the idea of 'primitive languages'. Comparative philology was naturally closely tied to the Indo-European language group during the nineteenth century, but Müller always stressed that his 'science of language' concerned all tongues. He even described the Aryan languages as *monstra*, domesticated as a result of literary tradition and political concentration and, so, untypical as compared with the mass of wild tongues in the world. This was one of the reasons why he regarded the collection of evidence about the languages of savage peoples as so important. Even in the late nineteenth century educated opinion — including ethnologists — accepted the existence of primitive languages so rudimentary as hardly deserving to be called articulate. Spencer's *Descriptive Sociology* series contains fascinating data on this. By contrast, Müller claimed that when one took into consideration all that language implied, the very expression 'savage language' was a contradiction *in adjecto* (1888b:xxv).

Linguists no longer even pose most of the questions to which Müller gave such easy answers a century ago. Still, as our attention is more and more focused on the symbolic qualities of discourse with which the anthropologist is concerned, it is instructive to hear him suggesting that probably 'we can form no correct idea of with what feeling a savage nation looks upon its language: perhaps, it may be, as a plaything; a kind of intellectual amusement, a maze in which the mind likes to lose and to find itself' (1855:124).Müller, unlike his ethnological contemporaries, clearly had a rich 'anthropological theory' of language (Henson 1974:38) of a scope and kind that is still relevant.

THE SCIENCE OF RELIGION

It is not entirely surprising that the beginnings of a sustained comparative investigation of religion were made by an age facing a profound crisis of faith. There will always be dispute as to whether the analytical advantage in the study of religion lies with the insight of a believer or the neutrality of one without particular religious convictions. The ethnologists were mostly atheist or agnostic in outlook and so suffered one kind of disability. Similarly, in discussing Müller's work in this field, one should not forget his simple but strong Lutheran faith. To an extent he used the literary materials available without abandoning any of his philosophical or religious presuppositions. Moreover, the sheer range of his interests prevented his making that kind of lasting scholarly contribution that many of his Orientalist colleagues did. Nonetheless, Müller has a unique relationship to the new discipline of comparative religion — his place in its history being secured by his editing the *Sacred Books of the East* series alone.

Müller shared the ambition and developmental orientation of the ethnological tradition of his time, yet his writings on other religions reveal some fundamental differences. His was not an evolutionary scheme like those proposed by the ethnologists — more a theodicy. He did not accept that the Jews had received a special disclosure, because for him the whole of man's history was a divine revelation. His was the Pauline view that God had nowhere left himself without a witness. Hence, no religion was entirely false. So, no matter how imperfect the sacred literature of other faiths might be, it expressed real truths. All religions represented, though in different languages, the same search after God. They were different expressions of one fundamental human faith springing from human nature — a universal religion — which in an age of doubt constituted an impregnable basis (1891a: 333).

This nineteenth-century theological liberalism exerted a tremendous influence on Müller's writings. But it is difficult to imagine an outlook which would have contributed to a more sympathetic study of other faiths. His work generated a considerable amount of hostility, many feeling that the suggested comparison of Christianity with other faiths was blasphemous. But Müller never doubted the superiority of his own religion, claiming indeed that the 'science of religions' would show its true place in the history of man and so indicate what was meant by the 'fulness of time' (1867: xx). After all, his series of Gifford lectures concludes with reflections on Christian theosophy after a vast survey of the other ways — in nature, in man, and in the mind — in which other religious traditions had glimpsed and expressed their sense of the Infinite. Man's whole history was a divine education, and these other faiths were an essential part of that growth. His view, therefore, gives expression to that limited tolerance of the 'embryonic' which contrasted the historical outlook of the Victorian age with the rationalism of the Enlightenment.

Few anthropologists seem to have grasped the premises on which Müller's work on comparative religion was based. Some think he regarded religion as a 'fabric of errors' (Lessa & Vogt 1972: 9). And given his symbolist and emotionalist stance, Evans-Pritchard's listing him (1965) with the intellectualist ethnologists, whose theories he severely criticized, is very misleading. Much misunderstanding also surrounds the idea of 'naturism' with which Müller is always associated.

Müller rooted all religions in a sense of the Infinite. By this term he did not wish to suggest a highly abstract conception, but merely to point out that man had a vague and almost instinctive sense of the Beyond. He first spoke of this *sensus numinis* as a 'faculty of faith' (1873a). Later, however, he abandoned this idea of a separate faculty for apprehending the Infinite and suggested that sensory experience itself gives an intimation of the Beyond (1878a: 22ff.). Nature itself was a revelation — witnessing nature stimulated man's religious sensibility. Natural phenomena also supplied the first terms by which the Divine was named. Originally man used the concrete symbols which were 'ready to hand' (ibid.: 121). Thus the deities in Vedic literature were known collectively as the *devas*, from the root *DIV* meaning 'to shine'. For Müller, it was a 'happy grasp of language to express the aweful feeling of the existence of a divine power by a word which meant light' (1851: 42).

This view is clearly a long way from that 'naturism' to which many of Müller's critics made objections, and it makes nonsense of the idea that he believed in any 'worship of nature'. (Frazer, by contrast, over half a century later (1926) was uncritically compiling examples under exactly this term.) Müller never suggested that God was identified with the sun or the sky. These phenomena were merely the first terms in which man spoke about what cannot adequately be stated in any language. What Müller in fact did was to express that characteristic 'preference for the concrete, [the] attachment to material symbols in primitive religions (Lienhardt 1956: 313). His 'naturism', therefore, is substantially a version of that idea of 'concrete logic' to which Lévi-Strauss has recently directed our attention. Müller did actually argue that the concreteness of the different systems of logic in Indian thought was in no way inferior to the analytical nature of Western thought (1853a).

Müller approached the growth of religion as the development of language — the choice of predicates used in religious expression. Vedic 'naturism', for instance, was the employment of natural names which metaphorically and approximately conveyed a sense of Divinity. In the absence of a more adequate symbolism, the sun and the sky were the best emblems available which possessed those characteristics of regularity and intangibility suitable to express the Infinite. In Vedic literature, it is those grand and orderly spectacles that are theogonic. After the physical predicates of the Rig Veda, there is a repudiation of this language in an evolving tradition of religious sensibility which culminates in the elevated Upanishads, where the applicability of attributes to Brahman is denied.

One is never sure exactly how Müller uses the term 'origins'. While he admitted that the Rig Veda was far removed in time from the beginning of even this one course of religious growth, he also thought it displayed a phase in the history of the human mind not preserved in any other literature. Hence a tendency to use these sacred texts as if they gave a privileged glimpse of the origin of religion in general. Subsequent research (and much contemporary opinion also) has shown that these Sanskrit works will not carry the speculative load that Müller made them bear. Much of the literature had only recently become available to Oriental scholars, and its chronology and translation were still the subject of considerable disagreement at the time Müller wrote. For instance, his 'henotheist' phase — a plurality of deities all share the attributes of a Supreme Being since there is as yet no established pantheon — was queried during his lifetime. Also, Müller quite evidently found the Vedic theogony so intelligible because he ascribed to the early Aryans that naturalistic pantheism which he himself acutely felt. Certainly he relied too much on a hymn-book (the Rig Veda) when there was other Vedic literature available from roughly the same period containing evidence of

24

a whole host of savage beliefs and customs which he all but ignores completely. There is thus much justification for Lang's dislike of Müller's account of the 'sweetness and light' in the early history of his chosen race. As he said, awe before the Infinite was very much a sentiment of modern Germans (1884a:233).[4]

What is undeniably a gain from Müller's personal involvement in his writings on religion is his acute sense of the intricacies of language and symbolism in this sphere. Here he contrasts starkly with the literalist interpretations of primitive religious expression given by the ethnologists. Tylor, for instance, regarded primitive religion as an explanatory metaphysics 'quite really and seriously meant' (1871:258). It was not a matter of poetic fancy, so it was unreasonable to look for symbolic meaning in their childish primitive rites (ibid.:431). For Lang, 'the vein of symbolism is so easy to work that it must be regarded with distrust' (1884b:150). Similarly, Spencer claimed that the distinction between fact and metaphor could not be expressed in savage languages, and that no savage was able to conceive a symbol or had ever adopted one (1876:362, appendix A).

Müller believed that in the religious sphere one could not really speak of 'knowledge'. The history of religion was in this sense a succession of struggles to express the inexpressible. So, the central difficulty in interpreting other faiths was to grasp the meaning which lay beneath the symbolism: literal translation could easily produce nonsense. Ancient language frequently carried both material and abstract senses, so to take the language of the Old Testament, for instance, solely in the former sense would lead to serious misunderstandings. The Hebrew word for 'bone', for example, had a spiritual as well as physical sense. The creation of Eve from the rib of Adam therefore signified that man and woman were of the same essence (1873a:32-4). Müller also suggested that the 'virgin birth' story could only be understood symbolically. He regarded the Johannine idea of Sonship as the essence of Christianity. Christ was a man, but also the embodiment of the Divine ideal of humanity. 'Sonship' was the most elevated metaphor available to express the intimacy of this relationship. There was thus no contradiction between the two statements that He was of human parentage and that He was the 'Son of God'. The story of the virgin birth he regarded as a mythological degeneration and elaboration, when 'Sonship' had ceased to be understood as a spiritual claim (1893a:final chapter). Whatever the accuracy of any of these particular examples, Müller's symbolist stance would in general command more respect today from anthropologists than the literalist interpretations offered by his ethnological contemporaries.

MAX MÜLLER AND THE ETHNOLOGISTS ON RELIGION

One of Lang's major objections to Müller's account of the growth of religion was that he rested it on the literature produced by a semi-civilized people. The ethnologists, in contrast, sought origins by looking to the beliefs and practices found among the lowest savages, who were taken to be the best representatives of primitive man. Such an equation — though often qualified — was fundamental in the work of the ethnologists, for it permitted a taxonomy to generate history. But Müller, though a developmentalist, would not accept this equation, and protested against the ethnological image of the 'savage' (1885). He argued that savages had had as long and complex a history as civilized men: they had not been preserved statically for the benefit of anthropological theorists. If he were restricted to the Indo-European world, basing his work on the literary record of a developed culture, at least his evidence was genuinely over three thousand years old: anthropologists used nineteenth-century savages.

It would be an oversimplification to call Müller a champion of the degenerationist school, but certainly there is a strong 'corruptionist' streak in his writings.[5] He did accept the reality of large-scale cultural regression. Some races were progressive, and others, whose history included a great deal of decay, were basically non-progressive. It was with these latter that the ethnologists wished to construct the progress of their ancestors, but in reality they were the worst possible specimens with which to do this. Müller's racism is undoubtedly an important factor in his stance here (1897:175), but the outline of his argument and its consequences would definitely be accepted by us now. The logical structure of Victorian ethnology astounds by its circularity. The basic equation of primitive and savage allowed the universal comparative method; the doctrine of survivals — a notion never really extracted from the domain of metaphor (Hodgen 1936:38) — proved the reality of progress.

Müller placed ethnologists in a 'theoretical' school and himself in a different 'historical' school, although these schools were not wholly antithetical (1892b:ch.8). Clearly, he was not content simply to collect and translate texts as were so many of his Orientalist colleagues; but he thought it preferable to begin the comparative study of religions on a narrower basis with high quality materials, rather than engage in uncontrolled speculation and unlimited comparison. At the very least, theoretical schemes should agree with what scholars knew about the actual historical growth of different religious traditions; otherwise 'evolution' would merely displace history. One should argue from the more known to the less, and not the reverse, as the ethnologists tended to do (1884:ix). Savages tended to become like India-rubber dolls which could be forced into any shape to fill the airy structure of ethnological psychology (1885:142;1891a:128). Müller constantly remarked on the unreliability of ethnological evidence, urging exactly the sort of caution and making the sort of objections which we would all now echo. 'What I have ventured to say on several occasions is, let us wait till we know a little more of Hottentots and Papuans, let us wait till we know at least their language, for otherwise we may go hopelessly wrong' (1892b:216).

One of the cautions Müller especially urged was over what he termed the 'ethnological -isms' used to describe primitive religions (1892a:appendixes iv,vi). We are now aware of the gravity of the error involved in using comparatively native terms like *tabu*, or creating categories like 'fetishism' or 'animism'. Müller thought such a practice thoroughly unscientific (1892a:409), and argued that if studies of savage races were to be really useful we should try 'to free ourselves from all preconceived ideas and instead of looking for idols or for totems or for fetishes, learn to accept and to understand what the savages themselves are able to tell us' (ibid.:292). There was no point in taking a native term like *totem*, adding an -ism, and then applying it to the diverse cases of animal symbolism. 'In order to secure clearness of thought and honesty of reasoning in the study of religion ... these terms (animism, fetishism, totemism) ought to be sent into exile. They have become dangerous' (1892b:159-60). Müller thought that a totem was a distinguishing clan mark, a case of the animate symbolism so widely used by the Red Indians for the expression of abstract ideas (1892a:407-8). He suggested that beliefs in descent from the totem, and about its sacredness, were secondary growths. The sign chosen became 'surrounded as the colours of a regiment are even now, by a halo of many recollections' (1892b:522) — exactly the example Lévi-Strauss uses in his recent dismissal of the totemic illusion (1969b:75-6).

Müller was by no means alone in making this type of criticism. Many Orientalists and philologists complained at the onset of the totemic epidemic in ethnology, and protested at the way fetishism was used as a panacea for all mythological problems. Müller himself was unquestionably inflexible over many issues; but when we realize his sophistication in ethnological matters (Dorson 1968:167-8), and note how he anticipated some of the lethal shafts which modern anthropology has directed at the tradition of the preceding century, we must regret that the ethnologists did not respond more positively to his writings. There are aspects of his work which make him nearer our present position and needs than his ethnological contemporaries. We need not, of course, go back to all the errors that accompanied Müller's insights, but it is worth knowing that some of the problems to which we must now address ourselves have been raised before by scholars we have seriously undervalued and who have not even been accorded a place in our history.

THE SCIENCE OF MYTHOLOGY

The enormous interest of the Germans in mythology and folklore during the nineteenth century can partly be explained by that same passion which led to their pre-eminence in comparative philology. Müller introduced to English intellectual life in 1856 the style of mythological interpretation based on philological analysis, and it was this approach which the ethnological tradition had to displace in order to establish itself. At one time constituting orthodoxy, Müller's system, by the time of his death, had been seriously eclipsed.

Late in his career, Müller admitted to youthful overconfidence, but he never lost his conviction that the philological approach to comparative mythology was established on a sound scientific basis. It was precisely because of the absence of rigour that he did not grant Sir William Jones the status of a pioneer in the field (1870:285ff.). But from the numerous satires written during his lifetime one might well be tempted to conclude that Müller spent a great deal of energy on a nonsensical enterprise. Naturally such essays scarcely reveal the complexity of his analyses; but more serious critics have not grasped the true nature of his writings on myth either — probably because they have failed to appreciate the extent to which this work is a part of a much larger whole. Only when one has appreciated the assumptions he makes about language, thought and symbolism, does his work on myth become intelligible. It is perhaps only now that we are looking again to language that his effort can appear in a more favourable light. Müller's thesis basically concerns how language carries and disguises symbolic structures, and how it may be treated as a key for unlocking other symbolic forms (Henson 1974:23).

For Müller, part of the importance of being able to provide a satisfactory account of mythology was that failure to do so would leave the continuity of reason in human history in doubt (1897:44). It was extremely problematic that so rational a civilization as that of Greece should have possessed such seemingly absurd myths. Müller hoped that comparative mythology would 'discover reason in all the unreason of mythology and thus...vindicate the character of our ancestors' (1895:xlii). His solution was that the meaning of a mythological formation was not on the surface. There was a *hyponoia* (an embedded 'under-meaning') which had to be extracted by analysis: language carried a significance which had to be deciphered. In order to show that myth masked a rational structure, its phraseology needed to be 'rewritten': full verbs, for instance, should be replaced by auxiliary ones (1856:46). Müller — like Lévi-Strauss — thought that under all the chaotic content of myth there was a definite order.

Müller approached myth as an inevitable by-product of the growth of language. In his view, language derived from 'roots' which had possessed an original 'active' significance. The initial poverty of linguistic resources required such elements to be used to describe occurrences other than human activities, and this was the source of the reason for the widespread dramatic quality of early expression. Language grew by means of metaphorical extensions, terms being forged to express abstract conceptions out of what had previously had a more concrete sense. With the passage of time and the changing signification of words, language became a repository of faded metaphors and fossil poetry — a common Romantic view.[6] Such poetry was unconscious — the metaphors constituting new concepts and not deliberately linking two notions already formed (1886:621-2). Polyonymy (where one object having many characteristics is known by many names) and homonymy (where different objects are called by the same name because they have qualities in common) were further sources of difficulty. Grammatical gender was also an important factor, though Müller did not place much emphasis on it.

Such features in the growth of language, and the influence of language on thought, yielded a genetic account of mythology. 'Personification', 'animism', 'anthropomorphism' were all mere labels for a phenomenon which still required an explanation: it became intelligible in terms of linguistic history (1892b: 313,341). This is the background to Müller's famous phrase the 'disease of language' (1861:11) — an expression which was meant to be provocative and to attract attention to a new style of interpretation. It was because of the large shifts in its development that language could achieve an independence of its speakers' intentions and so mislead them. Mythology was a shadow which language threw on thought, and which could never disappear 'till language becomes commensurate with thought which it never will' (1871:353). It is therefore the result of a pathological relation, where language forgets its past so that the sign (language) can react on the signified (thought) (1897:37-8).

In view of the degree of hostility it aroused, Müller probably regretted his striking expression, 'disease of language'. It is certainly misleading to refer to something as a disease when by one's own view it is inevitable; but the phrase does usefully emphasize the formal nature of his definition of myth, and so exposes the inaccuracy of the opinion that he was simply a solarist. He quite knowingly gave myth a very much broader definition than his predecessors, arguing that it should be regarded as a *quale* and not as a *quid* (1856:87). He compared it to an avalanche carrying within it all manner of different items and able to affect any subject whatsoever (1895:v). Our own scientific concepts like ether and gravity were mythological. There were poetry, allegory and history in myth, but 'we ought to look not so much to the matter as to the form. Myth may comprehend anything and everything, whether religion, philosophy, nature or history: but what is peculiar to mythology is the form under which it exhibits these various subjects' (undated MS on 'Epic Literature', Taylorian Library, Oxford).

It follows from this formal definition of myth that many of the criticisms levelled at Müller were illegitimate. Some argued, for instance, that by giving naturist interpretations to Indo-European myths he denied them any historical basis. Certainly he would have nothing to do with Euhemerism, partly because other civilizations did not share our kind of historical awareness. On the other hand, while he gave an elemental interpretation to the *Iliad* he did not deny that there may have been a real siege at Troy. But a pre-existing mythological framework would act as a structure to absorb or crystallize historical events and persons (1897:64,631-2).

Similarly, myth for Müller extends far beyond religious matters. Nonetheless, since all religious expresssion must necessarily be inadequate, this was an area particularly prone to misunderstanding. The passage of time had an 'oxidizing' effect on religious expression: myth was a parasitic rust (1891a:290). Myth arose when the emblematic use of concrete symbols (such as the sun or sky) ceased to be felt as symbolic; for then *nomina* were transmuted into *numina.Dyaus* became a mythological being when religious expression degenerated, emblematic attributes becoming substantive nouns. The 'disease of language' was thus clearly not a matter of minor linguistic confusion, but the death of symbolism, which was part of a large-scale historical semantic process. According to Müller, ancient Sanskrit actually provides a record of the way in which an increasingly liturgical society became unable to understand the simple poetic expressions of the Rig Vedic hymns.

It is the generality of these processes that Müller stressed, and in this way his work resembles aspects of modern linguistic philosophy. There is a mythology in our own language (1864:last chapter) which can deceive us just as did that of the ancients. This makes it doubtful whether Müller believed in a chronologically bounded 'mythopoeic age' (ibid.:357). No doubt myth was rife in ancient language, but there is no language where the possibility of bewitchment is completely absent. Linguistic philosophy is not a historical mode of analysis; but the similarities between 'disease of language', Wittgenstein's 'bewitchment' (where philosophical problems arise from failure to grasp the logic of language), and Mauthner's 'word superstition' are very close.[7] Certainly Müller's account of mythology could fairly be summed up by Waismann's comments about the 'fight of thought with the obtuseness of speech' and on language as the medium that 'pervades and warps our very thought' (1968:201,176). Similarly, we could see myths as cases of what Ryle termed 'systematically misleading expressions', 'category mistakes', or errors in 'logical geography', although Ryle seems to suggest that only philosophers are really deceived by language (1932: 13-4, 22). Müller in fact wrote specifically on psychological and philosophical mythology. There was a psychological polytheism (1878b: 487; 1899) which transformed activities into nouns, so that 'remembering', 'reasoning', and so on were regarded as separate faculties. Language, by a secret cunning, revenges herself when she is violated; errors are inevitable whenever philosophers forget how their language is constructed (1876: 349). Mind, reason and understanding are simply different aspects of language (1887: x), and this is why language itself is the best, though usually overlooked, evidence as to mental life. The 'true philosophy of the human mind...is the philosophy of language' (ibid.: 291-2).

Müller's approach to myth was a part of a much larger conceptual system. Having outlined it, it is possible to discuss the actual procedure of analysis employed in his writings. Just as the different Indo-European languages pointed to an *Ursprache* from which they had all diverged, so the many mythological dialects found in the literatures of ancient India, Greece, and so on, implied an original Indo-European mythological tradition. As philological problems could be solved by resort to cognate languages, so understanding a Greek myth, for instance, was helped by investigating the collateral evidence of the Vedas. In Müller's case, just as Sanskrit played a harmfully leading role in comparative philology, there was far too great a reliance on Vedic literature to construct the common mythological system. But he thought that the Vedas revealed a unique picture of such a system still in the process of formation. For instance, in one context *dyaus* is simply the sky; elsewhere it is a fully-fledged mythological agent.

Müller's analytical procedure consisted of locating in Sanskrit a name identical to that of a Greek mythical personality by using the laws of sound-change by which the Aryan languages had diverged. Etymological analysis of the latter then yielded a meaning from which could be inferred the natural phenomenon which had given birth to the particular mythical personality. These name equations (*Zeus* and *Dyaus*, for example) proved that Greek and Vedic myths had had the same source. Names were important in interpretation because mythical agents are personal names constituted when concrete symbolism is misunderstood.

In retrospect, Müller's system strikes us equally by the vast learning which went into its construction, and by its fragility at every point. Quite apart from the gross historical conjecture on which it was based, there was an immense disagreement among philologists over which name equations were acceptable, which phonetic laws were scientifically established, how rigorously these laws should be applied, how to infer

31

elemental origins from etymology, and so on. Clearly, however, it would be wrong to equate the philological approach to mythology with solarism. Tylor, for instance, did not like the philological method of interpretation, but acknowledged the widespread existence of solar myths.[8] Some philologists, by contrast, favoured meteorological interpretations. Müller himself favoured — though not exclusively — solar interpretations, since the natural language most fit to be a concrete symbolism for the Infinite would have to be suggestive of order. His position here is interesting in view of Durkheim's objection to naturism — that monotonous regularity could not possibly have generated the idea of the sacred (1912:119). It is now known that primitive thought decidedly does find natural regularities 'good to think with', since it calques endless symbolic orders on them.

MAX MÜLLER AND THE ETHNOLOGISTS ON MYTH.
The most general criticism the ethnologists made of Müller's approach was that it made a study of mythology a mere appendix to a 'science of language' (Marett 1936:45). It was, besides, a type of interpretation restricted to the Indo-European family. (Müller did in fact use his analytical scheme on ethnological evidence (1882a.)) Frazer thought the 'disease of language' theory so obviously absurd as not to deserve refutation (1927:329). Tylor never engaged Müller in controversy, so it was left to Lang to put the ethnological case. His attack began in 1873 and continued almost until Müller's death. Müller regarded anyone who was not a Sanskrit scholar as unqualified to offer an opinion, and for many years refused to respond to the criticisms of one he regarded as little more than a flippant journalist. This was certainly unfair, since Lang's articles made many penetrating points about philological analysis. Even so, the standard view that he demolished Müller is far from true. When Müller eventually replied, Lang (1897) was in turn forced to defend and modify several key points of ethnological theory.

Müller might have been spared the sort of rude remarks his assailants levelled at him, had his work been more clearly constructed and had they acknowledged the limitations which *he* admitted in his approach. He never claimed, for instance, that philological analysis could account for all the details of a myth. Comparative mythology was concerned with 'germinal' conceptions (1897:xiii,609). Hence, Vedic literature could only throw light on the basic structures of Greek myths. Further, he did not equate *Zeus* and *Dyaus*. After the Aryan dispersal there had been a great deal of separate development in the once common tradition: Müller only equated names. Most importantly, he did not claim the philological approach to be the only valid method, and explicitly discussed other schools of interpretation (1892b:chs

17,18). He had criticisms to make of them, but he did not deny their legitimacy.

Müller's work was part of the 'historical-genealogical' school. Confined to specific language families, it was based strictly on the principles of comparative philology. There was at the same time the 'analogical' school, also working on a limited scale, which looked to morphological comparisons rather than the equations of Müller's own writings; and it was the members of this school who, by their excesses, were responsible for much of the derision which fell on the far more cautious philologists. Of the ethno-psychological school to which the ethnologists belonged, Müller had mixed views. He was aware of the potential value of its work. If the widest comparison could show what was universal — Tylor's effort (1865) to distinguish between parallelisms which were the result of history and those which were direct expressions of human nature was such a search — the ethnological method had a real importance (1895:xxxiii). But for Müller, the trouble with this folklorist approach was that comparison was useless unless the facts were really understood, which could not be the case where the scope of inquiry meant a loss of control over sources. Comparing savage and civilized customs might be useful, but the results were no more than curious unless one knew that the resemblances were more than superficial (1897:226,290). Since Müller worked so closely with texts, ethnology seemed to him the result of too easy a resort to snippets of evidence from societies whose languages were not known. He could not understand why ethnologists refused to use the kind of literature he regarded as so valuable, nor could he see why, in order to explain the beliefs and practices of Vedic society, preference should be given to modern savages rather than to the native commentary on the Rig Veda (ibid.:451).

There were considerable disputes over assumptions and procedures in the study of folklore during the late decades of the nineteenth century. For Lang, myths were essentially to be explained by savage thought-processes, and not by linguistic developments. Thus, a Greek myth obviously out of phase in Greek civilization should be traced back to a condition of society and intellect in which it would be natural. The grotesque aspects of mythology were survivals of a time when the Greeks had themselves been in a barbaric state, and were therefore made intelligible by reference to contemporary savages. The Prometheus legend, for instance, was a survival from a stage of Greek culture when, just as one had to steal a wife, so one had to steal fire when one's own was extinguished (1897:193ff.). In the interpretation of myth, as in the field of religion, the divide between Müller and the ethnologists was greatly a matter of symbolism as opposed to literalism. Müller gave a symbolic analysis of the story of Chronos swallowing his children. For Lang it was evidence that the Greeks had once been cannibalistic — a kind of interpretation Müller saw no reason to accept, especially since 'swallowing' quite obviously has so many metaphorical employments (1895:294-6). Lang complained that the philologists resorted to 'the first theory of symbolism that occurred to the conjecture of a civilized observer' (1884a:118), probably never suspecting that a time would come when the easy resort to literalism would appear no more acceptable. As the autobiographical aspects of Müller's writings have been referred to, it is fitting to do the same for the ethnological tradition which displaced him. Folklore was essentially savagery still alive in the midst of culture: the peasant had been left behind in the course of social evolution. Studies of racial stereotypes in the nineteenth century have often been made, but the civilized/savage opposition is only part of a larger ideological formation. The image of the peasant adds the contrast 'progressive urban/static rural', with which are concordant such divisions as middle class/working class, and educated/illiterate. The thesis that ontogeny recapitulates phylogeny added the adult/child distinction — confirmed by the image of the childish savage. The primitive state of mind was to be found 'among untutored European peasantry, and among the children of the educated classes' (Lang 1901:345). Folklore was thus a constant reminder to Victorians of the existence of working class culture (Dorson 1968:160), and in some of the writings of the ethnologists (Frazer 1908) there is a direct expression of the fear that culture belonged to the few and that there was a deep savagery underneath civilization which could only too easily sap its strength. After all, Tylor called anthropology a reformer's science which exposed survivals and marked them out for destruction (1871:410).

Marett spoke of how Lang had rescued him and many others from the Germanic obsessions of Max Müller (1941:84), but of course the collective representations of the ethnological tradition which ousted him now also belong to our past. Anthropological traditions inevitably have limited life-spans, like all other socially-rooted conceptual systems. In view of the nature of our present difficulties in a discipline in process of transition, it must, however, be a matter of regret that Müller's work has been so forgotten. Some vaguely remember him as a fanatical solarist; but it has been recognized of late that, of the Victorians, only Müller had a remotely modern approach to myth (Ardener 1971b:lxix). There are certainly features of his work on both myth and religion which are not without relevance today, and ways in which he used language which are still suggestive. Müller wrote of Sir William Jones that 'it is the fate of all pioneers, not only to be left behind in the assault which they had planned, but to find that many of their approaches were made in a false direction, and had to be abandoned' (1870:301). Time has been very unkind to Müller in this respect. He tried to express some very important ideas before an adequate language was available to frame them, and his consequent eclipse has hidden much of value from our view. We are forcibly reminded by his example just how much we may have lost — and may still lose — by our lack of interest in the way the discipline developed, and by a narrow-mindedness over the breadth of context in which it might grow.

3   The Structuralism of Claude Lévi–Strauss

The 'science of language' of Max Müller, and the structural linguistics of Lévi–Strauss, belong to two very different scientific ages. But the work of these two men is related by this one stress on the vital importance of exploring links between anthropology and language. A critical analysis of Lévi–Strauss' structuralism shows, as did the examination of Müller's work, how the use of linguistic models may yield important insights, but also how it may produce error. We shall also see below that such models can deflect us from a semantic anthropology altogether.

One of the consequences of British social anthropology's lack of familiarity with other disciplines during the functionalist period has been its inability to react confidently to the work of Lévi–Strauss. The time has long passed when one could simply ignore his ideas, yet criticisms continue to be made which betray a failure to understand the nature of structuralism. Clearly, however, if we are to explore links with language in an attempt to further a shift from a functional to a semantic identity, we cannot avoid assessing the value of structuralism in this transition. We might well wish that in the last decade Lévi–Strauss had had a more even impact here, instead of just being an inspiration to a few British anthropologists; but it may be that we have already learned enough from that experience for structuralism *per se* now to constitute an impediment to our further development. One cannot sensibly express this problem in terms of whether one is for or against structuralism — this would merely obscure the fact of Lévi-Strauss' vital place in the growth of anthropology. Thus it is regrettable that those who have in fact benefitted most should now make exaggerated denunciations of structuralism, try to deny its pioneering role, and, in the case of Leach, even try to claim a functionalist identity (1970:9).

Structuralism is itself a conceptual system, and hence it is important to grasp its presuppositions and goals in order to locate correct principles of criticism. Structuralism is evidently not a part of a structural–functional discipline. It belongs to a different 'epistemic paradigm' (Scholte 1966). That Lévi–Strauss has constructed a different type of anthropology should in itself be an invaluable education for a community firmly wedded to one self–image. But there is a corollary, namely that one should not judge his work by the internal standards for evaluating a functionalist social science, as if they constituted universal criteria for scientific acceptability.

The task of approaching Lévi–Strauss' writings as a system is not an easy one. In the first place, into his works flow at least two distinct traditions — French sociology, and American cultural anthropology. Secondly, there is his avoidance of methodological statements and his reluctance to engage in what he regards as sterile philosophical debates about his work (1973a: foreword) — as if one could justify structuralism by regarding it as 'a way of doing things'. Thirdly, Lévi–Strauss does not so much establish links with other disciplines as raid other fields to both formulate and establish structuralist goals, and in such a way as to leave unclear how crucial it is for him to have understood his sources.

On the other hand, he has spoken of the strong unity in his work, claiming that for all his career he has been pursuing the same end (1970b: 9–10) of formulating the basic structural laws of the human unconscious. In this task the work on totemism and on the 'science of the concrete' were mere pauses between the two major assaults in the fields of kinship and mythology. The goal throughout was to make an inventory of those mental constraints which reveal that the seeming arbitrariness in such fields is part of an illusory liberty which really rests upon logical necessity.

Some aspects of this severe programme become clearer when one looks at *Tristes Tropiques,* which seems not to fit into such a scheme. Structural analyses are supposedly apersonal, yet this work is autobiographical. Here is a picture of the anthropologist, uncomfortable in his own society, working as an amputated human being (1961: 58) in a science which is an attempt to redeem a civilization which, by raping half of humanity and reducing them to the status of objects, made anthropology itself possible (ibid.: 381ff.). Lévi–Strauss' own field experiences have obviously been crucial in one sense, yet structuralism is clearly not a fieldwork enterprise. It is an essentially detached analytical procedure, providing intelligibility at a distance. Lévi–Strauss had been in contact with native peoples, but he was not thereby able to understand them (ibid.: 326–7). For him, Rousseau was the founder of the human sciences precisely because he saw that to know Man one had to view him from a distance (1962: 47,50).

Possibly this combination of humanism and remoteness betrays a profound inauthenticity (Diamond 1974), which leads Lévi–Strauss to transmute his own personal marginality into analytic universality. Structuralism thus is a highly 'unreflexive' anthropological tradition

(Scholte 1972) – an effort to attain understanding at a distance, without reflecting on the personal source of this form of enterprise. Clearly, understanding here must be of a special kind. It cannot be a case of the anthropologist as an individual subject translating the messages of subjects in another culture. Subjects must be replaced by 'objects'; we must sink to the level of the unconscious where science locates truth and where communication between self and other is ensured (1950:xxxi).

LEVI-STRAUSS' EXPLORATIONS OF THE LINKS BETWEEN ANTHROPOLOGY AND LINGUISTIC MODELS

In order to appreciate the nature of the system to which such a notion of communication belongs, it is necessary to survey that mental Odyssey upon which Lévi-Strauss set out in 1945, striving for a fruitful view of the relationship between anthropology and linguistics. Some of the earlier efforts were clearly misguided. Indeed, one is struck forcibly by the narrowness of his initial vision. After all, he was not looking to semantics, nor to anthropological linguistics, but to Prague structural phonology.

To understand this choice, it is certainly important to recall the impressive achievements of structural linguistics at that time. But we must also realize that the role linguistic models were to play had already been worked out to a large extent. Lévi-Strauss was not contributing to the 'language and culture' tradition. For him, linguistics was above all the social science which had first reached the unconscious realm in which invariants could be detected. In this sense, linguistics was 'good to think with' because suggestive of how an anthropological science should view models, the unconscious, explanation, systems, reduction and universals. Also, Lévi-Strauss' search did not begin from any really developed linguistic tradition in French sociology. Meillet and probably Saussure were indebted to Durkheim. Mauss several times remarked on the value of linguistics to the human sciences, though he scarcely made anthropology a part of linguistics as Lévi-Strauss suggests (1945:52n7). Indeed, Lévi-Strauss remarked on how timid ethnologists in general had been in working out links with linguistics (1949:20) — a fact true even of Boas, whose stress on the unconscious nature of linguistic categories was to anticipate the theoretical development of linguistics and thereby 'a future whose rich promise we are just beginning to perceive' (ibid.:19). Lévi-Strauss himself did not come to linguistics until a whole decade after his fieldwork, and seems to possess only a slight knowledge of his sources of inspiration (Mounin 1970).

During the nineteenth century there had been many parallels between anthropology and comparative philology, but for Lévi-Strauss the structural revolution in linguistics transformed the situation. With such a

39

close methodological analogy existing between the two disciplines, anthropologists should examine how the new methods applied to the phenomena with which they dealt. It was in part because he was creating a new field that his earliest papers on anthropology and language were evident struggles to find valid and fruitful links, and there was present in them considerable confusion as between the legitimate general principles involved in the analogy and misleading special applications of them (Ardener 1971b: xivff.). The idea of the 'social phoneme' as the elementary unit of kinship was one manifestation of this, as was his scarcely credible suggestion of detailed correlations between kinship systems and the structure of language families (1951: 63). No matter how valuable it may be to conceive of culture as a communication system, it is crucial to distinguish between these general principles and the particular characteristics of a single communication system such as language. Failure here could easily discredit a truly semiotic approach. Pike's 'unified theory' of human behaviour, for instance, is little more than a proposal for cultural analogues of linguistic units (1956); it certainly reaches no satisfactory analytical level.

It was not long before Lévi-Strauss' vision went beyond anthropology and language to the more general framework of cybernetics and communications systems.[1] His concern then was more with the links beneath anthropology and language rather than those between them. Economic and kinship structures were thus regarded as being *like* language. If a reduction to unconscious laws were possible with these social phenomena, it would be proved that all these facts were of the same basic nature as projections of such laws (1951: 58-9,62). The real parallel between anthropology and linguistics would then be that they both dealt with structures built out of constituent units. On this basis they could cooperate in an investigation into the working of the human mind (1953a: 71, 80).

The larger context of Lévi-Strauss' search received another formulation when he defined anthropology as a semiological discipline. No one, he claimed, came nearer to the appropriate view of anthropology than Saussure who ignored it when sketching the foundations of a general study of sign systems. Anthropology should be absorbed by semiology, and direct itself to those areas which linguistics had not yet occupied (1968a: 16-7). Language, economics, and kinship were the three fundamental sign systems — communication with messages, goods, and women, respectively (1953b: 296ff.). Other phenomena (myth and cooking, for example) could likewise be seen as communication structures, but were less easily analysed (1958a: 84). If language existed solely to signify while other sign systems did so only partially (1945: 48), nonetheless all the symbolic organizations of a culture belonged to the same field. Developments in mathematics, economics, biology and linguistics were of such a similarity that a common language might even be found in which to express them all (1954a : 581-3).

Lévi-Strauss viewed these sign systems as partial expressions of the social system (1953a : 85). Although he accepts the primacy of the infrastructure (1966 : 130), society is seen as a set of different types of lived and thought structures — an 'order of orders'. In his view, these were basically the terms in which Marx conceived of superstructures, although he had hardly begun to plot the relationships of homology, transformation and contradiction existing between the several ideological spheres (ibid. : 130).

In future years we may look back on these semiological ideas as Lévi-Strauss' most seminal suggestion, and it is a pity that his recent concentration on mythology has prevented further development along these broader lines. We have not yet been presented with any extensive demonstration of the notion of an 'order of orders'. Several important sign systems have been little more than hinted at. He has made a few remarks on material culture, some general comments on the semantic nature of art in pre-literate cultures (in Charbonnier 1970 ed. : 60-2); but perhaps the most important omission from Lévi-Strauss' writings to date is the subject of ritual. He seems to regard ritual as an attempt to escape from the categories of myth, and thus to be free of the discontinuity necessary for all signification (1971 : 603) — scarcely a convincing view of any human action, least of all one where formality is at a maximum.

SOME FUNDAMENTAL CONCEPTS OF STRUCTURALISM

We have now charted a sufficient stretch of Lévi-Strauss' explorations of anthropology and language to be able to compile an inventory of the more important elements of his conceptual system — concepts like 'model', 'unconscious', 'science' and 'reduction' — and to show how they fit together.[2]

The unconscious very early assumed a central importance for Lévi-Strauss. Indeed, he opposed anthropology to history in terms of the fact that the latter addresses itself to the conscious expressions of social life, whereas the former seeks for fundamental and unconscious forms (1949 : 18,24). It was for this very reason that Mauss brought the discipline to the edge of a new era in his essay on exchange. But he only began to sketch the lineaments of that deeper reality which lies beneath the empirically observable, since he allowed himself to be distracted by native ideas (1950 : xxxiiiff.).

The unconscious gives direct expression to the laws of the mind without interference by the misleading secondary elaborations which consciousness builds. Conscious models may be instructive, but being normative their primary function is to perpetuate and not to explain phenomena (1953b: 281–3). Native models, therefore, to the extent that they disguise reality, are sources of mystification to the anthropologist. Dual representation, for instance, may mask a real asymmetry in the social structure (1956). The human sciences must regard consciousness as their enemy (1964: 537). Hence the value of linguistic models — the governing principles of a language are not known to its speakers.

Lévi-Strauss did not choose the most helpful expression when he said that his structural models had 'nothing to do with' empirical reality (1953b: 179). He meant only that models of social structure do not describe concrete social relations, although to be true they must economically account for all the facts. They are not models *of* the empirically observable, but models built *on* such data, which refer to the underlying unconscious foundations. Unlike the case with British social anthropology, 'social structure' in his work is not of the empirical order. Unfortunately, however, he has not really clarified what he means by the term 'unconscious', even saying that whether it refers to a reality, a model, or a principle of intelligibility, is for psychologists to decide (in Rossi 1973: 40). Clearly in his writings it has little in common with the Freudian unconscious, since it is not an affective system at all. It is more an intellectual process of imposing forms on content(1949: 21).

Lévi-Strauss had explicitly expressed his debt to geology, Marxism, and psycho-analysis for the principle that scientific explanation consists in the reduction of one type of reality to another (1961: 61). Such a decomposition is the technique whereby structuralism locates the invariants of any domain. The charge of impoverishment has often been made, but structuralism as a search for fundamental properties is not meant to give an exhaustive account of social phenomena (1958a: 82). This is precisely why primitive forms of social organization are of such value: here the logical structures built by the unconscious mind are more evident (1969a: 268).

The stress on universals and the unconscious, when combined with a reductionist view of explanation, conflicts radically with the most familiar approaches in the study of man. The debate with Sartre, in this context, is not an inconsequential philosophical distraction, for Lévi-Strauss is here stating what he regards as essential before anthropology can be accepted as a science. He regards as false the distinction proposed by some between explanation in the physical and human sciences (1968a: 15). Science requires objects of investigation and these are not provided by the 'subjects' of existentialism. The advantage of the unconscious is precisely that at this level the subject is eliminated (1947: 527).

It is an axiom of such philosophies as phenomenology that there is a continuity between experience and reality; but for Lévi-Strauss, if appearance and reality were the same, there would be no task left for science. If experience is a starting point, it cannot be the goal. Science must decompose the empirical and recompose it on a truer level (1966:250). Philosophers merely allow the idea of the human subject to captivate them. Imprisoned by intuition and cultural idiosyncrasy,[3] the development of a real science of social phenomena is then prevented (1971:563,570,614-5). Science concerns 'Being' in relation to *it*self not in relation to *one*self (1961:63). It is the lesson of Marx and Freud, argues Lévi-Strauss, that when man reflects on his own meaning he always arrives at meanings which are false (1971:253); and it is the task of structuralism to grant the social sciences the status of the physical sciences by unveiling to their practitioners a realm of objects such as true science requires. The anthropologist may work 'from a distance', but he has access to a vast wealth of human experience. The philosopher, not knowing 'the other', possesses no true understanding of himself.

For Lévi-Strauss, an agnostic who studies man scientifically should regard the objects of study as if they were ants (1966:246).The ultimate goal of the human sciences, indeed, is not to constitute man but to dissolve him. In that sense, structuralism is anti-anthropological (Simonis 1968:344).[4] It is a stern attempt to place man in nature, by an ethnological investigation which first establishes the invariant foundations of that realm called culture. If nature is opposed to culture, in a wider sense culture is a part of the natural order. That distinction which is the basis of primitive thought is, for Lévi-Strauss, but one discontinuity among others in the laminated structure which is the realm of nature (in Charbonnier 1970 ed.:151-2). It is for this reason that he declares the nature/culture distinction to be of primarily methodological importance (1966:247n) — culture being produced by a process which scientific knowledge will eventually explain. Anthropology simply takes the human world of language and symbolism as given. It is not its task to explain that evolution in the nervous system which constituted the process of hominization and created the system of powers which made society possible (1968a:24). Lévi-Strauss is thus a transcendental materialist. Man is not an original creation. The human may be resolved into the non-human, just as one day life may be decomposed into its inorganic conditions (1966:246-7). The world appeared before man, and man will disappear before its end: man and all his meanings is only an ephemeral efflorescence in the larger course of nature (1971:621-2). Physical laws dictate that ultimately culture must sink back into the natural world; anthropology is thus 'entropology' (1961:397).

However, Lévi-Strauss is also insistent that this kind of reduction must not be an impoverishment (1966:247). To establish man's place in nature is not the same task now as it was for the Enlightenment philosophers or for nineteenth-century evolutionists. That the decomposition in structuralism is not a simple matter is evident from his work in kinship. Kinship is a fundamental structure of the cultural realm. The incest taboo constitutes a realm of communication rules which establishes an exchange organization which is not found in the animal world. Consanguinity is a natural fact, whereas affinity is a cultural fact. What makes kinship a cultural fact is how it diverges from nature and not what it retains from it (1945:50).

Nevertheless, kinship and culture in general are only opposed to nature in a limited sense, for both are creations of the human intelligence, and the human brain is a part of the natural world because a product of the natural world. Human thought resembles nature and can understand it because the human brain is governed by the same laws (1966:263). Possibly, therefore, the essence of our species would be more revealed by a mineral than by any work of man himself (1961:322,398). The human mind creates by using the world of which it is a part. It generates structures which are an image of a reality which is already contained within the structure of the brain (1970b:341). Nature and thought are hence manifestations of the same laws (1971:605). This is why Lévi-Strauss tries to show that myth rests upon a logic which is a 'rationality' immanent in the universe. To show that all the complexities of the cultural realm rest upon simple laws of the unconscious mind is to have placed man in nature. If culture is the result of the laws of the mind, and such laws are but expressions of that order from which the brain evolved, then culture is shown to be of the natural realm.

LÉVI-STRAUSS AND MEANING

We are now in a position to see what role the links between anthropology and language that structuralism values might play in our shift from 'function' to 'meaning'.When Lévi-Strauss first declared that anthropology aimed to be semiological science, he claimed that meaning was its guiding principle (1954b:364). In linguistics it had been shown how to pass from elements in themselves devoid of meaning to the semantic systems built upon them (ibid:368). Thus it is clear why Lévi-Strauss uses a phonological model, and why his main semiological concern is to establish the minimal features which constitute different types of communication systems.

Meaning is commonly associated with freedom, but for Lévi-Strauss this is an error. Meaning in structuralism is a product of logical laws. Structuralism (like linguistics) advances under the assumption of determinism (1970b:27). Human societies, like human individuals, do not create absolutely; all they can do is to choose certain combinations from a repertory of ideas which it should be possible to reconstitute (1961:160). Structuralism is thus a transposition of Kantianism into the realm of ethnology — that is, the attempt through empirical science rather than introspection to reach the constraining structures of the mind (1970a:59). No one could possibly deny the importance of focusing attention on the finite code instead of on the diversity of content. Nonetheless, many doubts can be expressed concerning the status of his claims. Chomsky, for instance, assigns very little value to structural phonology as a model for investigating the nature of the human mind, even making the dismissive comment that Lévi-Strauss' work shows no more than that human beings classify (1968:65).

But the nature of Lévi-Strauss' interests and assumptions make problematic what could count as a criticism of his work. It is reasonable to suppose that linguistic semantics will not find useful those organizing principles that are so vital on the phonological level. But if binarism seems a grossly inadequate approach to semantics, Lévi-Strauss is not concerned with any ordinary idea of meaning. For him, meaning is a secondary and always reducible phenomenon: meaning rests upon non-meaning (1970a:64). Out of a limited number of laws of thought the human mind creates significance out of non-sense. These laws of mind are the same as the natural laws of a cosmos which for Lévi-Strauss has no inherent meaning.

This view that meaning is the result of an articulation of the insignificant has been criticized severely by Ricoeur, who suggests that Lévi-Strauss merely elaborates the syntax of a discourse which says nothing. Structuralism opts for syntax rather than semantics (1963:607). But Lévi-Strauss retorts that the phonological revolution has shown that there is no choice, since language is built out of the relations of meaningless elements (1970a:64). Ricoeur, he claims, wants some mysterious meaning behind meaning. Clearly they are speaking of different phenomena. For Ricoeur, meaning is primary: human beings have a capacity for 'mean-*ing*'. But this power is possessed by the 'subject', whom Lévi-Strauss specifically wishes to leave out in his descent to the unconscious. In reply to critics who allege that structuralism destroys meaning, Lévi-Strauss asserts that in reducing something to a structure one does not lose meaning but rather finds details significant in ways one would not have thought possible (1971:242). But this 'significance' and Ricoeur's 'meaning' are hardly the same.

We must be careful how we express our criticisms of Lévi-Strauss here. The result of his endeavour to make linguistics play a fundamental role in the human sciences has in one sense been anti-semantic. Yet, in most ordinary senses, 'meaning' is not part of the structuralist universe of discourse at all, so we can hardly speak of his shortcomings. Lévi-

45

Strauss' 'significance' is part of a total system. We can accept this world-structure or not, but we have few terms for criticizing it precisely because other structures are built with a different language. On the other hand, one can draw attention to a semantic feature of structuralism itself. Given the discontinuity of nature/culture resting on symbolism, structuralism is an effort to establish a continuity. Yet it inevitably speaks in metaphor since it is itself a part of the world of language and symbolism. The work of Lévi-Strauss therefore, according to Simonis, has to be a kind of aesthetic perception (1968 : 311) rather than a 'natural science' of man.

TOTEMISM AND 'LA PENSÉE SAUVAGE'

The importance of Lévi-Strauss' analysis of totemism does not lie in the fact that he took to the point of dissolution a problem of nineteenth-century ethnology on which others had made only small analytical advances. It lies rather in the manner by which the decomposition was brought about. Regarding culture as a set of communication systems, Lévi-Strauss destroys 'totemism' by applying to it a thesis about translatability. Structuralism here is both a theory about the conditions for translation, and itself an instance of this kind of communication. The demolition of totemism in effect opens up a channel of communication between the primitive and ourselves, by dismantling a phenomenon into elements where the equivalences required for translation are found.

Totemic theories had defined as essentially alien an institution and set of beliefs which separated the primitive from civilized man. There was no way of converting it into anything our own culture possessed. What Lévi-Strauss shows is that 'totemism' is not a semantic field which we cannot match, because it is not a field at all. It is not even a 'mode of thought', merely a 'species' level in a much larger classificatory system (1966 : 62,218) from which it had been illegitimately ripped by the prejudice and incomprehension of ethnographers and theorists. More formally, it plays the role of a logical operator for converting messages on either side of the nature/culture distinction (ibid. : 91).

In this light, totemism is a system based upon the same logic of opposition and association which underlies our own thought; dissolved in such a framework, 'totemism' therefore becomes intelligible. There is no postulation of strange connections between social groups and animal species, but two complete homologous series of discriminations — one from the cultural realm and one from the natural. It is the differences and not the similarities which resemble each other (1969b : 149). In other words, a system of natural discriminations is being used as a coding device to make statements of social significance. Significance rests upon organization, and as a system of differences animal species are formally appropriate to play such a role (ibid.:135). It is neither utilitarian value nor objective similarity which explains their usage. The aptness is internal because the real link passes through the human mind (ibid.:81): animals are 'good to think with' (ibid.:162). With the birth of the human intellect everything acquires significance. Meaning is not decreed, but once it is anywhere it is everywhere (ibid.:163). Thus, nature herself supplies the human mind with endless materials with which to construct signifying systems.

By being shown to possess the minimal features of a language, 'totemism' is understood, since it can be converted into other systems. Complex cultural content is emptied by structural analysis until it becomes a logical form. So, a stark intellectual schema takes the place of a complex and affectively rich mass of data.[5] Criticisms have been made of this procedure; but we should recall that structuralism aims at intelligibility, and so Lévi-Strauss achieves his goal once he has shown to be present those minimal logical features required for translation. This indeed is the point of his attempt to transmute a totemic into a caste structure (1966:122ff.). In his view, if a phenomenon is a language it should be possible to state its code in another language (ibid.:75) Given certain elements in common (such as social groups and media of exchange) it can be shown that these elements, with a few simple rules of substitution, allow one to pass from one sign system to another.

Since the study of 'totemism' is concerned with translatability, the meaning of the expression *la pensée sauvage* is problematic. This is not the difficulty concerning the relation between collective ideational categories and the thinking of individuals. And clearly his 'untamed' mentality does not distinguish the thinking of primitive from civilized men. The problem arises because Lévi-Strauss is not essentially concerned with how human beings think so much as with the formal conditions for converting one system of 'objectified thought' into another. He has himself said that *la pensée sauvage* is not predicated of anything. It is a set of axioms and postulates required to establish a code which allows the least unfaithful translation possible of the 'other' into 'us' (1970a:62). The concept therefore really names a translational meeting-point: it states the basic requirements of a communication channel. What the relationship is between his 'fundamental structures' of the human mind and the processes studied by psychologists and neurologists is hard to say, yet perhaps the problem is not insoluble. If one has outlined a channel for converting systems of objectified thought, this will itself be an example of human thought. To speak of the conditions of translatability is thus to talk metonymically of the nature of thought. Translation, after all, is one of the activities of the human mind.

The study of totemism was a historical introduction to Lévi-Strauss' more general study of classifying activity in *La Pensée sauvage* itself. Ethnographers, he claims, have neglected primitive man's search for knowledge. Unless we grant this inquisitiveness, the Neolithic revolution is unintelligible; for agriculture and the domestication of animals could only have been the result of patient observation and experimentation (1966:13ff.). Primitive man, in fact, has an extensive knowledge of his natural surroundings, which is framed into large, internally coherent, taxonomic systems based upon universal logical principles.

For Lévi-Strauss, man has always been thinking equally well (1968d:33). Primitive thought, whether it be manifested in magic, myth or 'totemism', is founded on the same demand for logical order as is modern science (1966:3,10). But there is a very important difference between the savage and the civilized mentality. The savage has a consuming symbolic ambition, but his attention is directed entirely to the concrete (ibid.:220). Nature is accessible to inquiry at two levels — our science operating at an abstract level, the savage building a 'science of the concrete' out of sensory qualities and concrete objects. Our science creates events out of theoretical systems of concepts while the savage constructs structures out of events (ibid.:22). He is a *bricoleur,* with no special tools for his intellectual operations, who is consequently forced to use 'odds and ends' that have already been employed for other ends (ibid.:15ff.,33). A 'science of the concrete' produces myth and magic; nature approached on the other level yields physical science.

Some, for instance Bachelard (1970), would certainly view Lévi-Strauss' 'science of the concrete' as a misnomer. Natural science is essentially the overcoming of a number of epistemological obstacles, such as familiar metaphors and immediate experience. But it is precisely in the realm of analogy and the sensory that the savage mind works with elements which are signs half way between percepts and concepts. But natural science, in Lévi-Strauss' view, is merely a 'domestication' of a universal rationality (1966a:219). The style of thought which developed in ancient Greece and which is so important in the history of Western civilization, was a contingent event. Western science and concrete science are systems based on the same logic and are both valid in themselves. Nothing requires that the savage reorient his mind (1973a:474).

La Pensée sauvage is a landmark in the growth of anthropology, representing as it does a conception of the discipline as a study of the human mind. Between the Frazerian view that savage thought was erroneous, and the specious pragmatic justification of it by Malinowski, there was room for a new enterprise (1966:74). However, Lévi-Strauss' interest here is only a part of wider logical ambitions, as is clear from his work on myth. Evaluation must therefore wait till his mythological analyses have been discussed.

THE ANALYSIS OF MYTH

That Lévi-Strauss should have turned his attention in such a resolute fashion to the subject of mythology should occasion no surprise. Basic principles discovered in the analysis of kinship might be influenced by the exigencies of social life. Myth, on the other hand, is a privileged domain for structuralism, for here the mind only converses with itself, and so must reveal specifically mental laws.

In 1955 Lévi-Strauss declared that the study of mythology was in a state of chaos like that obtaining in linguistics before it achieved scientific status (1955:207). However, one feature of myth possibly offered a way out of this situation. Although the content of myth is very diverse and seems arbitrary, nonetheless certain patterns have a widespread occurrence (ibid.:208). Myth narrates a sequence of events, but its significance, suggests Lévi-Strauss, lies in an atemporal structure which can be likened to the harmonic structure of a musical composition. To extract the sense of a myth one must reach the code of the system, not remain on the superficial level of sequence. Myth, like music, occupies time yet also denies it (1970b:15-16) and so must be read both horizontally and vertically like a musical score.

This approach required a myth text to be reduced to sentences (1955:210-11). Each of these 'mythemes' is a relation and must be combined with similar mythemes to produce 'bundles' of relations. In the Oedipal myth, for instance, murder and incest are coded by that semantic impoverishment which accompanies the reaching of the logical level (1966:108) as 'underrating' and 'overrating' of blood ties. Myth proceeds from the awareness of oppositions to their mediation (1955:224). It is a logical model designed to overcome contradictions (ibid.:229), which it obviously cannot do if the contradiction is real. With the Oedipal myth the problem is that of the origin of man: the issue of being born of two parents versus being autochthonous.

For Lévi-Strauss, a myth has a layered structure. It states a message several times in different terms. It is this multiplication of levels which makes the structure clear (ibid.:212). All levels are equally important since the significance resides in the logical structure that is common to all (1970b:340-1). A myth, thus, is all its variants (1955:216-17), and its significance lies in the 'law' of the permutation group (ibid.:223,228). These ideas were elegantly used in analysing the Asdiwal myth. Here, a problem concerning the difficulties of combining a certain type of marriage system with a specific residence rule is stated in at least four different ways. Geographical, economic and cosmological codes are used, besides the statement of the dilemma in a sociological language; but all codes share an underlying logical structure in which is encapsulated the formal expression of the message (1958b). What is crucial is to avoid confusing the terms of any one code with the communication that the myth is making. Max Müller rightly noted the widespread use of astronomical codes in myth, but, according to Lévi-Strauss, in failing to see that myth uses several codes simultaneously he incorrectly interpreted such myths as actually about natural phenomena (1971:38).

Lévi-Strauss with these ideas unquestionably opened up in a provocative way a field which had long been stagnant; but there were no extensive demonstrations nor major theoretical advances until 1964, when the *Mythologiques* series began. Here his initial task was to reduce hundreds of South American myths to an economical coding scheme by which one myth could be transformed into another. Thus his aim was to constitute a 'mythological syntax'. He hoped to show how simple empirical categories such as 'raw' and 'cooked' could be combined as logical signs so as to form abstract propositions (1970b:1). This would prove that underneath all the seeming freedom and chaos of myth there were at work very definite constraining logical rules (ibid.:10).

The progress of Lévi-Strauss' analysis resembles the adjustments one can make on a microscope which bring into prominence different levels of organization (1973a:473-4). Thus, after examining the opposition of 'raw' and 'cooked' (one concrete means of stating the nature/culture distinction) the focus shifts to the 'environment' of that pair in the opposition of honey and tobacco. Honey is consumed as a raw product, though it is manufactured in nature by bees. Tobacco, on the other hand, is consumed only when burned. Honey is thus 'infra-culinary', while tobacco is 'meta-culinary' (ibid.:17,20). This pair elaborates the nature/culture division — myths concerning honey, for instance, being about man's connection with nature. In later analyses, the initial division is shown to be statable in an endless variety of concrete codes — astronomical, anatomical, zoological, and many others. And, by increasing the 'power' of the structural method, a simple opposition like that of noise and silence discovered at one point, at a deeper level becomes part of a very complex acoustic code (ibid.:328), just as the raw/cooked opposition itself can form an element of an elaborate culinary code (1968c:369ff.).

It is essential to Lévi-Strauss' approach that all these languages can be 'intercoded' (1971:38): that is, any message sent by one code can be stated in any other. Ideas like periodicity can form the basis of homologies between different realms (1968c:92). Cosmic and cosmetic codes can duplicate each other (ibid.:328). An abnormal relation between social categories — for instance, an unacceptable marriage — can be paralleled in the astronomical code by a rare event like an eclipse, and in the acoustic code by a noisy outburst, as an intrusion of nature to signify that the social order had been violated. Myths show the *bricoleur* at work using and re-using concrete materials to construct endless codes.

The *Mythologiques* series also contains a major surprise, for the study which began with the aim of eliciting the syntax of myth in tropical South America ends by exploring the myths in regions of North America. Although this suggests several historical hypotheses, these are not Lévi-Strauss' real concern. The shift is required as a source of new data with which to confirm his logical claims. The myths in the second area do not resemble those of the first in their content — raw/cooked becomes naked/clothed, for instance. But below this level is a logical scheme to which the myths of both areas belong which makes them part of one closed transformation set. The myths of North America thus furnish a proof 'at a distance' (1968c:11) of earlier analyses. Lévi-Strauss even claims it possible to predict the existence of certain myths (ibid.:449,407).

The aim of structural analysis in the field of mythology is to produce the optimal code for the inter-conversion of myths. Just as myth is a second-order code to language itself, so these analyses may be called the 'myth of mythology' since they constitute a third-order discourse (1970b:12). However, whereas Freud's interpretation of the Oedipal legend can be regarded as just a variant of the myth itself (1955:217), structuralism is not part of this kind of infinite regress (1971:561). Other authors try to translate myth into other terms, and in interpreting one myth they merely create another. Structural analysis does not try to give the meaning of myth — it simply allows the intrinsic organizational properties of the mythic domain to reveal themselves (ibid.:560). It is for this reason that there is an effacement of the author in the *Mythologiques:* the anthropologist is just an object through whom the myths can reveal their own logic (ibid.:561).

SIGNIFICANCE, RIGOUR AND LOGIC: STRUCTURALISM EVALUATED

It is upon the subject of myth that Lévi-Strauss has carried out his latest and most extensive structural investigations, so it is appropriate to assess structuralism as a system by criticizing his work on this topic. And it is not irrelevant to begin by remarking that the supposed semiological framework of the *Mythologiques* is nowhere clearly set out. It is a provocative notion that myth, like music, communicates by structure. Myth is also, like music, untranslatable; so in order to understand a myth one can only show how another myth constitutes a transformation of it (in Steiner 1966:38). Yet the musical parallel is clearly also something of a joke. In the same way, the linguistic nature of myth is not adequately discussed. We are told, for instance, that myth works in language at a high level where meaning almost 'takes off' from its linguistic foundation (1955:210). Myth is composed of words, but as signs in a meta-

51

language they act as elements of a 'super-signification' (1960a:148-9). Unfortunately, Lévi-Strauss concentrates so resolutely on the analyses of the myths themselves that we are provided with no more than such cryptic clues as to the assumptions on which he proceeds.

For example, the difficulty concerning the meaning of the expression *la pensée sauvage* presents itself again. For Lévi-Strauss the analysis of myth does not show 'how men think', but how myths work themselves out in men's minds without their knowledge (1970b:11-12). To critics who allege that he imposes an interpretation on the data, he replies that it does not matter whether native thought takes shape through the activity of the analyst or vice versa (ibid.:13). Of course, we are dealing with the unconscious mind; and if the goal is to increase the intelligibility of 'objectified thought', his comments make some sense in that his 'untamed' rationality is something which both anthropologist and native share. But if the aim is to produce a code for the conversion of myths into one another, in what sense does structuralism reveal *mental* constraints? One can readily see how Chomsky's linguistic work bears on various cognitive problems; but Lévi-Strauss works on mythical 'objectified thought', which is merely *in* language in no clearly specified way.

Something of the difficulty here is involved in that excessive binarism for which he has frequently been criticized. This characteristic of his work derives from the idea of 'distinctive features' in the Prague linguistic model, and many have protested that it is quite incapable of registering the subtleties of human thought. Natural communication combines both digital and analogue features (Bateson 1973:262), and the concept of binary opposition clearly conflates a range of relations like difference, contradiction, contrariety, and so on (Wilden 1972:9). Such a concept is patently inadequate for the analysis of symbolic structures; yet if structuralism is not concerned with 'how men think', the relevance of reminding us that men do not only think digitally (Leach 1964) is not entirely clear.

The general semantic inadequacy of Lévi-Strauss' myth analyses has been a topic for much comment. It has frequently been argued, for instance, that he only provides a grammar and not a meaning. But structuralism does not attempt to give 'meaning' in the sense that these critics demand. It merely sets out to reveal the fundamental organizing principles of a sign system. This is why Lévi-Strauss is essentially concerned with relations. With myth, the semiological principle that the value of the sign is positional is taken literally. Indeed, Lévi-Strauss even applies it at a second level: each whole myth is itself a sign whose significance only emerges at the level of the set.

In the structuralist programme, myth is just one realm where the *bri-*

coleur can be seen at work. His activity confers significance on anything, so mythology is like a kaleidoscope in which bits are combined and recombined endlessly (1966 : 22,33, 36). But a structuralist is only interested in showing that this process — however chaotic it might appear — is governed by strict logic. Even at the set level, therefore, Lévi-Strauss finds no 'meaning'. His task is to prove another realm to be law-governed. It is the issue of being and not being which sets the human mind in operation and generates all the other oppositions which appear in myth (1971 : 621). The whole of mythology is therefore just an endless elaboration of the problem of human identity — an endless calque upon the nature/culture disjunction. Since structuralism shows the whole structure to be constituted by a logic which is one expression of those laws of the natural world to which man belongs, the analysis denies the very distinction which myth itself presumes.

Many other criticisms, besides that of semantic inadequacy, which have been levelled at Lévi-Strauss' work have entirely failed to grasp the nature of structuralism, although in some cases the very unclarity of his writing is partly to blame. One such complaint is that structuralism is speculative and unempirical. Of course, because of the wide comparative nature of his work, Lévi-Strauss is quite capable of simply misreading his ethnographic sources. But actually the simple and endless application of a few principles to a mass of data is the most striking characteristic of structuralism. Lévi-Strauss himself has constantly stressed the need for detailed ethnography. Indeed, for his ends this is vital. In concrete logic anything can be significant, and signs may be linked by many connections simultaneously (1966 : 58ff.) so that one cannot know in advance the basis of any classification. It is true that structuralism is interested in 'logical relations devoid of content' (1970b : 240), but it would be wrong to infer from such a remark that Lévi-Strauss' work was unempirical. He has often emphasized the gulf between structuralism and formalism : structuralism does not separate form and content since structure *is* content viewed as a logical organization (1960a : 122)

The very extent of these sorts of misunderstandings means we must attempt to locate a standard which Lévi-Strauss himself values, so that his performance can be criticized by internal criteria. Since he strives to find logical necessity, and since envy of the precision of linguistics was a major part of the initial impulse to explore linguistic models, rigour suggests itself as a valid standard for evaluation.

Even so, we must be careful to apply the correct criteria of rigour. For instance, it does not matter that Lévi-Strauss gives no definition of myth. For some purposes, fidelity to native classifications of oral literature would be essential, and there the argument that it is necessary to know who owns a myth, how it is narrated, and so on (Hymes 1971a : 61,79), would be perfectly valid. But where the aim is to locate unconscious constraints, this is not so. One can treat myth as a linguist treats language: to produce a grammar one only requires a sample, it is not necessary to know who spoke it. Other niceties of mythography similarly do not apply. For example, a structuralist need not be concerned about the 'original' version of a myth, since in his analysis all variants are valid: every myth is original in relation to itself and derivative as a transformation of another (1971:576).

Also, there are kinds of precision for which Lévi-Strauss quite explicitly does not aim. Myth is a transformational not a metrical phenomenon and we must see that rigour and quantification are not synonymous. Lévi-Strauss himself has long suggested that the most appropriate mathematics for the study of human phenomena would be such branches as topology and set theory, which deal with qualitative, non-metrical precision (1953b:283): the realm of necessity is not necessarily that of quantity (1954a:585). Instead of trying to mimic the methods of the physical sciences, which might not produce any significant results, the social sciences, he has argued, should go straight for a different type of mathematics (ibid.:581).

We can now examine directly how Lévi-Strauss' work measures up to those standards which structural analyses must display if they are to attain their goals. There is a shock at the very outset of the *Mythologiques* where we are told not to take seriously the logico-mathematical symbols employed in the analysis (1970b:30-1).[6] Lévi-Strauss tells us that this is but a first attempt at scientific analysis, and that a genuinely logical and exact treatment will only come after considerable progress (ibid.:39). Presumably, therefore, the field of mythology is still in a pre-scientific state even after his efforts — which is a sad testimony to the success of his application of structural linguistic models which supposedly possessed the rigour of the natural sciences.

Lévi-Strauss says his symbols mean a load of relations vaguely perceived to have something in common. Certainly notions like 'homology', 'transformation' and even 'opposition' itself, are put to very diverse usages. And the signs (+) and (–) borrowed from the Prague school stand not only for 'presence' and 'absence' but also for 'more' and 'less' (1973a:90n12). Lévi-Strauss' analyses therefore lack an unambiguous principle of logical exclusion, and one wonders what level of logical necessity can be charted by employing such a heap of vague concepts. The *Mythologiques* series falls so far short of that linguistic rigour which prompted Lévi-Strauss' Odyssey, that it is probably not unfair to suggest that we should put the term 'logic' along with those other virtually meaningless metaphorical renderings of scientific concepts which he scatters through his writings (see Régnier 1968).

Yet a terminology of precision is used throughout these studies. Lévi-Strauss speaks of algebra, for instance, and of topological transformation (1968c: 155). The very assumption on which the whole analysis is based is technically expressed in the concept of mythical thought always forming a 'closed system' irrespective of the extension of its dispersal (ibid.: 160,388). If there are ambiguities or anomalies, this simply reflects the fact that there has been too hasty a formulation, or that the analysis has not been taken sufficiently far (1970b: 162 ; 1971a: 240). But a great many difficulties arise if one takes these linguistic suggestions of rigour seriously. Structural analysis is justified only if it is exhaustive. At the same time, the analysis of myth is declared interminable (1970b: 147,6). In a rigorous exercise one would expect a set to be defined and then analysed, but Lévi-Strauss' shift from South to North America very much suggests that in his work the 'set' is ready for extension at any time in order to solve particular difficulties. True, the move is accompanied by 'proofs' of its validity, but the meaning of this term is not evident here. The logical status of the 'moral proof' of which Lévi-Strauss once spoke (during an Oxford seminar in 1970) is scarcely clear.

Having respected the fact that there will be different criteria for evaluating different types of conceptual structures, the conclusion seems inescapable that Lévi-Strauss' analyses nowhere manifest that level of rigour which they must do in order for talk about logical necessity to be warranted. When evidence of an association of honey and sperm is not taken as upsetting a general relationship between honey and menstrual blood, but as adding a new dimension to it (1968c: 340nl), one wonders what type of ethnographic discovery *would* upset an ongoing structural analysis. If precision is merely metaphorical, the goals of structuralism cannot possibly be attained. And even were this not the case, Lévi-Strauss could not demonstrate the existence of a realm of impeccable logical order, because presumably his work would fall foul of Gödelian incompleteness.

Perhaps it is most fitting to conclude by looking back to the original source of Lévi-Strauss' vision, to inquire whether the idea of a semiological science seems capable of underwriting the goals of structuralism. Lévi-Strauss has stated that he has been applying Saussurian principles to the subject of mythology (1973a: 421), but problems arise even in this claim since the basic notion of the 'arbitrariness' of the sign cannot be invoked. Mythical thought as a species of *bricolage* uses elements that have already been used and so have acquired a meaning (1966: 19, 156).[7] This problem apart, it is difficult to accept that the idea of a system constituted by relations of difference, implication and association, suffices for Lévi-Strauss' stern logical aims. Resemblance, for instance, is regarded as an instance of difference tending towards zero (1971: 32), but as this point is never reached, all signs must have an associational element, which suggests that his semiological semantics lack a principle of logical exclusion. Moreover, it is hardly proven that Saussurian paradigmatic relations — the dimension of association and metaphor — form a rigorous and closed logical structure.

Few would deny that there are strict laws governing some aspects of language; but we have no warrant for thinking that semiology establishes 'signification' as a domain of such a kind. Barthes has claimed that it is not yet even known which kinds of oppositions will be important in this discipline (1967:82). Lévi-Strauss has treated metaphor[8] as a kind of logical relation between two realms (1970b:339), but his extensive mythological analyses fail to convince that metaphor can be subordinated to the idea of logic. The *Mythologiques* series for that reason alone does not form a proof that myth is a realm of *a posteriori* necessity. He certainly has not constructed a code of logical necessity to carry out the investigations. And we should surely remember that Saussure himself, while accepting the existence of syntagmatic rules in language, said that the terms in associational relations 'ne se présentent ni en nombre défini, ni dans un ordre déterminé' (1949:173).

Lévi-Strauss' work on myth clearly rests on some dubious assumptions. Moreover, it could not possibly attain the required rigour owing to the very imprecision of his own method of procedure. But his work as a whole, as a journey through a territory initially inspired by an interest in the relations between anthropology and language, is undeniably impressive. By it the discipline has been immensely enriched, even if our conclusion must be that linguistic models cannot possibly play the role Lévi-Strauss hoped they would.

Since structuralism itself constitutes a conceptual structure, it would be naive to expect it to suffer any wholesale refutation. The anthropology we can now do will simply be part of a different enterprise, gaining from it even when directed against it. Lévi-Strauss once commented that it was the task of structuralism to find levels of reality which had a strategic value (1953b:284). If this is a self-justification, it also legitimates other approaches. Structuralism, as he has himself admitted, does not affect one's perception of concrete social relations (1960b:53). No doubt science should not be constrained by common sense, but where human beings are the subject matter of a science they themselves engage in, a perspective which presents its discoveries in terms which they can hardly recognize is in a strange position. Whatever the view of the 'subject' and 'meaning' in the structuralist universe, they are basic facts in other maps. Even if some conceptual systems regard them as errors, they must even there be accepted as 'true' errors. Whenever men speak about themselves, their errors have meaning; and as their errors are part of what they are they cannot be entirely false. There is a sense in which the nature of human action implies that the facts with which any human science is concerned are substantially constituted by ordinary human perceptions, In common with other recent trends, semantic anthropology assumes that these more ordinary terms of human self-understanding have a most strategic scientific value.

4 A Critique of some Recent Developments in American Linguistic Anthropology

One has only to mention names like Boas, Sapir, Kroeber, Hymes, to realize the important contribution the anthropological community in America has made to linguistics. In the period of 'taxonomic' linguistics anthropologists even led some of the developments, and much of the teaching of linguistics in the United States is still conducted by anthropologists. Perhaps it is because the idea of an integrated science of man has not fallen away there that the study of language continues to be central. Certainly no introductory textbook would be conceivable without a discussion of linguistics, which contrasts strikingly with the position in this country. None of the standard introductory works in British social anthropology has a chapter on language. Indeed, in the majority of cases, a British training normally brings the anthropologist into contact with linguistics for the first time in the course of preparation for fieldwork.

This chapter is not concerned with the purely descriptive linguistic work of American anthropology, but with evaluating recent contributions to the field of 'language, thought and culture' studies. Clearly it would be inconceivable to deal with anything like all the work which might be subsumed under even this label, so a few areas of growing interest have been selected in order to assess how valuable this type of link between anthropology and linguistics is. There is no consensus over the names of these developments — ethnographic semantics, the 'New Ethnography', ethnoscience, formal semantic analysis, cognitive anthropology, sociolinguistics, the ethnography of speaking, ethnolinguistics, are the most familiar — so excessive scrupulousness has not been exercised in distinguishing between the various trends.

It would be irresponsible at this time to dismiss any of these applications of linguistics as simply false trails. One must obviously judge by substantive results, and as some growths are little more than a decade old, programmatic articles in some cases still outweigh detailed studies. How detailed work will modify the approaches one cannot predict, but in view of the great enthusiasm which has been aroused — some see the developments as revolutionizing cultural anthropology and making it an empirical science of meaning (Goodenough 1956:195) — there is a pressing need to assess the results achieved so far, and to subject their assumptions to critical scrutiny.

So far, however, this work has met with more than the normal degree of British indifference to American anthropology. For us, language has attained what prominence it now has largely as a result of the idiosyncratic vision of Lévi–Strauss, not as a result of any linguistic anthropology. That these American trends do involve technical linguistics will presumably disqualify most British social anthropologists from making a positive contribution, but to date there has scarcely been any reaction at all. But an anthropological tradition which finds itself in transition between a functional and a semantic identity cannot avoid inquiring whether this work really does constitute a major semantic advance.

This task is the more necessary in that, besides praise, some of these growths have provoked angry outbursts from some American anthropologists. Some dislike their implied 'idealism' (Harris 1968:586ff.). Others find their triviality an*emic* and em*etic* (Berreman 1966). Obviously linguistic methods cannot possibly be a curative for all the ills of ethnography, but this extreme language hardly makes the point most effectively. Linguistics has made such dramatic advances of late that Hymes has suggested that the diffusion of the tools of modern linguistics may be the hallmark of the second half of the twentieth century (1962:100). In view of this prospect, any unreasoned detraction from moves which might lead this way would simply be irresponsible. Some of the criticisms offered below have been made by contributors to the field themselves, but despite a rapidly growing literature we still lack a general critical survey which gathers together these noticed deficiencies which so centrally affect the semantic value of the trends. This is the task undertaken below.

THE SAPIR–WHORF HYPOTHESIS

Most of the literature considered in this chapter has been published within the last fifteen years, but one must begin by returning to an earlier phase of American linguistic anthropology — to the suggestive work of Sapir and Whorf. No criticism of the field of 'language, thought and culture' would be conceivable without first mentioning their contribution. For although recent ethnographic semantics often fails to make clear its ties with this earlier period, it is certainly part of a tradition[1] and weaknesses found there are relevant when considering the latest developments.

Neither Sapir nor Whorf fitted the severely scientistic and restrictive anti–semantic climate of Bloomfieldian linguistics. Indeed, Whorf once declared that the quest for meaning was the very essence of the discipline (1956:79). Unfortunately, from their compressed essays it is not always easy to see exactly what they meant. As with so much other work connected with the thesis of linguistic relativity, one simply is not sure what is being claimed. There have been attempts to formalize the Sapir–Whorf hypothesis, but long after the deaths of its authors a conference meeting to evaluate it (Hoijer 1954 ed.) still could not produce consensus as to what the hypothesis was. Continued disagreement concerning its interpretation and validity seem assured.

Some of the basic ideas of linguistic relativism are reasonably clear. What is less certain is whether they imply all that they are commonly supposed to, and whether writers like Sapir and Whorf really believed them. A 'new principle of relativity' (Whorf 1956:214) was announced, for example, and language was said to determine perception, and to embody a metaphysics. Language was a creative symbolic organization — the Humboldtian idea of language as *energeia* — so speakers of different languages were not equivalent as observers. Reality was built up largely on the unconscious language–habits of the speaker (Sapir 1929:162). A speaker was therefore at the mercy of his language, for by virtue of its form being projected onto reality, he was predisposed to certain types of interpretation rather than others.

Sometimes, Sapir and Whorf definitely speak as if language played a determining role, but the consequences of this position appear to be untenable. Indeed, it does not seem logically possible to state the hypothesis in this strong form. If language were the determining factor, one would not be able to understand a second language in order to see that there was a 'lack of fit' between them. But it seems unlikely that they wished to maintain the relativist position in this radical form. Whorf, indeed, was deeply concerned with the problem of international understanding and perhaps wished to draw attention to the subject of mismatch simply in order to face it more realistically. In this way, we might see his speaker 'at the mercy' of his language as actually a caricature of traditional grammarians who could not free themselves from the perspectives of their own language (Percival 1968). Certainly his very notion of 'fashions of speaking' goes against the idea that there are specific correlations between culture and particular levels of linguistic organization (1956:158); and he once even stated explicitly that language was but 'superficial embroidery' on deeper processes of consciousness (ibid.:239). Sapir too spoke of language as the most autonomously organized aspect of culture, as a 'selected inventory' of experience, so again no determinism seems implied.

Experimental work on cross–cultural cognition seems to undermine extreme relativism (Lloyd 1972:40–4). It simply is not possible to make

61

those inferences from linguistic to non–linguistic culture which one should be able to if the hypothesis were correct. We cannot, for instance, infer the absence of perceptual discriminatory ability from the lack of a certain colour term. Nor, on a more general level, will the idea that there is a metaphysics in language bear close examination. If by this term is meant an articulate system of abstract propositions, the contention is absurd and obviously belied by the fact that the most diametrically opposed philosophical systems have been written in the same language. In any other sense of the term the issue tends rapidly to become one of mere popular impression. Many critics indeed still refuse to accept the Sapir–Whorf hypothesis as scientific and declare further discussion to be pointless until it is clarified (Black 1968:75). Others have regarded it as no more than unspectacular old–time ethnological philology, stressing that it has never received other than anecdotal illustration (Lounsbury, in Hoijer 1954 ed.:270;1969:4). Yet others regard it as a valuable thesis which has stimulated much empirical research, even if it is unclear whether the results confirm or refute it.

Some of these difficulties were probably unavoidable. Whorf's work, after all, was not based on prolonged fieldwork among the Hopi but on interviews with a native informant in New York. Yet points like this do not help us greatly. More suggestive, perhaps, is the view of Kroeber that there could be no final verdict because the hypothesis is true and false at different levels. What was needed, therefore, was a new framework altogether (in Hymes 1964 ed.:698). In short, we could entertain the idea that something is formally wrong with the whole approach. This shows itself, among other ways, in the mere fact that very often the only evidence for linguistic relativity are linguistic facts. There is then access to only one end of the suggested link, and language clearly cannot be an adequate test for a thesis about linguistic relativity.

One way of advance beyond Sapir–Whorf may be to take this difficulty seriously, and to suggest that the whole approach in 'language and culture' studies is wrong. A second strategy is to adopt limited relativism as a framework in which to seek for universals. Considerable diversity — in colour classification, for instance (Berlin & Kay 1969) — may mask invariant structures. The relativity theory of Einstein was similarly not relativistic: stress on different frames of reference can yield systems which transcend those particular frames. Here it is useful to remember how strongly the histories of linguistics and anthropology resemble each other in certain features (Casagrande 1963:281). The ethnocentrism of Victorian ethnology paralleled the dependence of comparative philology on the classical languages and Sanskrit. The relativism and functionalism of anthropology appeared in linguistics as the stress on the uniqueness of each language. Now in both disciplines there is an interest in universals. We should therefore stress that 'Whorfianism', which was certainly a provocative link between anthropology and linguistics, lay at the high point of relativism in both. It is therefore doubly appropriate that the whole area now be recast. There should be no more facile pronouncements on the relations of language and culture. This is why it is important that researches in ethnoscience, and so on, be not hostile to comparative work (Kay 1969:9,13). Certainly the relativism of earlier linguistic anthropology in America has now lost its linguistic foundations.

LANGUAGE IN SOCIETY

Those modern linguistic inquiries, such as sociolinguistics and the 'ethnography of speaking', which have aquired 'social foundations', are clearly important advances on the earlier 'language and culture' studies, even if they do not represent the radical departure for which one had wished. To a large extent the field has grown up because of the restricted interests of Chomskyan linguistics (Hymes 1971b:269–73). 'Competence', and the relation of linguistics to a study of the human mind, have been so stressed that much of what is legitimately regarded as 'knowing a language' — for instance, the ability to switch between languages in different cultural contexts — has been cast out as a problen for other disciplines to deal with. Such a linguistics works in a virtual sociological vacuum. Indeed, Chomsky once explicitly claimed that his theoretical interest was in the ideal speaker–hearer in a homogenous speech community (1965:3). No doubt multilingualism is found in an extreme form particularly in areas of rapid social change; but there is some truth in the view that as all languages comprise different dialects, registers, and so on, all situations are multilingual (Whiteley 1971). So much of the history of linguistics saw a stress on 'autonomy' that many now think it vital to rectify this deficiency by giving linguistics a strong social component (Hymes 1964:6–7, 41). For them it is a severely impoverished approach which does not regard knowledge of the relations of speech to social context as a part of linguistics. After all, when one speaks of 'acceptability', far more than grammatical considerations are relevant (id. 1972b:4).

No doubt a comparative ethnographic study of communication — how speech functions in different contexts in various cultures — could be very revealing (id. 1966:114, 158). And much work has already been done which shows, for instance, how language variations can be markers for aspects of social structure. We possess impressively detailed studies by scholars like Labov, and anthropologists will be familiar with the way in which speech registers status differences (Geertz 1960;Albert 1972) or demarcates ceremonial occasions (Rivière 1971a).

No one will deny that language can mark social categories, or the fact that choice in a manner of speaking may be a way of claiming and maintaining a certain social identity. If British anthropologists would include such data in their monographs it would be a gain. What is debatable is whether a new sub-discipline is required to handle such facts (it is true that some contributors like Fishman see the 'sociology of language' as only an 'area of convergence'), and whether this institutionalization, with its attendant 'closing off' effect, may not be a perspective of limited value from which to view them. Certainly there are emerging several features of sociolinguistic inquiry which, from the vantage point of semantic anthropology, are far from satisfactory.

In the first place, much work so far has been simple descriptive studies of linguistic diversity of an essentially correlational nature. Many would accept that sociolinguistics is chiefly concerned with 'the systematic co-variation of linguistic structure and social structure...and perhaps to show a causal relation in one direction or the other' (Bright 1966 ed.: 11).[2] But there are several weaknesses in this scheme. Language and social facts are normally too inextricably bound up together for correlational studies to be feasible; they are not sufficiently independent. At the same time, language and culture do not mirror each other. All instances of linguistic variability need not be indices of social diversity, and it would be absurd to add social components to all the details of linguistic behaviour. Language is *in itself* a highly complex organizational structure, so talk of reconstructing 'linguistic theory on a social basis' (Hymes 1972b: 2) may be very harmful. Linguists might reasonably fear that such a 'social basis' will be added only with a great loss in descriptive precision.

Such a danger is the more real in view of the frequently crude picture of social structure presented in some sociolinguistic studies, and the often crassly simple interpretation of the relation of speech to cultural context. Indeed, since these studies are so concerned with actual speech behaviour, they risk resuscitating the sort of functionalism of the more '*parole*'–natured traditions in social anthropology (Ardener 1971b: lxxvi), which would be a misfortune in view of the opportunity that attention to language gives us to transcend such a framework. Hymes, for instance, has stressed functional considerations as the starting point in sociolinguistic inquiry, and even sees the shift from 'autonomy' to a socially based linguistics as a transition from structure to function (1972b: 6,9). There is a place for such functional studies certainly, but it should also be recognized that a field growing out of the felt deficiencies of the Chomskyan tradition almost deliberately looks away from those paradigmatic structures which, in language as in other systems of human action, are vital to understanding the nature of the phenomena which the recorder of events — in this case speech behaviour — registers. The sociolinguist will not reach these by setting out the use of speech in different cultural contexts, or by correlating verbal and social variation.

Although sociolinguistics is still very much concerned with linguistic variation, many contributors to the field would certainly not accept that this sort of correlational study adequately defined their subject. This is particularly so in view of the marked increase in attention given to pidgins and creoles over the last few years. These languages, for so long the unwanted step-children of linguistics — indeed even fairly recently regarded by some linguists as 'degenerate' — are now claimed by some to possess considerable theoretical significance. In these languages one has in an extreme form the sort of interrelationships of language, culture and socio-historical processes (Tonkin 1971b) with which those interested in the sociology of language are concerned. DeCamp has suggested that if a genuine sociolinguistic theory emerges it will be heavily in the debt of pidgin and creole studies (in Hymes 1971 ed.: 14). Hymes has even expressed the hope that these researches will widen sociolinguistics into a general study of the maintenance, transmission and transformation of the social and symbolic order (ibid.: 5).

We shall have to wait to see whether in fact this field possesses such a theoretical potential, although a widening of sociolinguistics along these lines would clearly be a welcome advance. Whatever the future shape of sociolinguistics may be, these ambitions do raise an important general issue. If we are to deal adequately with the 'social and symbolic order', surely we need at least a semiological approach and not just an expanded sociolinguistics. Language, obviously, is not a complete inventory of culture, but always a selective metalanguage. As Mauss put it, there is always 'a divorce between linguistic forms and the substance of thought...because language is but one of the means of expression of collective thought and not the adequate expression of that thought itself' (1923: 125). Not all that is of cultural significance will be registered in language. Cultures will vary over how much they store in language. Some, for example, may have a very strong non-verbal inclination, embodying their collective categories in other sign systems. What is a 'matter of language for one culture may be a matter of gesture, plastic art, ritual for another' (Hymes 1966: 122). Language may universally store information in different systems of beliefs and values concerning these other symbolic forms, although clearly the value of language as a key here will vary from culture to culture. But if sociolinguistics were to block the way of a broader study of cultural signs it would be regrettable. Ethnography without linguistics may be blind, and linguistics without ethnography may be sterile, but we must also see the vital importance of recognizing that language is only one of culture's semantic systems. Linguistic anthropology must be less fruitful than a broader semiological framework: it could certainly never furnish an adequate basis for a semantic anthropology.

Hymes has valuably emphasized that anthropology has its own interests in speech, and so should formulate its own questions about it (1962:133). Unfortunately, his colleagues have not responded as warmly as one would have wished to this suggestion. In fact, at the moment the 'sociology of language' bears the rather disconcerting marks of an infant social science. Over the last decade the number of studies has grown enormously, jargon has proliferated, questionnaires and quantification have already appeared giving those precise answers to probably insignificant questions so typical of social science. The very way of framing investigations often seems to prevent the asking of just those questions which would shed light on the really important cultural facts, the result being an apparently detailed, but actually superficial comprehension.

A complicating factor here, undoubtedly, is the fact that multilingualism, on which sociolinguists have done so much research, invariably constitutes a serious social and political problem. Its involvement with issues of language planning and social engineering may easily divert the discipline from its descriptive and theoretical task and make it a tool of applied social science. The sociolinguist would then be, not so much a theoretician as a 'political commentator' (Webber 1973:35) — a state of affairs which, by tying inquiry to extrinsic interests, could well seriously impede the development of a fruitful anthropological study of language. Of course, this is not a necessary consequence, but the theoretical gains accruing from 'applied anthropology' should not lead us to entertain high expectations here either.

Possibly the 'sociology of language' will make a more useful contribution to the growth of a semantic anthropology by focusing rather more on emic matters. Hymes, for instance, has often urged that work be done on 'folk linguistics' — the beliefs about, and attitudes to, language in different cultures (1972a:39). Such phenomena, after all, are universal cultural facts, and an 'anthropology of language' must take seriously the point that people not only speak but also speak about language itself. It is strange, in view of the intense interest in ethnozoological domains and the like, that linguistic anthropologists should have so seldom explored the subject of cultural views about language (Hoenigswald 1966:17). For all the modern use of language and linguistic models to investigate classificatory systems, it seems to have been overlooked that language itself is a social fact and that one might therefore reasonably expect verbal activity to form such a symbolic structure. Indeed, there are some very clear demonstrations of how language as a system of collective representations shares the organizing principles of other symbolic systems (Gossen 1974:230). This being so, there is a concordance which gives language an even greater value in the investigation of symbolic forms.

Investigations of this type have not yet excited great interest, although valuable work has been done on 'oral literature'. Perhaps one reason for this is the fact that the literate/pre-literate divide is still surrounded by a host of prejudices, and still the subject for precipitate generalization (see J. Goody & Watt 1963). Now that communications technology has brought our own culture to a 'post-literate' phase, perhaps we shall see more clearly what consequences we can attribute to literacy itself, but we certainly cannot simply assume that it caused an intellectual revolution of such scale that we look in vain for abstract thought and so on in primitive cultures. Nor have we any warrant for thinking that other societies lack elaborate and insightful conceptions about language (Finnegan 1973). To take one instance, the Limba define themselves by language and are extremely interested in dialectal differences (id.1969a:63-4). Speech they regard as a basic social activity, and they are acutely aware of its 'performative' aspect. For them, to speak is to establish or maintain a social relationship (ibid.:72-4;1969b). It may even commonly be the case that in pre-literate societies such facts are well known, and language use seen as the paradigm of social exchange.

Such investigations rest on a rather different type of question from that normally found in sociolinguistic literature; but obviously a culture's view of its own and other languages must have a central place in any ethnographically based linguistics. We must know how a culture discriminates various types of verbal acts, and what classification of oral literature it possesses. Using our own terms like 'myth', 'religious poetry' or 'proverb', for example, may violate some crucial cultural distinctions. A more adequate anthropological study of language therefore has a basic import for the general problem of understanding another culture. We shall never know the size of the loss caused by the fact that the functionalist fieldworkers for the most part did not make the investigation of language in this sense a topic to be written up in their monographs. It may well be that we shall discover significant differences between cultures in their attitudes towards language and symbolism. Some cultures might have a strongly expressive bent, while others could well be highly pragmatic and instrumental. For these latter, of whom the Mandari are one, it would be an error not to emphasize the instrumental aspect of prayer and ritual (Buxton 1973:415-6).

That there are significant variations in views of language is clear from the history of our own culture. The attitude to language during the Enlightenment was not that of the Romantics of the early ninteenth century. Urban has generalized this point and spoken of high and low evaluations of language (1939:32) — two opposed views regarding the relation of language to reality. It is no coincidence that, at a time of grave crisis in Western history, philosophy should have so resolutely turned its attention to linguistic investigation. If conceptions concerning language do provide clues about a culture's relation to symbolic systems in general, then help will be available on some of the larger analytical problems of cultural interpretation. This will not be an adequate key on its own by any means, but to appreciate differences even in terms of features like relative instrumentality will be to have gained some insights. It is to be hoped that investigations of 'language in society' might develop in these anthropologically fruitful ways.

COGNITIVE ANTHROPOLOGY AND ETHNOSCIENCE
Some developments in recent American linguistic anthropology do not share the express discontent of sociolinguistics with the Chomskyan framework. Ethnoscience has even been called a 'competence' theory, in that it concerns models of knowledge (Werner 1969:350; Durbin 1966:25). Its aim is to elicit the rules underlying cultural action, and Tyler has argued that cognitive anthropology requires a rethinking of the concept of culture itself on the premiss that it does not refer to behaviour but to a deeper conceptual organization (1969 ed.:1-3, 13-14). This difference between these trends and sociolinguistics certainly exists; but we should be wary of using a Chomskyan terminology to describe it, for the very reason that so much of this work is based on the pre-Chomskyan taxonomic linguistics which was leaving that discipline at the same time as anthropologists were beginning to be attracted by it (Keesing 1972:299).

Behind ethnoscience, formal analysis and cognitive anthropology, lies the general inspiration of the scientific precision achieved by linguistics, and the belief that similar rigour is attainable in dealing with other cultural phenomena (Goodenough 1956:195). Undoubtedly, certain of these movements — the 'New Ethnography', for instance (Sturtevant 1964:99) — are very important. It is ironical that despite the lack of theoretical interest in language in British social anthropology, we have possibly shown a greater concern for 'knowing the language' as part of our fieldwork than has been the case in America, where the tradition of short periods of field research has had a greater popularity. Consequently, the new American stress on detailed ethnographic inquiry is a gain — especially the stress on 'emic' (culturally meaningful) units. It is obviously right to point to the fact that in ethnography it is important not only to get correct answers, but also to ask significantly framed questions (Frake 1964:132). This explains the emphasis placed upon 'validity' in much of this literature. Indeed, it is a useful protest against traditional ethnological categories, rather like the 'rethinking' of British anthropology in the 1960's (Kay 1969:8). There is also certainly some resemblance between the 'ethnography of speaking' and that linguistically orientated ethnomethodology which has proved to be such an important advance in sociology.

Even so, such a single-minded concern with rigour and validity may be attended by grave risks. Already the insularity of cognitive anthropology is stark: reference is hardly ever made to the work of Lévi-Strauss, or to the British work on symbolic classification. Such evidence of sect development within linguistic anthropology is no more acceptable than that 'closed systems' mentality which excluded language from functional anthropology. Especially troubling here is that some of the pronouncements about detail and rigour seem to enshrine an unrealistic vision of ethnographic omniscience. The idea that access to the deep cultural rules which generate social events will give the anthropologist the knowledge to act like a culture bearer is a nonsense. An anthropologist cannot even 'know the language' like a native speaker,[3] let alone culture as a whole. Of course it is desirable to aim at descriptive methods which prevent the gross discrepancy of interpretations which have sometimes strikingly occurred. But it is harmfully illusory to think there is a method available which will provide the anthropologist with the same understanding as a native, or permit complete replicability as between two anthropologists working in the same culture.

A more serious shortcoming, from the viewpoint of a discipline wishing to concern itself with semantic issues, is the impoverished view of the data to be found in much of this work. Quite irrespective of whether a label like 'cognitive' can be justified, one may doubt the value of such a narrowly conceived enterprise. That multidimensionality of the social, which must be recognized if there are to be advances in anthropological understanding, is often lacking, and no gain in rigour can offset this loss. That richness of the British work on symbolic classification — largely due, no doubt, to its links with the French sociological school — is absent in the American literature. Indeed, its restricted perspective is implicit in the very name 'ethnoscience'. One should seriously query whether construing animal symbolism as 'ethnozoology' really does represent an increase in exactitude, whether regarding ritual practices in a primitive society as 'ethnomedicine' may not so much mislead as to the nature of the activity as constitute the very opposite of cultural validity. After all, one seriously fails to grasp the total semantics of exchange if one thinks of Mauss' work on the gift (1969) as an essay on 'ethnoeconomics'. Sturtevant has himself suggested that the term 'ethnoscience' is something of a misnomer (1964:99), though he does not elaborate why this is so. But this is a very important point, and the issue it involves contains the seeds of that suspicion that some of the basic features of the approach may impede understanding rather than the reverse.

Few anthropologists would now accept the thesis that categories of collective thought are causally generated by social life (Durkheim & Mauss 1963). On the other hand, it is of vital importance to appreciate the all-pervasiveness of the social in primitive thought. Such categories are replete with meanings from many dimensions: seemingly innocent taxonomies carry a 'heavy social load' (M. Douglas 1973 ed.: 11). Therefore one of the greatest dangers which semantic anthropology must avoid is an over-reaction to that functionalist reduction of meaning by completely severing meaning from its social context. One must escape the functional framework without forgetting the social location of meaning. Douglas' work has recently become more Durkheimian in its stress on the link between symbolism and social structure; and she has pointed out the semantic failings of her earlier asociological structural analysis of the abominations of Leviticus, which rested content with discovering taxonomic principles (1966: 55) and making no reference to social experience. She now declares that is it quite unacceptable to conduct such an analysis without showing the relationship to the social life of the people who think with such a category system (1970b: 303). It is certainly a useful corrective to have it stressed that a classificatory system is lived and used although we should also be wary lest this turn back into an advanced form of functionalism.

It is a well known fact that in primitive cultures the nature/culture distinction is often stated by a whole homologous series of discriminations from other symbolic systems — sexual opposition, colour contrasts, orientational symbols, and so on. By such means, a social message about the difference between insiders and outsiders, for instance, can be expressed and elaborated by several orders of symbolism, the valency of each expression being supplemented by its concordance with the others. Colour categories in primitive societies (Conklin 1955) in this way invariably embody far more than colour information. Similarly, the classifying in Karam thought of the cassowary in a taxon of its own rather than as a bird, is not a comment on its appearance but a symbolic way of pin-pointing the important social relationship of 'cross-cousins' (Bulmer 1967). The category 'cassowary' is thus multi-dimensional in a very important sense. To have approached the problem as one of 'ethnozoology', with complicated social metaphors added, would have been a semantic nonsense. An ethnographic semantics which regards words as labels for pieces of reality and forgets the immensely complex symbolic load of primitive categories (Rosaldo 1972: 83) will not make much of a contribution to semantic anthropology. Animal categories have been shown to be homologous, not only with kinship categories, but even with the physical structure of the house (Tambiah 1969). What one might have regarded as discriminations in a domain, therefore, are actually partial refractions of larger socio-conceptual schemes.

Similar criticisms can be made of 'ethnomedicine'. It has frequently been observed that the disease categories of primitive societies rarely overlap with those of Western science (Frake 1961), but it is extremely questionable whether these discrepancies can be adequately registered as the difference between medicine and ethnomedicine. In cultures where the 'personal idiom' is so pervasive, 'illness' is so intertwined with social values that the term 'ethnomedicine' will obscure the symbolic weight that such notions as 'symptom' carry. As far as symptoms and cures are concerned, Mandari are prepared to incorporate knowledge from their neighbours as well as Western principles (Buxton 1973: 324). But while theirs is not a 'closed system', it is nonetheless built around stable 'symbolic centres' (ibid.: 326). In a similar way, the Safwa taxonomy of disease and cure is related to a classification of social relationships (Harwood 1970). But then the analytic problem arises of the propriety of using aetiological categories as translational equivalents at all.

Some anthropologists have taken the often insightful and effective beliefs and practices in primitive cultures regarding psychosomatic disturbances as evidence that primitive thought can be very closely compared to Western scientific models (Horton 1967: 53). But our culture is so typified by large areas of socially autonomous thought — that is by scientific maps languaged by one-dimensional discourse — that this parallel is not very happy. Even though there are aspects of Western medicine which have a social component, we could never say as Turner does of Lunda medicine, that healing procedures 'are governed by the same principles and modes of classification as their religious rites and moral concepts' (1964b: 300). Anthropologists must clearly exert themselves rather more to find the conceptual resources required for translating this type of multi-dimensional category which is so basic a feature of primitive thought. Whatever gains there have been from ethnoscience, it simply shirks this task and so falls far short of semantic adequacy.

One of the assumptions of ethnoscience is that a culture possesses a set of articulate domains. In assessing the possible value of this development, criticisms made of 'semantic field' theory in general are therefore highly relevant. There has been great enthusiasm about this intersection of Saussurian structuralism and von Humboldt's idea of language as *energeia* (Ullmann 1972: 370); but whatever its fruitfulness, there are some dangers which should not be overlooked. There may firstly be a temptation to regard domains as more articulate than they really are. Ullmann, for instance, has expressed doubts as to whether the structural

71

approach in semantics could possibly reach the same degree of exactitude as has been attained with other levels of linguistic organization (1958:6). It seems highly unrealistic to regard the whole of a vocabulary as a mosaic of tightly structured fields, which is an important reservation when some anthropologists have spoken of regarding the whole lexicon from a structural point of view (Lounsbury 1968:224). Native taxonomies are neither exhaustive nor strictly hierarchical (Conklin 1962:423) — a fact to which should be accorded more import than is commonly the case. We should not forget, either, that the very insistent pressing for data by ethnographers intent on discovering articulate domains may yield a structural fullness which comes into being only under those abnormal conditions. In the ordinary course of social life the significance of a concept may be located precisely in its ambiguity: the most vital parts of social knowledge may lie in relatively unstructured areas between two taxonomies.

We may of course expect there to be highly articulated areas in all cultures, but we should always regard their location as a matter for detailed research. There is little point in stressing 'emic' units if domains themselves are unthinkingly thrust on other cultures. It is relevant that linguists who have pioneered the structural approach in semantic inquiry (Lyons 1969) commonly begin with a basic knowledge of the field they investigate. The anthropologist is in quite the opposite position. Certainly some of the domains we regard as 'natural' will have such a wide cross-cultural recognition as to qualify as universals. But the problem of where the areas of articulateness and relative lack of structure will be found in each culture must be approached in an empirical manner.

But there is still that difficulty noted in the case of the Sapir-Whorf hypothesis. In so stressing lexical domains one may forget the extent to which ethnographic semantics is dependent on language in the narrow sense, and thereby overlook the fact that linguistic registration of conceptual fields may be very partial (Kay 1969:2, 2n). Studies by ethnographic semanticists themselves have shown that 'covert categories' — a notion suggested by Whorf — often have great taxonomic importance (Berlin *et al.* 1968). The significance of this type of consideration can well be appreciated for a subject like ritual. There is no reason why the units of ritual action need all have corresponding terms in language, so a linguistically based approach here would be seriously defective. We have to appreciate that inter-lingual translation is only a part of the process of anthropological interpretation. There is also the problem of rendering in one's own language symbolic forms which are not fully expressed in language in the culture one is studying. Many of the shortcomings of Turner's analyses of Ndembu ritual symbolism derive precisely from insufficient caution over this difficulty. By failing to distinguish between linguistic and ritual signs he too hastily unpacks the latter into language, producing heaps of polysemous symbols (Ardener 1971b:xlii-iii). Clearly, 'semiotic transmutation' (Jakobson 1959:23) is a vital part of semantic studies, but it is missing from the horizon of linguistic anthropology.

Attention also needs to be given to rectifying that deficiency of cognitive anthropology which springs, no doubt, from its interest in 'competence', that setting out abstract taxonomies without indicating the nature of the cultural life in which the thought they embody is located is of very limited value for understanding another society. In this respect the British work on symbolic classification, which constituted such an area of advance during the last decade, is also very inadequate. We do not want a functional account of knowledge here, but some notion of 'contextual grammar' by which we can give a more discriminating account of the relation of thought and action. It may well be that in some societies—those with prescriptive marriage rules, for instance—a fundamental duality in social structure (wife givers/wife takers) may lend a thoroughly binary character to the whole symbolic order. But as basic as the principle of complementary opposition may be, symbolic grammar never exists at just one level, and so to set out a series of homologous pairs could at best be only a start. Whiteley's linguistic study of Gusii colour symbolism, for example, shows that a colour may have several symbolic values: semantic associations present in a ritual field are different or simply absent in another context (1973:146, 157).[4]

We cannot know how complex this contextual grammar will be. Certainly context here cannot be taken in a behaviourist sense. Conceptual structures themselves may act syntactically by affecting the principles of symbolic association, valency, equivalence, and opposition of other structures. These relations have been underemphasized in much work on symbolic classification, although the fact that they have semantic consequences is obvious. After all, one of the basic errors of the Victorian intellectualists was not to see that concepts which were associated with each other under certain circumstances could well have no particular link under others (Evans-Pritchard 1973:140). Consequently it is not a sufficient basis for structural deduction merely to establish the pervasiveness of binary opposition. Thus, although the cumulative evidence in Needham's analysis of Nyoro symbolism is impressive (1967), we cannot rule out the possibility that his conclusions may be unwarranted because there are at work contextual principles which are not evident in the available ethnographies. Such factors might not only alter symbolic associations, they could actually restrict the principle of binarism to limited semantic fields. One could not then set out the dualisms as if they formed one system, and homology would allow inference only between pairs in certain symbolic sub-sets. Binarism might well formally unify a set, but other syntactic principles could well fragment such a system. We could even envisage contextual factors recomposing the membership of different sub-sets.

Studies in dual symbolic classification have been the victims of much misunderstanding (Needham 1973), but they will need to be much improved if anthropology secures a more semantic identity. The British work, since it studies collective representations and not individual thinking, has never aimed to be 'cognitive' (ibid.: xix-xx). By contrast, American ethnographic semantics, whilst sharing the sort of weakness just discussed, has an added problem, since it does specifically construe the activity of investigating the systems of meaning by which a people organizes its world as getting 'cognitively salient' findings (Kay 1969: 1). But to set out a taxonomy as the 'cognitive' organization of a culture obviously raises the query as to whose knowledge this really represents (Goodenough 1965: 259), and the general issue of the extent to which what we call culture is shared.

It seems quite reasonable to assume that two individuals in a culture could have significantly different views about a taxonomy, or even that one individual might have more than one version. When anthropologists have talked of systems of thought or symbolic structures, they seem to have taken for granted cultural homogeneity. This may be the result of some prejudice about the wholly socialized nature of primitive thought, but whatever its source it constitutes a serious ethnographic deficiency. Consideration of socialization might almost lead one to predict diversity. For instance, in a stratified society one would not expect all to perceive the social structure in the same way. There are several other loci besides hierarchy where one might expect variation of this sort. Recent work on the 'problem of women', for example, has shown how anthropologists have tended to construct symbolic systems out of 'male models', analytically leaving out half the population (Ardener 1972). Because women are a 'muted' group, they may tend to express their self-identity not directly in language, but in other symbolic forms which the investigator has not accorded the import they deserve.

This sort of analytical difficulty we could take right down to the level of the individual. There is no omniscient informant who could impart data about his culture from no particular viewpoint. It seems entirely reasonable to suggest that there are believers and sceptics, or philosophical and pragmatic types as Radin argued (1953), in all societies. We cannot assume that literacy/pre-literacy correlates with the presence or absence of individualism, the secular outlook, or abstract thought. Conceivably all societies have their literalists and their symbolists — 'twins are birds' may mean different things to two Nuer, just as to a group of Melanesians *mana* may mean all the things that diverse ethnological theories said it did. An anthropologist encounters not a culture but particular human beings who are liable to have different views about their society. We cannot generate 'culture' simply by erasing all these differences. American linguistic anthropology, for all its talk of psychological salience, has not produced a more adequate framework for handling these issues than any other anthropological tradition.

FORMALISMS AND SEMANTICS

One of the recent ways in which anthropology and linguistics have been linked in America is in formal analysis. I shall concentrate on its use in kinship studies, since it is upon kinship terminologies that most such work has been done, though even here analyses are hardly numerous. Many have been impressed by the elegance and precision of these works, which were almost the first to apply linguistically derived techniques. Kinship, however, might well be a special type of domain, so that a successful application of, for example, componential analysis here would be no grounds for thinking that similar results could be attained with other cultural phenomena. But the value of the formal approach even in the kinship field has been greatly exaggerated, especially when we point out its specifically semantic shortcomings.

Kinship has often been regarded as the very basis of primitive societies — which has some truth in view of its 'totality'. However, formal analysis deals only with nomenclature, and whilst this bears some relationship to the way kinship actually works in a society, it may be slight and very variable. The rigour of formal methods, in other words, is achieved by a loss of the 'social semantics' of kinship. Colby's comment that componential analysis has contributed more to semantics than to cultural understanding (1966:15) is therefore rather revealing. If anthropology aims at greater semantic insight in order to attain a better understanding of culture, then a 'semantic' contribution which can be opposed to 'cultural understanding' can hardly attract us much. There is good reason, in fact, to regard these linguistic approaches as far more theories about scientific description than about culture or meaning.

This view must be coupled with the fact that while ethnographic semantics aims at the culturally significant, the very procedures of formal analyses seem to create a framework more hostile to this 'emic' goal than less technically explicit methods. The aim is to construct the 'inner form' of a kinship system (Hammel 1965 ed.:3) after employing the genealogical method to collect all the terms which belong to the universe of kinship (Goodenough 1956:198). From the system, the components ('dimensions of contrast') constituting the domain are extracted. Yet, as

75

these principles need not be lexical, there is clearly the possiblity that culturally familiar components like generation or sex will be given an analytical role. Moreover, there is the initial supposition that kinship is a domain at all. Because the bounding problem is so difficult, ethnocentrism must be a constant source of danger. It is not only a term like 'uncle' which we cannot assume to be universal. Genealogy may simply be a part of our particular kinship ideology, and 'kinship' itself need not be a cultural universal.

There is grave risk, therefore, that along with methodological enthusiasm may go a severe lack of 'model consciousness'. This well reveals itself in the way the results of formal analyses are interpreted. In his paper on Crow and Omaha systems, for instance, Lounsbury concludes that the analyses 'predispose us rather strongly in favour of an "extensionist" theory of kinship systems' (1964:243). As formalism thus supports Malinowski's position that kinship is basically genealogical and family-centred, he dismisses Leach's symbolic analysis to the Trobriand category '*tabu*' as totally erroneous (Lounsbury 1965; Leach 1958). But the 'results' of Lounsbury's study prove nothing since his conclusions only replicate the form of the assumptions underlying the analysis itself. Moreover, if we are to accept that the approach is genuinely semantic, it is not enough for Lounsbury to speak about accounting for a system with as few postulates as possible, or to say that a combination of simple rules make formal sense of the system as essentially genealogical, or that the most elegant results are obtained when the analysis is based on such assumptions.

This objection is strengthened when one realizes some of the other restrictions which accompany formal analysis. All the terms in a domain are assumed to have one feature in common, and for the purposes of the analysis each is given a basic non-connotational definition which both makes it a member of the set and also distinguishes it from all the others. But kinship words like others have many meanings, as those who do formal analyses are well aware (Scheffler & Lounsbury 1971:2), although they are not taken into consideration. In the Iroquois system, for example, the term for 'grandmother' also means 'moon'; yet Lounsbury argues that the structural analysis of semantic fields must exclude metaphors (1962:1807; Goodenough 1965:198), since they are merely extensions from the basic field.

This view of metaphor is highly contentious; and since metaphor is so clearly important in cultural life one would expect it to have gained rather more prominence in the work of anthropologists than it has done. Recent studies (Fox 1971) have indeed shown such a symbolic idiom to be absolutely fundamental in some kinship systems, but our ability to handle such a concept in general remains inadequate.[5] The extensionist view adopted by Lounsbury strangely duplicates in a semantic realm the sort of ethnocentric error enshrined in the ego-centric approach to kinship in general, since it regards metaphor essentially as a 'mother's brother' in a litero-centric view of meaning. As we now see that the mother's brother is only a complicating addition when the basic unit of the system is not correctly identified, a similar perspective might suggest a more fruitful approach to metaphor. Just as the mother's brother is a basic part of the alliance structure which secures the exchange of women, so instead of regarding metaphors as additional elements in literal domains we could regard them as fundamental parts of larger semantic fields — perhaps even those with the role of exchange of meaning between two fields. Since most words do participate in several semantic areas, this suggests we might make metaphor central rather than peripheral.

Whatever the value of this view, one should recognize that there are already in existence approaches to kinship which far more deserve the label 'semantic' than do the linguistically inspired formal analyses. For well over a decade, Needham has been conducting a series of 'total structural analyses' of societies with prescriptive alliance rules. Such an effort has not been intended as a contribution to the subject of kinship, but rather as an elaboration of the thesis of Durkheim and Mauss that there is concordance between social and symbolic structure. He has suggested that this link may vary in intensity from a high level in those societies he has so closely studied, to a low level in societies with cognatic kinship (1960b: 105). The former here have a crucial status, since it is possible to treat 'kinship' as a refraction of a larger cultural classification, where indeed the 'totality' of the phenomenon is equivalent to its non-existence. Not suprisingly, such a project has now culminated in the analytical dissolution of the subject of kinship itself (Needham 1971b: 4–5).

This is a vital advance for several reasons. One is that it makes evident that a semantic identity will not be achieved so long as the basic shape of our subject matter remains the same. Our transition will require the territory to be radically recast. In such a move the very 'objects' with which the formalists work — 'unilineal', 'matrilineal', 'Iroquois system', etc — may well all disappear. Marriage, for instance, has been redefined as just one refraction of the 'total syntax' relating the categories male and female (Rivière 1971b). These are the sorts of steps which it will be important to consider if we are to talk with justification about anthropological semantics. Formal analysis excludes and ignores so much that we find we are not concerned with meaning at all. And it is pointless to pretend that more studies will rectify initial methodological problems, since, as the procedure leads away from semantic considerations, increased ingenuity would only make the deficiencies more glar-

77

ing. Formalization, besides, is a conversion which expresses a phenomenon in a language with which few anthropologists feel easy (Korn & Needham 1970). Essentially it is a species of translation which makes the subject less accessible rather than more. Moreover, once the analysis has been performed, the conclusions still have to be converted back to ordinary language. No one will deny that the efforts of the formalists have been interesting, but we might feel that all this expenditure of energy is not justified by the importance of the results. And, in any case, the formalists have still to show how their work makes for an advance in our understanding of social life (Needham 1971a:xxxi).

Finally we can return to the difficulty discussed with respect to ethnoscience, namely the employment of linguistic models to expose 'psychological reality'. Some have argued that one must aim at cognitive salience if the formalist approach is to be labelled semantic at all (Wallace 1965:230). But if we take only componential analysis it is clear that several solutions can normally be produced. It is not obvious whether psychological validity can be attributed to any one of these, and if so, how one is to choose between them (Burling 1964) — a difficulty which remains even if one could rule out certain of the formally possible solutions. If 'cognitive' in the expression 'cognitive anthropology' is warranted, we have to insist on some distinction between 'God's Truth' and 'hocus-pocus'. Psychological validity must be established independently of the analysis itself: predictive success, elegance, economy, and so on, are not enough. Indeed, research has shown that sometimes a complex schema is the more culturally appropriate model (Burling 1965). The general problem here is far more complicated than anthropologists have allowed. The meaning of 'psychological reality' itself seems to vary between disciplines. For some anthropologists it may be a matter of codes, but in developmental and cognitive psychology the concept of mind is altogether different (R. Brown, in Romney & D'Andrade 1964 eds:251). If anthropology is not, and has no means of, tackling 'thinking' as it is studied there, it is difficult to know what the contributors in these modern anthropological trends are aiming at.

The short history of anthropological formalism in America is itself revealing on this issue. For the last decade, the stress has been increasingly on formal solutions and less on psychological reality (Wallace 1965:229). Some now regard 'cognitive saliency' as the goal least likely to be reached by ethnographic semantics: and, as some grant this concept the same sort of status as the mythical frictionless plane in physics (Tyler 1969), perhaps it is now realized that the goal was always obscure. Clearly the new linguistic trends have not solved the basic epistemological problems of anthropological understanding as was hoped (ibid.:78n14). Indeed, there are those who claim that what anthropology can gain from linguists is their attitude to description — the effort of just formulating rules to fit data and generate more, without any concern over the psychological reality of these rules at all (Burling 1969:819, 825-6).

As was the case with Lévi-Strauss' work, it seems an inescapable conclusion that American anthropologists have also pressed linguistic models and techniques into tasks they cannot really perform, For many, ethnographic semantics is now only a bore. And cognitive anthropology, having failed, now produces erroneous and out-of-date descriptions of the nature of models in linguistics. After all, whatever the difficulty involved in the claim, it is a part of Chomskyan epistemology that linguistics is of relevance to psychology, even that linguistics is a branch of cognitive psychology. Part of his stress on explanatory adequacy is precisely the feeling that a scientific linguistics should be able to decide between competing descriptions. If anthropologists employing formal methods are unable to do this we might wonder, not only what the term 'cognitive' means, but also what 'rigour' means. Much linguistic anthropology has been inspired by the precision of linguistics; but if formal analyses do yield rigorous results, it seems not to have been asked whether such a rigour is one of any importance or relevance. We need to ask what human thought and action are like before we know what sort of exactitude to aim for.[6] We need to look far more closely at the topics with which anthropology is concerned, for only then will it become clear what we want our relationship with language to do, and where we shall most likely find in the many possible links those of most help in dealing with such a subject matter.

AMERICAN LINGUISTIC ANTHROPOLOGY: EVALUATION AND REORIENTATION

The sort of criticisms we have made in this chapter clearly illustrate that a large gulf separates linguistic and semantic anthropology. The sort of semantic deficiency we have discussed above makes it plain that a discipline concerned with meaning will not obtain a sufficient basis from the type of link with linguistics so prominent in the American work. Naturally there will be a place for technical linguistic skills in semantic investigations, but semantic anthropology is language-based in a broad and flexible way rather than linguistics-based. Indeed, to rectify the sort of shortcomings discussed above we need to go to a different sort of literature—that by linguistic philosophers rather than linguists. We can suggest something of the nature of semantic anthropology, therefore, to conclude this chapter, by showing how this other scholarly tradition makes good some of the leading deficiencies we have noted of the recent American trends.

Anthropological inquiry is, whether this is explicitly recognized or not, at all stages a matter of translation — and the translation of culture, not just of language. It is therefore of some import that in all the literature of ethnographic semantics—supposedly a major semantic breakthrough—there is scarcely any discussion of the complexities of translation at all (Colby 1966:14). Nor, somewhat ironically, has the notion of 'ethnography' received the attention it requires (Tonkin 1971a). The ethnographic basis of anthropology is a highly complex personal experience, as the more autobiographical classics of the subject reveal so well. But those contributors to linguistic anthropology rarely comment on the fact that their understanding is made possible by the setting up of a personal relationship with members of another culture. Indeed, their familiar expressions like 'eliciting data' and 'valid frameworks' seem quite likely to obscure completely what objectivity in their work means. Describing an approach as an effort to 'wring a small body of linguistic data dry' (G. Williams 1968:14) simply disguises the nature of anthropological inquiry.

A second major shortcoming was noted in discussing ethnoscience. Anthropology studies what Wittgenstein called 'forms of life' (1953: para. 23) — that is, complexes of thought, language and action in a shared cultural context. We cannot approach social meaning as if it were framed in rarefied theoretical systems. This is the value of Wittgenstein's stress on the relation between meaning and use, his insistence that to grasp the point of human speech we must site it amidst the rest of human activities (1969: para. 229). Social semantics are to be understood in the life of society, not in lifeless taxonomies: we are dealing with 'practical knowledge', which is based on theories of both formal and informal kinds which are themselves parts of the life of that society. And here it is important to realize that the process of communication between one person and an inquiring anthropologist is itself a cultural situation which will be governed by a set of cultural rules. This situation of exchange is itself a social episode of whose nature the ethnographer should be aware. Boredom, fear, resentment, and so on, may generate new facts in these situations. Perhaps what is said may have been intended simply to satisfy and remove an alien presence. We should not forget — and the linguistic anthropologists have not studied these complications or made them explicit — that while the anthropologist is theorizing about native activity, the native is equally theorizing about the anthropologist's purposes and actions. These anthropologists are striving for scientific rigour; but such a set-up is clearly unlike anything which occurs in the physical sciences.[7]

Anthropology deals essentially with cultural facts which occupy a region between pure theory and mere behaviour. It was towards the second pole that functionalists erred in defining away meaning by reducing it to social process. Some of the trends in recent American linguistic anthropology approach far too closely the first pole, thereby losing a vital dimension of the subject matter. The relative strength of these two affinities of social knowledge will vary from situation to situation. But some general indication of its nature can be given by remembering that, when we say language is a social institution, we are stating that language is a multi-purpose structure which is part of a total cultural system of communication. Language is not only the embodiment of 'knowledge' in the narrow sense, but a hightly complex and heterogeneous system capable of performing many tasks. To counter some of the weaknesses of the American writings, we can look to the work of linguistic philosophers on this point and remind ourselves of some essential features of ordinary social communication.

It was one of the important emphases in the work of Austin that a philosopher's interest should not be in language alone, but in the total 'speech act' in its cultural setting (1962: 147). Language use then becomes part of a more general theory of human action (Searle 1971 ed.: 16-17). Such action exists on many different levels of formality, with language merely a part of a larger conventional pattern. Some meanings are transparent; others are hidden in a complex set of rules. Some conventions are stated in language; others are known yet not explicitly stated. To use Ryle's terms, certain cultural areas are regions of 'knowing that': they receive explicit linguistic formulation. But there is also much in the life of society which depends on 'knowing how', for which no ready system of rules is available. This does not make it 'behaviour' rather than 'action', for even without definite rules we are still dealing with essentially conventional phenomena. These facts about communication force us, if not to a specifically semiological viewpoint, then at least far beyond language. There are some conventions which are fully unpacked linguistically; but so much in social interaction — including perhaps its basic characteristics — forms but a tacit background. The nature of the human powers which such facts reveal will doubtless some day be explained by other sciences, but if they are 'givens' for anthropologists that should not prevent our seeing that they lend the realm of human action certain logical characteristics. It is a major failing that so much linguistic anthropology does not consider this linguistic complexity of natural human communication with which we are all familiar.

We can see the importance of setting language in its social context by imagining an alien anthropologist trying to understand a culture solely from inadequate literary sources. If such a person were concerned with our own society, for example, he would encounter statements like 'A thought struck me', 'I was beside myself with joy', 'It's raining cats and dogs'. With such linguistic evidence, the anthropologist might be tempted to conclude that we had a kinetic view of the intellect, a dogma about bi-presence, and that we were obviously impermeable to experience. Of course, all these inferences would be absurd. These figurative expressions do not mislead their speakers, but one must understand the conventions of such constructions before one knows what 'evidence' language contains. And to have this grasp is part of what it is to know a language, and being able to employ it in the right contexts is part of belonging to a culture. Although we readily appreciate these facts and complexities as regards our own language, anthropologists seem less able to remember such commonplaces when dealing with a different culture.

In a related respect too, the work of linguistic philosophers on the logic of ordinary language is a useful counter to those strivings we have noted in much linguistic anthropology for an undefined rigour. It is with the resources of ordinary language that natives communicate ideas with the anthropologist and with each other; and it has been stressed that natural languages in fact have no strict logic and are not governed by strict rules. Austin has well shown that ordinary language contains some highly complex yet nonetheless organized conceptual fields, but he doubted that there would be present one overall coherent system (1956: 62). Again, no linguist would deny that there are many regular features in language; yet, as they could well be more orderly than they in fact are, Weinreich has proposed a principle of 'limited sloppiness' (1963: 190) to describe their composition.

One of the explanations for such a feature is certainly that language is a social institution that has not been *constructed* but has grown in the same sort of way that others have. The heterogeneity of its structure is therefore scarcely suprising, especially when we remember that stating facts is only one of the tasks of language alongside asking questions, performing actions, giving orders, raising emotions, and so on. The interests of logical positivists in the elimination of ambiguity from language would have led to a language which was 'ideal' only in a technical sense. It would be 'as clear and transparent as glass, but also as brittle' (Waismann 1968: 23). A calculus governed by exact rules is simply not a more rigorous form for a natural language to take: it just would not function if constructed in such a way. Most of our leading concepts have blurred edges (Wittgenstein 1953:para. 71), but this is a vital and subtle imprecision. A speaker of a language is aware of such vagueness; and there is no significant sense in which we can call such a characteristic defective, since there is no general standard of exactitude with which to compare it. It may well be true that in view of modern developments in logic we should not underestimate the complexity that formalisms can achieve, but we cannot usefully regard ordinary languages as more or less inadequate approximations to such systems since they have altogether different functions.

Because artificial languages are syntactically rich but semantically poor as compared with natural languages (Wilden 1972: 163, 168), we have good general grounds for doubting the value of formal analyses in a shift towards a semantic identity. Problems of synonymy and contradiction which are soluble for formal systems are highly problematic for natural languages. Indeed logic developed largely in relation to artificial systems and has only recently begun to concern itself with ordinary language. We have only to think of the diversity of employment in ordinary language of a term like 'is' — 'two plus two is four', 'God is good', 'rain is wet', 'black is beautiful' — to wonder whether any logical systematization could adequately deal with the intricate semantic overlaps and differences between them. Some have expressed the hope that generative semantics may help to establish the structure of our 'natural logic' (Lakoff 1972); but it is not clear that these post-Chomskyan developments will produce any greater semantic insights than their predecessors.

By contrast, Waismann's work is highly suggestive on these issues. He has stressed the 'elasticity' of ordinary language and the 'open textured' nature of its concepts (1968: 42). Logicians have typically envisaged a concept as a clearly bounded space—yet our notions have such ragged edges that the meanings of words overlap. Natural concepts thus participate in one another. Such a complex and ever changing structure possesses semantic spaces which our logics cannot adequately map. The logical spaces of natural languages, for instance, are not of the two-valued kind, and hence Aristotelian logic cannot register the contours of our ordinary thought (ibid.: 80). Our natural logic is indeed well illustrated by the very complexity of the modes of action of our terms 'true' and 'false': the subtle semantics of ordinary speech is conveyed in expressions like 'too true', 'barely true', 'half true', 'true enough', and so on. Just as we now know that Euclidean geometry is a less accurate representation of 'real' space than modern systems which challenged the classical axioms, it may well be that similar radical rethinking will be required if we are to map more efficiently the semantic spaces and structure of ordinary social exchange.

Such reminders as these are valuable when so many of the recent trends in linguistic anthropology have aspired to some general idea of rigour, and when they have so stressed logical articulateness. This work is thus reminiscent of those scientistic phases in 'constructionist' philosophy earlier in this century, and it is important to see that philosophy has now acquired other interests which are of far more relevance to anthropologists who work with and through natural languages. Since we are concerned with knowledge and communication in different 'forms of life', to overstress rigour at the expense of looseness and complexity is simply to put oneself on the path to an inexact precision. There are routes towards a more sensitive handling of meaning which are the very opposite of those recommended by linguistic anthropologists. Perhaps part of the difficulty has been that we have tended to be influenced too much by exact and specialized thinking, forgetting that ordinary thought is related to social formations, sets of emotions and values, and social action. Anthropologists in a post-functionalist situation must not forget that the 'knowledge' and 'meaning' which interest them are multi-dimensional social phenomena. The shift from 'function' to 'meaning' is not one where a semantic focus displaces a social one. In any adequate semantic anthropology the full social dimensions of the subject matter it handles cannot be omitted.

II Explorations in Semantic Anthropology

5 Ordinary Language and Human Action

Part two of this book consists in a series of semantic explorations of particular anthropological problems; but as semantic anthropology rests upon a certain conception of the nature of human action, it is important to begin by making some general philosophical remarks about the characteristics which the semantic powers of human beings must lend to any discipline studying human action. Some would doubtless think it rather odd that the topic of social inquiry should be approached in this way. Social scientists, after all, are not for the most part greatly interested in what philosophers do, and linguistic philosophy, the value of which I shall stress here, has even been dismissed as a socially irresponsible and pathological movement (Gellner 1968a). But Wittgenstein's view that language is *the* 'form of life', and philosophy essentially an activity, has led to detailed socio-conceptual inquiries. Since linguistic philosophy thus involves a sensitive study of conceptual systems — a kind of 'descriptive anthropology' (Hampshire 1970: 234) — our regret must rather be that its value has not yet been fully realized (MacIntyre 1971b).

As part of a general change in the climate of thought, there is now in process a paradigm shift whereby several distinct disciplines are moving by similar paths towards a new way of speaking realistically and scientifically about human beings. There have recently been developments in the social sciences with debts to both linguistics and linguistic philosophy similar to those of semantic anthropology. So although I have stressed the need for semantic anthropology to develop in a new intellectual context, continued dialogue with the social sciences will be beneficial, for some social scientists are clearly perturbed by the same sort of problems that lie behind our own rethinking. Even if our semantic identity is far from secured, the very difficulty of the discipline has ironically made us less able to avoid those semantic difficulties which in reality all social sciences must face. In our case, the difficulties of translation between different cultures are stark; but sociologists have often spared themselves the thought that complex problems of meaning are involved when one studies human action in one's own society. In some ways therefore, the social sciences have an even larger leap to make than anthropology.

And we must also provide the vital comparative perspective that is so frequently missing. There is a clear risk that the approaches to social phenomena which have a linguistic inspiration may overlook the fact that the social sciences have grown in a literate culture, and that this may have destroyed some of the fullness of our non-verbal capacities — or at least blunted our consciousness of non-linguistic signifying — so that we now only speak metaphorically of gesture, for instance, as a 'language'. So here anthropology has a special obligation to remind others of our semiological powers.

SOME RECENT SEMANTIC SHIFTS IN THE SOCIAL SCIENCES

We can usefully approach our general topic of the nature of human action by briefly contrasting some of the recent semantic trends in the social sciences with the old style of inquiry. The new social psychology and the new sociology put great stress on the centrality of language in social life (Cicourel 1973; Lyman & Scott 1970) — something which the social sciences seemed to have forgotten, since language was rarely considered a subject for close investigation. With the new emphasis, there has been a shift to the view of social life as the creation and negotiation of meaning; and around this theme some hope for a general reconstruction of sociological knowledge (J. Douglas 1971 ed.). In the new paradigm, human beings are convention-making, theory-constructing, rule-following creatures — premisses which are clear in the ethnomethodology of Garfinkel (1967) and the dramaturgical sociology of Goffman (1959,1967). The invaluable service has now been performed by Harré and Secord (1972) of gathering together the scattered manifestations of the new position, and constructing out of them an elegant and clear 'ethogenic' conceptual system.

Basic features of these developments can be grasped by seeing how they parallel the Chomskyan revolution in linguistics. Chomsky has in effect challenged the very conception of science that existed in his discipline. He has argued that the restrictiveness of the behavioural methodology, which left out some of the most basic characteristics of language (like 'creativity'), has made a nonsense of the subject and so of science itself. Whatever difficulties may be involved in his distinction between 'competence' and 'performance', many criticisms of it have been wrongly directed in that they have failed to see how it expresses a fundamental shift in the notion of what constitutes an adequate explanation (Fodor & Garrett 1966). This same concern for explanatory adequacy has been strongly expressed in the social sciences by the abandonment of a hopelessly inadequate positivistic view of scientific method (derived not from the actual practice of natural science but largely from philosophers like Mill) in favour of a realist conception of science.

The methodology of the old paradigm in social science was bound up with a 'mechanistic' model of man. Skinner, for instance, uses a stimulus-response model because he feels this kind of framework is necessary in order for his practice to be called scientific. In adopting an 'anthropomorphic' model of man, ethogenists are making the general point that the work of Goffman is not only not less scientific than that of behaviourist psychologists, it is, from a more valid view of science, considerably *more* scientific than the latter. Much social science does not give significant accounts of social phenomena simply because it is mistaken as to what it is to provide an explanation of something (Louch 1966:xi). Ordinarily the concept means 'to make intelligible or clear', and the social sciences have often failed because they have been attracted by a deductive-nomological schema which was presumed to be the form for which all respectable inquiry should aim. But, as is by now obvious, this has led to such grotesque parodies of science when emulated in sociology that the study of human action has been almost completely crippled. Many — for instance those in the *Einheitswissenschaft* movement — have commented unfavourably upon the achievements of sociology and have suggested that its failings were the result of not being sufficiently scientific. From the viewpoint of the new paradigm, their criteria were scientistic and the developments they would have liked would merely make the inquiry of social facts *less* scientific. What was required rather was a fundamental change in outlook regarding the logic of investigating human beings.[1]

Strong evidence of the depth of the errors on which the old paradigm was based is contained in the fact that the exactitude at which its methods aimed, and which it was thought its conceptual apparatus would bring, has been exposed as completely illusory. To take an extreme case, in his famous review of Skinner's *Verbal Behavior*, Chomsky (1959) shows clearly how when one uses a behavioural repertoire to describe human speech, the concepts are employed figuratively, inconsistently and nonsensically — a good indication that such a conceptual framework is basically inappropiate. It is certainly true that many of the concepts in ordinary use to describe human activities are vague, but the widespread use by social scientists of specially devised technical terms has not constituted an improvement. Indeed, we are fully familiar with the vagueness and flexibility of these ordinary concepts; and since they clearly fit in social life itself, they in many ways qualify as exactly the sort of resources out of which a good scientific model of social life should be constructed. What the old-style psychology gave us,

89

in the main, was a quasi-precise knowledge of less than we already knew as agents ourselves. Such a strange mixture of experimental methods and conceptual confusion (Wittgenstein 1953:232) cannot be regarded as science.

The Durkheimian premiss that social facts must be regarded as 'things' was one way of stating that science requires one to adopt a certain attitude towards one's objects of study. Such a premiss does not entail that restrictive method and positivist outlook which virtually regards human beings as if they were themselves things — an outlook which merely caricatures science. The subject matter of social studies are persons who use language, construct meanings, follow rules, give accounts of their actions — beings, in short, who have considerable insight into their own nature. Such powers [2] cannot justifiably be excluded from any adequate science of social life.

It is because human agents are able to use language, and because their knowledge about their own action is substantially contained in ordinary language, that the work of the linguistic philosophers has such a value for social inquiry. Austin, for instance, has shown what an immensely rich stock of subtle distinctions ordinary English contains relating to human responsibility (1956). In natural languages, as he emphasized, are embedded those associations and discriminations which generations of speakers have found it important to make (ibid:46). This does not mean that ordinary language should always have the last word. Our everyday concepts might prove deficient in certain areas — Freud, for instance, drew our attention to hitherto little noticed episodes for which the ordinary resources of language did not make adequate provision. Technical terms may be quite legitimate additions to the stock of ordinary notions, but inventions are far more likely to be inadequate than the readily available terms which are already a part of the social institutions which the investigator has to describe. As psychology deals with the same phenomena that Jane Austen wrote about, ordinary language should at least have the first word. This at least is a more realistic beginning for studying human action than that chosen by those favouring a 'physicalist' discourse who, embarrassed by the elaborateness of ordinary language, so often expressed pride in the number of terms they had avoided using (Neurath 1966:51).

A social inquiry which exploits ordinary concepts will not depart totally from our ordinary understanding of ourselves. If this seems unscientific, then we should recall that this ordinary understanding constitutes a great part of what we are. And the elaborateness of ordinary language is simply a scientific fact about human beings, not a matter to be disregarded. The new kind of social science is first and foremost a conceptual study of an intrinsically semantic subject matter — a fact obscured and often obliterated by the old scientistic desire for quantification. To depart from the conceptual system involved in a set of moral and evaluative notions by breaking actions down into quantifiable physical units of behaviour does not promote a more precise study of social or psychological facts, since the new units completely destroy the nature of the facts one is investigating (Louch 1966: 18, 54–5). No doubt, for some, the very familiarity of this 'anthropomorphic' approach will make it unacceptable, yet clearly scientific realism demands that an anthropomorphic model be used when a science actually is about human beings. It is hardly an adequate framework which excludes whole dimensions of what it is to be a human being and which discounts powers which the social scientist like everyone else knows he possesses. A social scientist has no more basic capacity to understand human action than the people whom he is studying, but it is clearly absurd that he should proceed as if he had far less. To dispense with the semantic resources of ordinary language can only produce nonsense descriptions of human activity. This is why so much social science has provided less understanding of human beings than they themselves display in the course of their lives. It leads, for instance, to the pathetic situation of Skinner wondering how his books can be regarded as scientifically valid if they were written as responses to environmental stimuli (1957: 553ff.).

THOUGHT, ACTION AND THE NATURE OF HUMAN STUDIES

We have seen that while a particular view of the nature of physical science produces nonsense when employed in the study of social action, this gives no grounds for thinking that there can be no scientific study of a phenomenon which is so much bound up with notions like meaning and rule. Since Winch has argued forcibly that human action is a subject matter to which the sorts of explanations given in the physical sciences are inapplicable (1958: 72), we can use his work to discuss in the most general terms what is involved in the study of such a phenomenon. Certainly his book omits a great deal that is a part of social science, but he states very clearly the basic logical features that an account of human action must have if it is to be reckoned appropriate.

Even if Winch is concerned only with a starting point, it is vital to see how important it is to begin social inquiry in the right framework. If such inquiry rests on mistaken assumptions, no amount of actual empirical research or quantification will rectify the initial mistake so as to produce meaningful results. No statistical flair, for instance, can possibly relieve the investigator of the necessary prior semantic inquiry: statistical significance can well be without significance in a significant sense. Even when one is dealing with so seemingly countable a phenomenon as a tribal population, in fact one is speaking of a conceptual entity with boundaries constituted by definitions (Ardener 1974). Numbers here are the 'surface structure' of systems whose deep structures are necessarily classificatory in nature. Failure to identify these underlying conceptual parameters is to miss the significant generative units, after which no study could be either exact or even empirical in the true sense of the word. There is no general form of precision at which all sciences should aim. With a conceptual subject matter, to be exact may just involve close attention to a semantic structure. Since social interaction is so much a matter of exchanging meaning, the precision of measurement of the physical sciences corresponds in the social sciences to a more minute conceptual delineation (Harré & Secord 1972:132).

It is facts such as these which constitute the correctness of Winch's insistence (1958:4) that social scientists cannot view the role of the philosopher as that of a mere underlabourer clearing up a few problems before 'research procedures' and the like can reign supreme. A great many issues concerned with human beings are intrinsically philosophical, and very often a particular difficulty requires to be met not with research so much as with conceptual clarification. This is sometimes true in the physical sciences also, but one can well appreciate its force for the social sciences since their subject matter is itself of a conceptual order. Errors here are like misunderstanding a language — this is why we can speak of 'linguistic' considerations as relevant in determining whether any proposed theory is, in general, suitable or not. For this reason alone, social scientists cannot brush aside as irrelevant the painstaking conceptual investigations of philosophers. It may be that, as a second-order inquiry, philosophy only makes explicit what we already knew rather than making fresh discoveries, but this reminding activity is not of less scientific import.

The crucial fact which Winch conveys by contrasting social and physical science is that, as social phenomena are meaningful, social action is a species of 'internal' relations, because the relations between ideas are of a logical kind (ibid.:123). This could be a potentially misleading way of expressing the point, but much of its power can be grasped by recalling the deep conceptual gulf in our language between 'reason concepts' and 'cause concepts'. Even if the gulf can be bridged conceptually, we are talking of two very different semantic fields. We can speak of a causal sequence as a matter of external links, but the connection between a reason and an action is not of this contingent sort: meaning is contained within action, since action expresses a conceptual schema. So, mental terms like 'motive' or 'intention' do not refer to causal forces (Ryle 1966:113) because their relation to any action is internal — they are a part of the action.

This important separation of two semantic fields is maintained in our ordinary everyday discourse, and is clearly embedded in legal proceedings, for instance. Normally, to call something an 'action' invites an explanation of a very different sort from that we give of a 'bodily movement' (MacIntyre 1966: 108). Obviously, therefore, the gulf between 'action' and 'behaviour' risks being obliterated by those social scientists who see their work as concerned with 'human behaviour',[3] and who view their task as giving causes of behaviour and setting out causal consequences of behaviour. We ordinarily only invoke causal factors when a human being is in some way less than a person — when his agency is destroyed by drunkenness or the compulsion of others, for example. When we are dealing with an 'agent', a causal account can never be adequate and may be totally inappropriate. By now it is patently clear how hopelessly a causal theory of language use fails us. It reads like a mythical description of a matter which we as speakers can already explain in more adequate ways. This failure with language is stark; and it is of the very widest significance, because speaking is a paradigm case of a human rule-governed activity. Gross deficiency in causal explanation here necessarily implies similar failure with other types of social activity.

This basic conceptual problem concerning the description and explanation of human action can be usefully stated by employing the distinction between 'transcription' and 'transliteration' from the theory of translation. Of course, the relationship between model and reality is not simple in the physical sciences; nonetheless the contrast between these terms well suggests the extra dimension involved in theorizing in the social sciences. We can say that theoretical statements in the physical sciences point to regularities in phenomena: such propositions register conceptually connections between occurrences. With social phenomena, however, such conceptual links already exist, because they are structured by virtue of the meaning they have for their actors. The physical sciences have to transcribe, in that they must devise a graphological set to systematize the sounds of a 'language' previously unrecorded. By contrast, the language which the social sciences investigate is already a system possessing a conventional orthography composed of human meanings. In such a case, one must transliterate — that is, descriptions in social science must preserve this structure as an important part of the facts being dealt with. When inquiring into human phenomena, we are not dealing only with our technical language but with the discourse of others too. Our facts are not only already classified, they are classifications. Human data are of a conceptual order, so they are destroyed if this pre-existing order is disrespected. In social science, one can explain only if one can describe, and this one can do only if one has grasped the concepts embodied in human action. If the investigator fails to understand the conceptual structures which compose the subject matter of his science, he does not have the right to speak of human action at all. Thus, he must build upon this semantic foundation, not violate it.[4]

We can elaborate the difference between human studies and the physical sciences by using the opposition 'internality'/'externality'. The social sciences deal with conceptual facts, so we can speak of 'events' and 'rules', and liken the procedure of investigation to a communication exchange. By contrast, we can say that the physical sciences are concerned with regularities in occurrences, and that they are observationalist in method. Social science cannot be observationalist in this latter sense because of the internal dimension of its subject matter. The grammar of action is not external in a simple sense: it is semantic, existing in language and other shared conceptual reservoirs. Discovering the structure of social phenomena therefore entails symbolic dialogue between investigator and other human beings.

This internal aspect of rule-governed phenomena has been well illustrated by Hart in his discussion of the activities of drivers at traffic lights. It would not take an observer long to notice regularities in the motion of vehicles, related to the colour of the lights. But the lights are not the causes of these patterns. The lights are part of a convention structure and do not have to be obeyed. They are quite literally signs — that is they have meaning for drivers. What one is witnessing is rule-following activity, not causal regularities. If one describes this situation in only external observational terms, a whole dimension of social life would be omitted (1961:55–7,86–7).

This sort of consideration is not of a mere abstract philosophical relevance, for the semantic nature of social events must intrude in all sociological descriptions. It is internal considerations, for instance, which determine whether two events are of the same kind, and even whether something is an event at all. We could imagine a Christian ceremony in which one of the participants sneezed, for instance. As far as the meaning of the situation was concerned this would literally be noise — a non-event. On the other hand, in a culture where there was a belief in disease caused by indwelling spirits, the same physical occurrence of a sneeze during a healing rite might well be the most central and significant event of the proceedings, indicating that the spirit had been expelled. Although a physical scientist has to formulate the theory he uses, he is not under the same semantic constraints as the social investigator. The anthropological failing of ethnocentrism — thoughtlessly imposing our own cultural categories on another society — is thus just one instance of a general epistemological difficulty in inquiries into social facts. Because an action has an internal connection with the meaning embedded in it, one cannot describe an activity as 'praying' or 'voting', for instance, unless the actor possesses these concepts or ones which substantially overlap with them. Voting does not bear the same relation to a specific human action as does gravity to the fall of a physical object, because the concept of 'voting' is part of the action itself (Winch 1958:51).

As semantics and not observation determine the nature and boundaries of events, so we should remember that a rule can create a phenomenon. In some cases rules merely regulate an activity which exists independently of them. But there are also 'constitutive' rules where rule and phenomenon are not at all separable. For instance, the act of mating in chess is the expression of the rule which actually establishes the move itself. The move did not exist first and then have a rule added to regulate it: it has no existence apart from the rule, and this rule no existence apart from the others which make up the game of chess as a whole. Thus, to return to the notions of externality and internality, an observer at a football match unfamiliar with the game could easily note patterns of behaviour on the field, but such regularities could not reveal to him the point of the game, nor could he understand what fouls or offside were or even that they were separate events. Lacking the conceptual system in which these notions have their place he might not have registered them at all. Because rules can create events, the observational ideology of the sciences of human behaviour is clearly logically inadequate. Just as an occurrence may be a non-event, so a non-occurrence may well be an event. For instance, saying or doing nothing can constitute a positive act of politeness if there is a rule that silence is a sign of respect in certain circumstances. Such a fact could well be exposed by a process of communication, but it would remain undetected by any purely observationalist method of inquiry.

In recent anthropology, some of the general dualisms upon which the discussion of this chapter has been based have appeared in Ardener's richly suggestive distinction between paradigmatic and syntagmatic structures (1971a).[5] His stress on the conceptual dimension of human facts involved in the analytical separation of a generative programme and a sequence of events (1973a) in effect inverts the structure of the functionalist ideology. For functionalists, the prime data to be recorded during fieldwork were the 'real' observable phenomena like economic, political and kinship behaviour. Values, beliefs and symbolic usages were also noted, and interpreted as elaborations of this primary social reality. They were located by reducing them to the needs of the social system, that is explained away as elements which served to make the society work better by integrating the diverse parts of the social structure, and so on. The general argument of this chapter should make it clear why the order of priorities enshrined in this positivistic scheme must be rejected. It is precisely the conceptual structures which contain the syntax of those events which the investigator can actually observe. It is the semantic structures which are generative, behaviour merely being the linear physical realization of these constitutive programmes.

Such a view does not mean that functional work was not valuable. Actions have consequences, and no doubt there are bonds between different social institutions. The deficiency has been that functionalism was coupled with a devaluation of semantic concerns. Clearly this has impeded the development of semantic anthropology; but the point also needs to be made that this prejudice cuts away the ground from underneath functionalism too. As it is a semantic foundation which constitutes the events the fieldworker detects, he cannot scientifically speak about the functional links between institutions until his data have been understood. Even functionalists, therefore, must admit the priority of conceptual structures. If they do not, they simply have no basis from which to pass on to their more sociological interests. Human action is a semantic fabric, so any social investigation must be a conceptual inquiry. Any other starting-point will make a nonsense of scientific method. Human beings are meaning-makers, and this directly determines what general form a science of social action must assume. Functionalism (just like the extreme case of behaviourism in psychology) was part of an observationalist ideology which rested on a fundamental epistemological error about the nature of human action. For those who fail to see the intrinsically conceptual nature of human social facts, real scientific empiricism would prove impossible.

Of course it is often said that what is 'internal' necessarily falls outside the domain of science, that science can only deal with the publicly observable. Hence, if sociological inquiries are to deserve the label 'scientific', they too must restrict their scope to what is external. This argument is perhaps the major factor lying behind the sad state of so much psychology today. Haunted by the problem of 'other minds', equating mentalism with non-science, psychologists in many fields retreated into a behaviourism which has left out some of the most basic characteristics of human beings. In so doing, psychology cut itself off from that conceptual system out of which a realistic account of human action could have been built. Such a strategy, moreover, was based on a series of profound conceptual errors, as recent linguistic philosophy has made very clear. When we speak of the 'internality' of social activity, we are not talking of a private realm — the concepts of 'meaning' and 'rule', in fact, only make sense given a public context.[6] The internal aspect is not observable in a gross sense, but it exists in language and can be located by communication — a shared method which is the basis not only of social life but also of social inquiry.

Wittgenstein constantly stressed this need for public criteria in semantic issues, and he used it against the ego-centric standpoint which lay at the root of so many classical philosophical problems. Language was not just a social institution, it was an *essentially* shared possession. The impossibility of a 'private' language thus establishes the strongest conceptual affinities between the notions of publicity, meaning and rule. There have to be other human beings if we are to follow a rule; and we could not speak at all if we could not speak to each other. This refutation of linguistic privacy, and the demolition of Cartesian privacy in general, is not only of philosophical import, but of the very widest significance to investigators of social life. Ryle's analysis of mental concepts, for instance, fully exposes the absurdity of regarding human action as if a person were composed of distinct mental and physical sequences (1966). But the crucial point to grasp is that the destruction of this dualism not only eliminates a certain concept of mind but also liquidates the corresponding concept of the human body. This is why the Rylean concept of action is not behaviourist. In the same way that internality is not synonymous with privacy, so publicity is not the equivalent of physical behaviour. When watching a human being in the course of a social interaction, one is not witnessing a body behaving and failing to witness a mind thinking, one is seeing a person in action.

While an 'inner' life is a basic part of a human being, we well know in daily life that for all ordinary people this internality in no way means inaccessibility.[7] Social life would not just be very different, it could not possibly exist were this not so. That we normally understand other persons is essential to their being persons and to our being a person. We cannot think of language, mind and meaning in an individual context, and then try to fit others into the scheme: they all three can only exist in a shared context. It is basic to everyday life that we can understand one another. We can do this even when we try to give misleading information about our motives. Concepts like 'bluff' or 'pretend' would not exist in our language otherwise. It is even a familiar situation for someone else to know one's mind better than one knows it oneself, as for example when one accepts another person's account of one's action which conflicts with the explanation one had originally given oneself. These are not mystical occurrences, they simply register basic powers possessed by human beings, and they give social life fundamental logical characteristics which any adequate account should accept as data. Some provision should be made for such phenomena in building a conceptual system to describe social interaction. To leave them out in an effort to be more objective leads to a scientistic metaphysics which is quite the reverse of true science. Those who wish to deny that we have these powers merely validate our contentions; for to challenge our position they must utilize their semantic powers even to frame an argument, let alone engage in dispute.

THE CONFIGURATION OF RULE SYSTEMS: A RECENT CONVERGENCE

The oppositions internality/externality and programme/event have sufficient generality to affect accounts of human action over a range of academic disciplines. It is therefore the more interesting that anthropology and law should recently have converged on a statement of these dualisms very similar to that most clearly expressed in modern linguistic theory. Possibly the parallelism points to a universal in the structure of rule systems. Language is after all a rule system *par excellence*, so we might well expect to find in linguistics clues about the form of other systems of rules. Even so, there are bound to be prominent features in the construction of language which will not be good guides to the shape of other rule systems, so it seems unreasonable to expect other forms of human action to be describable by detailed models of the transformational generative type (Lyons 1970:12). Chomsky himself is less than certain of their general applicability (1968:64), and since with the rise of a post-Chomskyan school of generative semanticists the form of these models in linguistics itself is still a matter for debate, now is not the time to attempt detailed comparisons. Nonetheless, it seems possible that we shall find socio-semantic universals of a 'grammatical' kind, and thus these recent convergences around a gross distinction between a deep and a surface structure may be important.

With Chomsky, the focus of description in linguistics changed from taxonomic concerns — segmentation of a corpus of language — to the investigation of a rule complex. For Chomsky, when one says that someone knows a language, this means a speaker has internalized a system of rules (ibid.:23). Furthermore, since it is an undeniable fact that we learn to speak a language from a very limited and degenerate sample, something is suggested about the nature of the rule structure involved. That an infinity of utterances can be generated by a restricted number of principles is a feature of organization which language need not possess, and it is one which Chomsky claims effectively rules out the possibility of any sort of behaviourist explanation of language ever being satisfactory. This is why he has rejected as logically inappropriate for linguistic description finite state models and phrase structure grammars. Such basic features as language displays can only be satisfactorily handled if we give the rule system at least two dimensions: one concerned with physical realization, and another of a more abstract character which the latest research suggests is of a logico-semantic nature.

The structure of a jurisprudential system, which like language is an essentially rule-governed framework, has recently been characterized by

Hart in strikingly similar terms. He argues that it is hopeless to look for the 'quintessence' of legal rules. Just as Chomsky rejects certain kinds of model outright, so Hart dismisses as wholly inadequate proposals that the nature of law is enshrined in imperatives, in force, and the like. This is so because the fundamental fact about a legal structure is that its rules are of two distinct kinds (1961:91–2). The dual dimensionality is present in the legal field in a primary set of rules which relate positively or negatively to different types of actions, and a secondary set which belong to a different logical type. They relate to primary rules, but over such questions as precedents, interpretation and changes in the law. This difference of logical type seems easily expressible in the language of deep and surface structures. After all, law is a limited set of principles generating a vast range of particular cases. The primary rules, moreover, do concern actual events, while the secondary rules play a basically semantic function.

This particular parallel suggests that it may be a type of generative model that we need to explain human action in general. Ardener's distinction between a programme and a syntagmatic sequence certainly separates a generative semantic system from its manifestation as a chain of events in a way which makes employing the imagery of deep and surface structures apt. Such a framework enables us to state the nature of the gulf between the newer anthropology and Radcliffe-Brownian structural-functionalism by comparing the latter to the taxonomic phase in linguistics, which was concerned with analysing 'immediate constituents'. That structural-functionalism had a stultifying penchant for taxonomy is not a novel comment, but the reference to immediate constituents points to a more general theoretical deficiency of the framework. In construing social structure as the totality of actual social relations, Radcliffe-Brown confines us to surface structure and is thus forced into trying to compose the syntax of a social system out of the observable events instead of stating the grammar of the events by constituting the logical form of the generative principles. Because the semantic form of social facts is constitutive, the significance of events is not a matter of the kind of observation contained in the scientistic ideology of Radcliffe-Brown. In other words, from the events alone one has no way of telling what their structure is. Human action is no more a succession of behaviours than language is a chain structure — despite its linear appearance as speech.

It is for this reason that those social scientists who are attracted by correlational sociology, or those functionalists who speak of their preference for explaining social facts by relating them to their social context rather than by reference to generative structures, are working with models which are logically inadequate. It follows also that those

99

anthropologists whose work belongs to the old style fail to grasp the importance of our emphasis on the semantic qualities of social facts if they see recent movements in the discipline as giving us an awkward dichotomy between systems of ideas and systems of institutional behaviour. The very concept of action makes such a division absurd. We are not now just writing less about function and more about meaning; and those whose perception of the latest trends leads them to adapt in this partial fashion are really missing the nature of the newer anthropology. Chomsky, after all, did not extend or elaborate a tradition so much as establish a different style of linguistics by rejecting some of the basic presumptions of the previously dominant outlook. For this reason, it is no exaggeration to say that *Syntactic Structures* (1957) amounted to a redefinition of the aims of linguistic theory. Obviously, because any new paradigm grows out of the deficiencies of its predecessor, and because the older style of inquiry will have generated information of value to the new, no shift in an intellectual discipline can be regarded as constituting a start from scratch. At the same time, to define semantic anthropology as post-functional and post-structural means that it cannot be seen as a mere refinement of either. A more radical shift is involved. We can speak of a new anthropology here because it rejects a certain epistemological space and a conception of science.

ETHOLOGY AS AN EXPANSION OF ANTHROPOLOGY: A CHALLENGE
The way in which human action has been discussed above suggests that anthropologists should look very critically at that ethological growth of the social sciences which has of late been so enthusiastically recommended by several colleagues. For one thing, the distinction between those who see ethology as of great value and those who do not is already supposed to constitute a major division in the discipline (Reynolds 1973:384). Naturally, no one could possibly deny that in our present state of knowledge the Durkheimian view of the 'social' as an autonomous domain is an unacceptable instance of a closed system. If there are cultural universals which can be grounded in some physiological basis, research is quite rightly directed to the links between the two realms. To leave such matters uninvestigated simply because they require one to go beyond the orthodox boundaries of social science would be absurd. At the same time, the very vogue of 'ethologism' — a combination of romanticism, gloom and science (Callan 1970) — in our culture suggests that there may be at work a fascination for animal studies which is not of an altogether scientific kind. This filtering of social concerns through the animal world — an employment of the natural realm to yield terms of human self-understanding just like the 'totemism' of primitive cultures — should at least make us wary as to

our reasons for being attracted by ethology.

The recent popularity of ethology has resulted in a great amount of poor work in a field which can boast the presence of a number of conscientious scholars. But the former work is not irrelevant to the writings of the latter because it is the same perception which builds the bridge that makes possible both types of contribution. When Desmond Morris declares in an untroubled way that he is a zoologist and man is an animal (1969:9), this is essentially the premiss from which the more sober approaches take their start. And one need not be a fundamentalist believing in the separate creation of man to feel sceptical about the framework of ethological inquiry which springs from it. Human powers which are exercised in social interaction (intersubjective understanding, the use of language, and so on) obviously have a natural basis, and an explanation of them will ultimately be supplied by sciences like neuro-physiology. But just as we must see that the severe naturalism of Lévi-Strauss' search for invariants involves the high cost of decomposing facts before their complexity is understood, similar considerations are relevant in assessing the work of ethologists.

Man no doubt cannot shake off his long evolutionary past, but to view our social behaviour as the outcome of natural selection and to speak of 'genetically programmed behavioural predispositions' (Tiger & Fox 1966:77) obscures a great many conceptual problems. Among others, only man has any knowledge of his biological history, and this knowledge must alter his relationship to it. The social sciences study people who not only live but also have a conception of life. Thus an account of human action must take into consideration the fact that we do not just behave, we act — that is we have conceptions of behaving. Our discussion above pointed to the logical gulf between action and behaviour, and we might therefore wonder by what means ethology can show us the links between customary activities and impulsive behaviour (Freeman 1966:337,340). One need only recall the pioneering work of Mauss (1936) to know that the human body is part of a system of collective representations and so a theoretical instrument. It is simply not possible to view human movement as if it were mere behaviour. Of course we are all subject to physical constraints, but no adequate scientific account of human action in its various spatial frameworks can ignore its profoundly semantic qualities (D. Williams 1974).[8]

No one would wish to prejudge the ultimate value of scientific attempts to place human culture in the context of evolutionary biology. But the conceptual character of human activity is itself a part of the natural history of our species, and so it is quite reasonable to insist that ethologists address themselves to some of the semantic problems concerned with human action before they can expect to capture our attention. In the hands of those like Tinbergen, ethology has been a tremendous advance on animal studies carried out in laboratory conditions; but the discipline is still an essentially biological explanation of behaviour. Those who advocate ethological approaches in the social sciences have still to produce a satisfactory conceptual bridge between the biological realm and the semantic sphere in which action occurs. Callan, who has cautiously set out some useful links between ethology and anthropology, has quite rightly claimed that the extent of this gulf between the two disciplines has been seriously underestimated by most practitioners (1970:34). Furthermore, ethological explanations tend to be functional (ibid.:71); so this extension of anthropology would return us to the framework from which other recent developments have been freeing us. Indeed, instead of meaning being reduced to social structure, concepts themselves now become functions as quite literal 'adaptational devices' (Tiger & Fox 1966:81n6). Conventions like rituals and symbols are shared modes of adaptation, the displacements of a pre-existing behavioural repertoire (Freeman 1966:339,340n). By this route the path from function to meaning is blocked by the advent of a biologist functional semantics.

The general problem involved in the ethological approach in social science can be stated in terms of a question: are we dealing with two systems (animal behaviour and human action) which differ only in degree of complexity but where the phenomena are of the same basic kind, or does the gulf register the difference between systems which are at two discrete levels of organization such that we have features on the higher for which no analogue can be found on the lower? If the words 'social' and 'language' cannot be employed of animals with the same implications that they have in a human context, they should not receive a dual use. If it is the case that only at a certain level of organization can the phenomenon of a rule or convention exist, we cannot regard them as just highly complicated behavioural regularities. Now it seems scientifically imperative that we regard language-users and those without language as belonging to different levels of logical complexity. There are features in the activities of rule-following language-users which are unique to them and which cannot be handled at all by conceptual systems adequate for describing other species. If we need to use different kinds of models, and even different descriptive terms, for the two levels of complexity, then clearly notions like a 'primate programme' in human beings will belong to a terminological limbo. Not only do they not form part of a conceptual system, they semantically violate the two types of description on either side of the gulf between human action and animal behaviour.

As has often been contended, language is really the crucial test here. It has become common to speak of 'animal languages', but there seems good reason to regard language as species-specific. Hockett has even suggested that a valuable way of searching for the universals of human languages is to contrast them with the communication systems found among animals (1963: 8ff.). The view that there is a difference of kind between animal communication and language is strengthened, should the suggestion prove correct that language is not the manifestation of a general high intelligence but of a specific language faculty (Lenneberg 1964). And of course Chomsky's stress on the fact that human speech is an open-ended system which is free of environmental stimulus would further widen this gap.

We already know that the stimulus-response model of verbal behaviour (itself extrapolated from animal studies) leaves out the most basic characteristics of human language use. If, by contrast to such language, animal signals form a behaviourally-rooted fixed repertoire, we have to say that the difference between an animal's screeching in the presence of danger and a grammatically articulate proposition that 'such and such is the case' is not a matter of increased complexity but a difference in kind. And those like Sebeok who admit that language is an unbridgeable gap 'between man and animals cannot solve the problem simply by recommending a wider zoosemiological framework (1973). Just as behaviourist accounts of human verbal activity fail, so projected behaviourally-rooted semiotic systems (see C. Morris 1955) seem grossly inadequate. Our non-verbal communication may be more like that of animals than our language, but we can still easily exaggerate the similarity between our gestures, for instance, and animal communication. After all, humans can perform semiotic transmutations; they can substitute a phrase for a gesture, for example. And if this equivalence is possible, our non-linguistic signs must partake of the same systemic complexity as language itself (Jakobson 1967: 673).

This conclusion suggests we should not use the term 'sign' in speaking of animal communication at all. Far from being biologically caused, in human conventional signifying activity arbitrariness is basic. A similar proscription seems advisable with the concept of a rule, which despite its great complexity and resistance to definition is a notion that is indispensable to the scientific description of human activity (Harré 1974). A rule implies semantic structures, publicity, and non-necessity. Just as free human action is something where the agent could have acted otherwise, so human conventions could have been different. When one describes an event as 'conformity to a rule', therefore, one is in a discourse of a logically different type to that of subsumption an occurrence under a general law typical of causal accounts in natural science.

If the gulf between man and animals has to be stated in terms of distinct types of powers, science demands that the difference be conceptually recognized. Indeed, ethology and social science should have very different characteristics, because if language separates the two realms it also significantly affects the nature of description in the two sciences. The social sciences study persons who have conceptual systems of their own actions. Language therefore appears twice. Firstly in the theory of the scientist, and secondly as part of the activity of the people studied by that science, who use language, among other things, to formulate explanations of their own. In ethology one obviously cannot begin by exploring the linguistic resources of those one studies, since animals do not possess the institution of language. As a natural science, ethology must content itself with external observation. The ethologist here is the only one to formulate a discourse for explanation, since animals do not give accounts of their behaviour. Language here merely makes for us a more general point. To be a person requires the exercise of considerable anthropological skills. It requires self-understanding, communicative ability, and other-understanding. Thus it is that in all the social sciences those being investigated possess exactly the same powers as those doing the investigating. This is clearly not the case in ethology, which is why it cannot be assimilated to any type of science which sees a man as a semantic creature.

There have been many poetic statements about language creating a distinctively human symbolic atmosphere. Müller, for instance, claimed that because of language 'we not only stand a step above the brute creation, we belong to a different world' (1861:364). What we need is a more scientific a way of expressing the truth contained in this view, and perhaps the notion of 'reflexivity' is valuable in this connection. Language both manifests and is an index of an organic system with highly reflexive abilities (Hockett 1963:13). Human beings not only speak, they can also speak about language. This capacity to operate on a meta-level — to communicate about communication — seems absent in systems of animal signalling, although claims have sometimes been made to the contrary. Here again then, we see that 'quantal' principle at work which gives us a hierarchy of discrete orders of logical complexity. Reflexivity is not a capacity which increases gradually, but is an instance of 'emergent' properties. In other words, there are critical points in levels of organization above which a creature may be described as a symbol-user, but below which there is no rudimentary analogue of such a power.

Clearly then, whilst zoosemiotics has greatly increased our knowledge of animal communication, this more general framework does not solve our analytical difficulties. There are 'design features' of a fundamental

logical kind which still separate our signifying capacity from any communication systems found in animals (Hockett & Altmann 1968:63ff.).
These cannot scientifically be characterized as merely cases of increased
complexity (Lenneberg 1968:598,611), so one is entitled to be sceptical
about a proposal for the study of 'communication in general'. Communication is one aspect of a whole mode of being, and we must be very
careful lest in concentrating on this single perspective we regard as
parallels what are very superficial similarities indeed (ibid.1969:136).
Nothing in animal communication resembles the semantics of being
human and of human interaction as realistically described by Goffman.
We may describe as a dance that performance by the honey bees which
signals the location of honey, but such an activity can neither state nega-
tives nor convey a message about the performance itself. Again, apes
under exceptional circumstances have been taught to combine counters
to make simple propositions; but a real demonstration of the reflexive
capacities of a language-user in such a creature would require it to state
such a proposition as 'I am stating a proposition'.

These examples demonstrate the value of Bateson's advice (1964) that
Russell's theory of logical types can enable us to appreciate fundamental
aspects of natural communication.[9] Man sends messages; but his brain
also allows him to frame messages which classify messages, and again
messages which classify these classifications. These three kinds of
message cannot belong to the same logical type. We can further use this
scheme to state the nature of the 'accounts' which are so important in
the understanding of human action. Accounting is an expression of reflexive powers, because the reports a human being gives on his own performances are not cases of mere verbal behaviour which belong to the
level of the action itself: they monitor the action from the framework of
another system. Not only do animals lack this power, human beings display this capacity on several levels. Thus, a human being not only processes information, he also processes the processing of information — he
can monitor the monitoring of his actions. This is the basis of the familiar
complexity in human semantics. Language can convey information; it
can also be used for pretending, lying to others, deceiving oneself, and so
on. Clearly, therefore, whilst it may be sufficient to regard animal communication as an information system, this cannot be so of human
language. Language is so much a part of our imaginative life, so much
geared to the creation of 'alternities' (Steiner 1975:222,218), that we
miss much of its genius if we do not also regard it as a system of mis-
information.

Our hierarchical framework has further elaborated the gulf between
human action and animal behaviour. It is clear that if we are to advance
our understanding of social interaction we need a better knowledge of

the basic properties which make human beings capable of activity of this logical kind. And this cannot come from studying creatures who lack these powers. Just as a constitutive rule creates a phenomenon, so we could say that a certain level of organization brings into being a whole new range of features. If animals lack our neural organization, we cannot regard language as a development of the communication systems of a lower order; nor can we think of human institutions as complex combinations of patterns of animal behaviour.[10] This stratification in nature has to be marked conceptually by natural science (Shwayder 1965). That is, we need a different way of talking scientifically about a creature who plans, has models of plans and models of those models (Miller *et al.* 1967). Some animals may be conscious of their behaviour, but human beings are aware of their consciousness, which profoundly affects the nature of their activities. Human interaction requires the activation of powers of mutuality: the understanding needed of oneself and another demands that one knows that the other knows, and so on. Of course, the potential for operating on this level is not always fully exploited by human beings, but the possibility of exercising these abilities must affect how we describe all their activities. Certainly, no natural science which studies animal behaviour has anything remotely like the necessary conceptual resources for doing this.

Wittgenstein made the philosophical point that there were certain concepts which could only be applied to a language-user (1967b: no.520). We have now seen many reasons why such a viewpoint must be respected by science, even those branches which wish to go beyond the boundaries of existing disciplines. If, for instance, it is correct to say that we are symbol-users because we are intentional creatures, the decision that only those who use language can be said to possess symbols rules out whole areas of human vocabulary as inapplicable to animals. These conceptual truths must be respected by science, since science cannot make sense if it violates the semantic conventions of language by the way it describes its subject matter. No matter how human the dance of the honey bee looks, it cannot be described as 'rational'; for there are such strong linguistic affinities between the concepts 'rationality', 'intention', 'rule', 'symbol', 'reasons for', that such a predicate is only semantically acceptable when one has a creature that can speak (Bennett 1971). We are therefore forced to give a different type of explanation, employing a different set of terms for human action from that we use when describing animal behaviour. Human activity is not pre-existing natural behaviour to which rules are added: it is the rule, and a being capable of following it, which create the activity.[11]

Because creatures with and without language have to be scientifically described by two different conceptual systems, ethologists themselves have a crucial problem of language in that they must find a system of concepts in which to express the parallels and links upon which their science is based. We cannot adequately describe human action with terms used to refer to animal behaviour, since we cannot link them to notions like 'rule' and 'intention'. This is why behaviourist accounts of our activity leave out its most basic characteristics. On the other hand, it is no less objectionable to employ action concepts to describe animal behaviour. For example, it has become commonplace to speak of the 'authority structure' of primate groups; but in a human social context authority is a notion linked to ideas of legitimacy and to systems of values and beliefs. If these circumstances do not hold in the animal case, it invites confusion to use the same term.

This problem is even more clear in the case of ritual. Whether one adopts the positivistic position of the functionalists that ritual is a special kind of behaviour — that related to 'mystical' beliefs — or whether one argues that all human action is ritual because all action is symbolic and patterned (albeit at different levels of formality), in the human context ritual is profoundly semantic. By contrast, in an animal context, the term is specifically applied to those biologically rooted performances of an impulsive and instinctive kind such as the attraction of a mate or the defence of a territory. But if such behaviour is spectacular, in common usage 'performance' means the very reverse of instinctual, just as human conventions are the reverse of impulsive (Leach 1966a). Even when we speak of a person indulging in an impulsive activity, we are referring to ritual which shares the symbolic nature of other human actions.

These examples carry a general warning. Unless ethologists are very careful, their approach to social phenomena could well remove them from the domain of science through failure to find a location in any acceptable conceptual system. As such, the enterprise could then only be a mixture of observational method and linguistic confusion. There are different levels of logical complexity in nature, and ethology cannot become a science if it disrespects the architecture of our language which registers these discontinuities. Ethologists cannot hope to convince us just by providing the findings of more detailed research, since we can only feel happy with these results once the ethologists have subjected their own science to conceptual scrutiny. In the meantime, social scientists should not forget that human beings are creatures who, possessing considerable self-understanding, can offer explanations of their own action. Perhaps it would be far more profitable to explore and make explicit the nature of this knowledge as a means of building the social sciences, than to observe rats and chimps.

If social scientists wish to advance their understanding of human action they might do well to look to areas where rules and meanings definitely apply — for instance, in law and language. It is an illusion, created by such edifices as the Comteian hierarchy of the sciences, that makes us think that animal studies will give us a 'deeper' understanding of social facts. Of course we commonly speak of animal 'societies'; but since 'social' is a term intimately bound up with other terms like symbol and language, it may well be that this usage, too, will mislead. We do not yet know what are the minimal features of the social, and what its systemic prerequisites; but there is no point in hastily handing over problems to other sciences, and speaking of 'social biogrammars' (Tiger & Fox 1972), if invariants can be located at the level of the social itself. If students of human action broaden their disciplines by scrutinizing linguistic theory and the philosophy of law they will at least know they are dealing with systems of the right level of organizational complexity. If ethology is partly a response to the past lack of theoretical growth in the social sciences, then it is certainly welcome. Yet we can possibly develop and even transform the disciplines concerned with the social life of human beings at their present level, instead of seeking to reinvigorate them by finding a route into biology. We have set out above some of the foundations on which a semantic development of anthropology and the social sciences in general could be built. We can now apply our orientation by exploring more specific topics.

6   Recasting Witchcraft

We have so far made but a few very general remarks on the differences between structural-functionalism and semantic anthropology. Of course, because the consensus in British anthropology has long been destroyed, many of the developments of the last decade have already shown us in concrete terms how two very different general outlooks concerning the nature of the discipline may manifest themselves. One spectacular instance has been in kinship studies. Descent theorists, traditionally emphasizing institutions and social functions, have signally failed to see that alliance theory is concerned with rules and categories and not with behaviour. This chapter takes 'witchcraft' as a subject where the same general cleavage has similarly already appeared. By showing below how deliberately following a new type of interest can considerably reshape this topic, the gulf between the newer and older styles of anthropology will be made that much clearer. Only detailed ethnographic analysis can establish the value of the proposals made below, and in this chapter little more than an outline framework for a new style of approach is given. Even so, the analysis (which makes considerable use of insights from linguistic philosophy) provides a useful and specific demonstration of that broad link which exists between semantic anthropology and language.

The topic of witchcraft is highly suitable for these purposes for several reasons. Firstly, the deficiencies of the functionalist writings are here very clear. Also, it has already constituted a bridge with other disciplines: philosophers have used Evans-Pritchard's Zande study to debate general issues concerning the nature of anthropological inquiry (Winch 1964; MacIntyre 1964); and historians have recently made extensive researches into the subject. Whilst we may feel flattered that other scholars find our work invaluable (Thomas 1971:436n), this interest places us under a particularly heavy obligation to look carefully at our achievements in this field. When this is done, it is apparent that anthropology has far less to offer these other disciplines than some obviously think.

TWO STYLES IN THE STUDY OF WITCHCRAFT

Evans-Pritchard's 1937 study of Zande witchcraft is an undeniable land-mark in the history of anthropology, but the last two generations have not greatly advanced our understanding of the problems he wrote about. His book concerned the sociology of knowledge and perception (Douglas 1970 ed.: xiv), and it would be an understatement to comment that subsequent work has not done justice to its theoretical pregnancy. Like some of the other early 'paradigmatic' writings, it has been emasculated by being converted into a functionalist framework where it was interpreted as about 'social control' and the like (Ardener 1971b: lxxvi) — exactly the sort of approach from which Evans-Pritchard continually distanced himself. The emphasis in most subsequent works in the field has been on the social locus of accusations, theories of 'social strain', and hypotheses concerning the dissolution of redundant relationships. The 'micro-sociological' conception of anthropology has almost completely submerged his most important ideas. From Evans-Pritchard's construction of the logic of the Zande conceptual structure which lay behind the perception and labelling of certain kinds of events, anthropology virtually went a full circle until it seemed to be suggested by some functionalists that witchcraft could be explained by misfortune.

Unfortunately, those historians who have lately studied witchcraft have failed to see the gulf between these two approaches. MacFarlane (1970), for instance, juxtaposes quotations from Marwick and Evans-Pritchard, seemingly oblivious of the fact that they represent two very different conceptions of a discipline. Thomas describes his work as 'mainly sociological' (1970: 47), and it is no surprise therefore that it is open to many of the criticisms which can be made of the sociological tradition in anthropology (Keynes 1972). These scholars cannot be blamed here since the semantic style of tackling witchcraft has not been much in evidence for them to use. Of the many recent books on the subject — many ironically dedicated to Evans-Pritchard — almost all have been representatives of the old approach.

Mair's general survey (1969), for instance, does not go beyond the functionalist perspective. And one can see here plainly, in the very arrangement of the material, how the fact that her main interests are in the politico-jural field necessarily affects the treatment of witchcraft. Marwick, the figure in the field most associated with the 'social strain' hypothesis, still sees studies of witchcraft and sorcery as contributions to behavioural science. His is an attempt at 'making generalisations about repetitive social situations and processes, and, within the range of statistical probability, at making predictions of the outcomes' (1970 ed.: 17; 1966: 173). His remarks on the inadequacy of the sociological analyses by those like Lewis are completely justified. But when he suggests that the difficulty here 'springs from the failure of anthropologists to quantify and objectify their methods rather than that they are stuck with too rigid or too simple a model' (1972:382), he evidently sees progress as consisting in the elaboration of a framework rather than requiring any substantial theoretical rethinking. A recent set of essays by Manchester anthropologists (Gluckman 1972 ed.) similarly represents that easy resort to sociological generalizations which has been responsible for the virtual stagnation of whole areas of the discipline over the last generation.

Lastly, the A.S.A. monograph on witchcraft (M. Douglas 1970 ed.), by its very title stresses aspects like confessions and accusations, and thus reveals the divergence of interest between most of the contributors and Evans-Pritchard. Certainly the 'boundarism' of Douglas's introduction is a step forward, and cannot be located in the old style, but Beidelman's severe comments on the continuing propensity for taxonomic and functional thinking makes a rather dissonant epilogue in a volume which contains very few new insights. Lewis, for example, gives an old-fashioned comparative functional study of the social correlates of witchcraft and spirit possession, which rests upon the most simplistic of assumptions concerning the link between belief and social structure (1970). In a similar fashion, Esther Goody offers the sociological hypothesis that it is the ease of terminating marriage which lies behind the fact that Gonja believe that it is only the witchcraft of women that is evil and should be punished, without even a minimal attempt to construct the symbolic syntax which relates the categories of male and female in Gonja society (1970). As Ardener makes very clear in his analysis of Bakweri witchcraft notions, it is pointless to try to account for such facts without first constituting the conceptual 'templates' (1970:156,159n15), that is without trying to specify the ideological structures which generate such events.

In trying to reframe the topic of witchcraft, considerable emphasis will be placed on underlying classificatory structures in order to stress one aspect of the reorientation which a semantic approach involves. Of course Mair is quite correct to say that to advance our understanding there is no need to scrap everything which has been done on this topic in the last thirty years (1972b:140), but no one would suggest this. On the other hand, there is a definite need for a 'rethinking of the approach itself, rather than simply more studies' (Beidelman 1970:356). Douglas has long criticized the narrow conception of the scope of witchcraft studies, and has suggested that advance to a broader frame of reference would require an atmosphere of debate and tension (1967:80). We have seen some elements of cleavage appearing, but this atmosphere has not been in evidence in the recent literature to the extent one would wish. It is to be hoped that the recasting offered here will make the opposition between the older and the newer styles of anthropology in this field more striking.

AN ANALYTICAL DISSOLUTION: SOCIETY AS A MORAL SPACE

One of the reasons for the shortcomings of anthropological discussions of witchcraft is the idea that it is a phenomenon which should be treated as a topic at all. So, following Lévi-Strauss' demolition of totemism and Needham's of kinship, my suggestion is that our understanding will advance when 'witchcraft' is analytically dissolved into a larger frame of reference. Some still argue that our first task is to define witchcraft, and then by comparison to see what the phenomenon really is (Standefer 1970). But it is vital to locate the nature and dimensions of the field by which 'witchcraft' is constituted. Such a location can then define the phenomenon away. Studies of witchcraft — let alone comparative studies — would then appear a semantic nonsense, and the mark of our better comprehension would be a decreasingly frequent employment of the term.

In this connection it is important to see that witchcraft may have become a separate topic for anthropology because of its appearance in the history of our own society. This occurrence, by supplying us with a ready-made term, would be sufficient to destroy those cautions we observe in the translation of culture in connection with other problems. The gulf between the intellectual structures of seventeenth-century England and Zande society, for instance, is vast. Moreover, Evans-Pritchard himself emphasized that our historical witchcraft was not like anything we so label in primitive cultures (1937:64) — a fact which historians should not underestimate the importance of when they use anthropological data in arriving at their interpretations.[1] English witchcraft existed in a culture which possessed such categories as 'natural philosophy' and a theological system upon which witch beliefs were partly parasitic. Great violence must be done to the conceptual structures of another culture in speaking of witchcraft if it lacks those environing categories which defined it in our own. Where the conceptual field is so different we could not reasonably expect to find the same phenomenon, and so the one term should not be used twice. This just becomes an easy way by which a whole host of labels can be illicitly employed in describing other cultures.

This point, though it may strike a social scientist as of rather little import, is crucial in semantic anthropology and affects all the topics with which it deals. As Dumont has rightly insisted, it is only by a painstaking investigation of details that the route to the universal is kept open (1961:37-8). We simply cannot confuse categories like 'caste' and 'hierarchy' with the general sociological notions of stratification and inequality. This 'smug sociocentricity' merely sacrifices the goal of understanding to the convenience of an immediate discourse (1972:261). Such social science does not even recognize the extent to which it is itself the product of a particular type of social system, and therefore uses almost unthinkingly the categories of thought which come most easily to it.

In the case of witchcraft just such a conceptual laziness has been at work. We require far more to observe the discriminations existing in the culture under study, instead of employing those which our own supplies. While doing this, advance can also be made by endeavouring to formulate a common framework which can absorb the details of particular cultural schemas. The common language used here to recast witchcraft seeks to sink beneath cultural terms which are not safely used in anthropology to an analytical level of sufficient depth that satisfactory commensurability between cultures can be attained. Indeed, the proposed framework may be a cultural universal.

Against those who associate convention with variability and nature with universality, one can argue that there are certain characteristics which are not optional for a culture because the idea of their absence is made unintelligible by basic features of the concept of the social life of human beings (Winch 1960:233). Because a society is a conceptual and normative system, students of human social life must deal with the 'actions' of 'persons' in an articulated 'moral space'. The total moral space of a culture will have many dimensions, each constituted by a system of collective representations. For dissolving witchcraft, only two primary structurings will be discussed: firstly, a system of concepts of human action and its evaluation; secondly, a system of person categories. Naturally, to understand any particular patterns of social action it would be necessary to relate these planes to the other classificatory structures.

ACTION AND EVALUATION CONCEPTS

Cultural classifications of human action and its evaluation have been little studied by anthropologists. Of course, data have been obtained incidentally; but, for want of the relevant interests, it has rarely been a subject for inquiry in its own right. Anthropologists thus have attempted to explain 'sacrifice' or 'ritual', for instance, without investigating systematically the concepts of action of the culture in question, and without grasping therefore the kind of principles on which the distinctions of such a system were based. Partly this may have been due to a scientistic presumption that human beings themselves have very little of any insight or worth to say about their own activities. Yet it is evident that there is a very rich and discriminating system of concepts concerning human action embedded in ordinary English, and there is no reason to

113

suppose that a pre-literate culture would be less well endowed. Indeed, folk systems there could well be more elaborate and insightful.

Despite efforts of philosophers and anthropologists to investigate fundamental categories of the human mind, we cannot afford to be confident that the candidates that have already been proposed are sufficiently well grounded empirically. Hence it must be admitted that while the articulated 'moral space' is offered as a cultural universal, the term 'moral' is clearly one of our own culture's action and evaluation concepts. Consequently it cannot be entirely free of the translational difficulties which beset other cultural concepts. The best we can do is to acquire as broad a perspective as possible, and this is why it is so unfortunate that philosophical discussions of morals have normally been conducted on such a narrow cultural and historical basis (Collingwood 1944:43,46; MacIntyre 1971a:1-4). We have often been given general theories of ethics, yet it is surely important to observe that our moral 'ought', for instance, first appeared in the eighteenth century (MacIntyre 1971a:165). Such a notion was absent in Greece, so it is only by a mistranslation that we can say that Kant and the Greek philosophers were arguing about the same subject. Moral concepts are so much a part of — indeed in large part constitutive of — different forms of social life that it is unrealistic to think in terms of a timeless discourse. What we need is less an abstract theory than a social history of moral notions — both a historical perspective on the basic items of our human vocabulary (such as 'person' itself) and the comparative data from students of other cultures. Only this kind of research can give us a better knowledge of what are social universals. Without such a perspective our interpretation is bound to be less refined.

Here perhaps is a role for the sociology of knowledge, for clearly there can be no history of ideas in a vacuum. The Cartesian *cogito ergo sum*, which has so little import for us now, can presumably be set against a general cultural configuration which made it of such concern to Descartes (Wilden 1972:212ff.). No doubt a certain type of social experience lies behind what may be our contemporary equivalent of his dictum — 'I speak, therefore I am a social being'. Mary Douglas has recently put forward the general argument that there is a concordance between social and symbolic experience: the image of the human body mirrors the perception of the body social (1970a). Such a thesis would naturally imply that very different ideas of duty, self, action, and so on, will be found under different social conditions. Durkheim made obligatoriness and desirability universals of morality, but he still suggested that their relative importance could vary considerably (1906:46). It seems feasible, for instance, that there are cultural conditions where Kant's imperatival view of ethics would be barely intelligible since it contains that notion of universalizability by which 'ought' is severed from particular social ties. If Kant's view was partly a response to a growing individualism, obviously it will not suit a culture where the stress falls upon social role instead of the individual who acts a role. Certainly, if we are to understand institutional facts about responsibility and punishment we shall need to uncover the conceptual systems relating to ethics and the nature of the 'person' which they embody.[2]

There is a place for vital research on these subjects, and anthropologists could contribute usefully by giving a comparative perspective on basic concepts in the field of human action. What the outcome of such work will be we cannot tell. Perhaps it is unrealistic to expect complete relativity in the field of morals; but Mauss (1938) has shown how those seemingly basic concepts which we feel ought to be *a priori* and timeless in fact are the result of a complicated history in our own civilization. And Lienhardt, discussing the Dinka concept of self-knowledge, has pointed out how the whole area of 'mind' and 'experience' can be construed differently from the way it is in our culture (1961:149-50). That there are pre-literate societies with extensive 'psychological' vocabularies is well known. What is not certain are the divergences we may find in the fundamental presuppositions of such domains. A comparative study of ideas of human action cannot be just a survey of different evaluations, since the basic concepts may be too discrepant. We already have ethnographic evidence of striking differences in moral consciousness and perception (Read 1955:226). In some cultures, for instance, there is purportedly not that clear differentiation between a 'person' and his situation or status that we find in our own (ibid.:196).

Such interests as these will require semantic anthropology to separate iteslf from that uncritical adherence to a Western philosophy of mind which has so impaired much of our work (Needham 1972:188). We need a broadly based empirical study of different cultural concepts of the human person and his powers. Some studies are already available (Geertz 1966), but research on this topic must be an intensive analysis of cultural categories. Writings under labels like 'culture and personality' studies, or 'psychological anthropology', by virtue of being culture-bound could not be adequate.

A SYSTEM OF PERSON CATEGORIES

The second primary articulation of the moral space we have proposed as a framework for dissolving witchcraft consists of a set of person categories.[3] It is a classificatory system through which is distributed a range of cultural predicates ascribing attributes and powers to different types of human being. Of course we have much data on this subject, but because it was not a leading interest of the functionalist field-workers, the topic was not approached systematically, and so our information remains inadequate even for those cultures best known to anthropologists. For instance, in order to define a 'witch' we should need fully mapped out the different symbolic definitions of those sorts of person categories normally translated as 'sorcerer', 'diviner', 'prophet', 'priest' and so on.[4] So often we have been told that a witch is believed to possess such and such 'supernatural' powers, without being informed as to what the culture in question regards as the natural powers of other categories of human being.

We may regard the 'person field' as structured like a chess board. It forms one plane of the many which make up the total moral space, and therefore cuts through other classifying systems in the culture. With this image we have a framework which makes it clear why witchcraft cannot be approached as if it were a separate topic. The identity 'witch' is only one on a board which contains other persons with differently specified characteristics. Moreover, this one system intersects with others — with concepts of human actions, evaluatory ideas, and other systems of beliefs. We could say that to tackle 'witchcraft' as if it were an isolable problem would be like someone unfamiliar with the game of chess observing a series of movements and then writing a book on 'bishops'. The point is that the 'bishop' cannot be understood apart from — indeed exists only by virtue of — the whole system of definitions and rules which constitutes chess. In Saussurian terms (1949:153ff.), the value of the bishop (or witch) derives from all the other pieces which the bishop (or witch) is not. Neither has any significance in isolation — a striking demonstration of the way in which anthropology is a species of inquiry into the nature of semantic identities and not a matter of that Radcliffe-Brownian butterfly collector identifying natural species.

No doubt such a scheme will seem needlessly intricate to some, but the deficiencies in the functional approach make it necessary to work out a new framework in such an explicit manner. And the scheme is designed to encourage a greater empiricism in this area than has been shown in the past. The structure of the person system is itself an empirical matter. Certainly one will expect there to be recurring patterns cross-culturally — among other reasons because of the appearance of formal categories like marginality in all classifying structures — but it is an ethnographic matter how many pieces each puts on the moral board and what type of discriminations it makes between them.

Undoubtedly one source of past empirical shortcomings has been the enormous influence of Evans-Pritchard's monograph on subsequent studies. This analysis was only an interpretation of a belief structure in one society, and there was no reason to presume that detailed features of Zande thought would be found elsewhere. Unfortunately, however, it has become almost a model for witchcraft studies in general. In many cases it is patently clear that ethnographers have had the Zande scheme in mind when organizing their own data. Gluckman even boldly claimed that Evans-Pritchard's argument applied to 'all African tribes who believe in witchcraft' (1944:61), despite the fact that one of his earliest articles on Zande thought specifically warned against the projecting of any one cultural scheme into a general model (1929:1-2).

It is unfortunately the case that a few excellent monographs have tended to become frameworks into which ethnographers could fit their own field material instead of paying more attention to the particularity of the culture they happen to have studied. Thus it is probably no exaggeration, in view of the enormous influence of Evans-Pritchard's study of the political system of the Nuer — although here too the most 'paradigmatic' insights were missed by his imitators — to suggest that a whole phase in British social anthropology of concern with lineage typologies would have been substantially different had he done his field-work elsewhere. In the case of witchcraft, the Zande distinction between the witch as the possessor of innate psychic power and the sorcerer who consciously manipulates objects, has clearly become the basis for ill-conceived taxonomic generalizations. Evans-Pritchard was not trying to impose on future studies a conceptual strait-jacket, yet this is what the distinction has become, despite protests from other anthropologists about the misguided nature of the enterprise (Turner 1964a). Middleton and Winter, for instance, argue that the witch/sorcerer opposition is vital for comparative work, although some of the cultures discussed in the volume where they make this claim obviously do not possess it (1963 eds: 2). Mair is even prepared to defend the distinction on the basis that the anthropologist is able to find physical evidence in the one case but not in the other (1969:23). It is not merely that the opposition is sometimes just imposed, or that it is normally presented along with suspiciously Western terms like 'spirit' and 'matter'; for even where a Zande-like scheme does appear, the difference between the witch and sorcerer only gets its meaing from the whole system of differences which makes up the set of person categories. Far from accepting this, some have even suggested that it is permissible to overlook the one opposition if it does appear in the effort to arrive at sociological generalizations (Marwick 1966:170). Yet others, given a host of cultural identities, think it sufficient to regard several differently named persons as different kinds of witch.

Clearly it would be better to follow the advice given by Leach in his attempt to rethink anthropology out of the taxonomic phase (1961:10)—

to take each case as it comes along. We need semantic analyses of conceptual fields of the kind Lienhardt made in his study of the terms related to the Dinka notion of *apeth* (1951). One need only think of whether the powers are regarded as hereditary or not, whether they are exercised consciously or not, whether the category is associated with 'foreignness' (Buxton 1963 : 105) or exactly the reverse, to see what a mass of disparate phenomena have been subsumed under the one label of witchcraft. It is not even the case that 'witchcraft' is always disapproved of, nor is the 'witch' always defined by a process of total symbolic inversion. Despite these well known ethnographic facts, some (Mair 1969) still persist in speaking of the 'universal image' of the witch.

Of course, because of their interest in the locus of accusations, the old-style writings on witchcraft have certainly established some patterns which definitely do recur in many societies. But the advantage of employing our framework of person identities and concepts of action is that we can go far beyond the functionalist statements about misfortune and social competition to make a more discriminating study of particular social ideologies. For instance, we can associate particular person categories with certain types of action and motivation. Among the Bakweri, for instance, there is a strong conceptual tie between *liemba* (witch) and *inona* (envy), and, not surprisingly for a people with an egalitarian ethic, a strong link between these and the possession of wealth (Ardener 1973a : 5). Witchcraft can only be understood when the complex which makes up the whole conceptual field in which a *liemba* acts is set out. For the Gonja we have evidence that the act of bewitching can be associated with two very different evaluations of action according to the sexual identity of the witch (E. Goody 1970). Thus, female witches engage in an activity which is disapproved of, while using these powers is actually an accepted convention in the competition between males for authority. Further significant variations are found in terms of the victims of evil-doing. For instance, some categories of person with powers to harm are thought to use their evil indiscriminately, while others aim it at well circumscribed sectors of the moral space of their culture, for instance those persons labelled 'affines'. Clearly it is by following up details like this that we shall be able to distribute those facts clustered into 'the witchcraft problem' into larger cultural schemes of action concepts, ethical theory, and person categories in ways which respect the particularities of each case.

One of the gains of the idea of a moral space is that it is a framework which can encourage an empirical approach to the cultural composition and full scope of the person system. For there is the danger that the alien nature of such categories as 'witch', 'diviner', and so on, because they are not part of the internal structuring of this classificatory plane in our culture, will lead anthropologists to close off this area as concerned with 'mystical belief' or suchlike. But this may badly disfigure the semantic structure of other cultures. Among the Lugbara for instance, the symbolism which defines witchcraft and sorcery is only a part of a larger schema applied to differences in social distance and social time in general (Middleton 1963:271). Among the Safwa, witchcraft and sorcery operate in affinal and descent relationships respectively, which suggests that they are both partial refractions of a larger classificatory system (Harwood 1970:137-8).

There is certainly much evidence that 'political identities' should be included in the same person field as the witch, and political action in the general system of action/evaluation concepts. Religion and political structure are often quite explicitly aspects of a single coherent ideology, so that 'government' is not a separate sphere but merely a dimension of a total symbolic classification (Hocart 1970; Coomaraswamy 1942; Dumont 1972). The outlook of the old-style British anthropologists — that political behaviour was 'real', and rituals and beliefs largely embellishments — obscured this vital semantic point. Hence the numerous instances where the two have been artificially ripped apart and then joined again by some functional hypothesis about the link between mystical beliefs and political structure, such as that ritual sacralizes political statuses and so supports the social order, and so on.

Nor is there any reason to presume that such explicit ideologies are confined to those cultures with an elaborate 'Great Tradition'. For instance, the Swat Pathans (who have been the central ethnographic case in the recent development of the transactional approach to politics (Barth 1965)) clearly display a cultural schema containing the oppositions of power/passivity, violence/mediation, wealth/humility, which subsumes both religious statuses and political action. In Africa too where the institutional-functional tradition has been so strong in anthropology, symbolic analyses have also proved fruitful. Needham has shown 'complementary governance' systems to exist among the Nyoro and Meru (1967;1960a). And among the Nuer, an analysis of the identities 'priest', 'prophet', and 'bull' exposes a larger scheme based on the opposition of violence and peace (Beidelman 1971).

Using this kind of framework for these examples clearly shows that it is considerably more instructive to analyse the collective representations of a culture than make easy resort to the familiar political rhetoric of our own society, or to be concerned with whether it is appropriate to speak of 'chiefs' or not (Needham 1960a:124-5). But to do this we also need analytic terms with which to construct our analyses which will not distort the nature of cultural categories while framing them. We have suggested that the notion of a 'person' system may be of general value here; but there are other general notions which provide conceptual strands of the total moral space. For instance, with the examples used above the male/female opposition seems a likely basic syntactical component. It is an opposition which in many cultures is concordant with the witch/sorcerer distinction; in the Hindu scheme it emerges in the idea of the 'marriage' between the king and the *brahmin* priest; in the secular-mystical dyarchy of the Nyoro it is present in inverted form as the maleness of the princess and the femininity of the diviner. Clearly, also, such a discrimination forms a basic part of the field of kinship classification.

It may well be, then, that the general framework outlined for reshaping witchcraft has a value far beyond this problem. It may provide a scheme in which a good many other traditional areas of the subject can be recast. After all, it is a fairly obvious fact that other cultures are not organized along the lines by which the social sciences are taught in our universities, even if our introductory textbooks frequently give the opposite impression. Having sketched this analytical scheme, our semantic investigation can turn to some ideas from linguistic philosophy to aid our comprehension of the facts now that they have been rearranged.

TYPES OF DISCOURSE; THE 'POINT' OF THE RULES; SPEECH ACTS

A natural language is not a homogeneous structure. In English there are moral terms like 'good', for instance, which do not behave like ordinary descriptive words; and some would argue that there is a 'naturalistic fallacy' which acts as a general boundary marking off the ethical domain, so prohibiting the transmutation of moral concepts into naturalistic discourse about 'effectiveness', 'utility', and the like. There is no reason for thinking that a similar heterogeneity does not exist in other languages. The idea of different 'domains of discourse' may therefore be of wide value, especially in reminding us of features to remember when looking for the appropriate concepts in our own culture to translate those of other societies. If it is accepted here that ethical utterances may not be recast as scientific propositions, or judged by the same types of criteria, it is obviously vital to respond to the existence of corresponding prohibitions in other languages. Naturally, these domains and prohibitions will have to be established empirically; but if there are invariants to be discovered in comparative work on the moral field, we may presume that some of the deepest distinctions on which the configuration of our own domains are based may find parallels elsewhere.

These considerations are even more important when dealing with such problems as witchcraft, because ethical discourse is so closely bound up with human action and evaluation. This is why Wittgenstein's notion 'form of life', which emphasizes the relation of speaking to non-linguistic action by locating language in its broader cultural context, is so useful. Concepts, says Wittgenstein, express our interests (1953: para.570). Thus, in order to understand a mode of discourse we must not only grasp the rules but also the 'point' of those rules. Meaning is part of a game whose conventions have some purpose (ibid.: paras 564-5;Winch 1964:26-7). Consequently it is vital to study the part which concepts play in the life of the community. In other words, if we wish to explain types of discourse we must do it 'by reference to the in-stitutions and forms of social life with which they are associated' (Hampshire 1970:14). By stressing rules and the relation of concepts to action we are able to make our explorations semantic rather than func-tional.

Zande moral concepts are social in a rather different way from that in which the theoretical terms of science are, for instance, because the links between concepts and action are different in the two fields. Perhaps cer-tain of the 'unscientific' aspects of Zande thought become more intellig-ible, therefore, when we look at the relation between 'social knowledge' and 'social interests'. We know that Zande witchcraft beliefs have a practical point, also that the system is not logically complete, in the sense that there are problems an anthropologist could raise which have no interest for the Azande themselves (Evans-Pritchard 1937:24-6). The anthropologist can expose 'conceptual synapses' — beliefs which are not brought together, ideas which are not pushed to a conclusion, ques-tions that are not asked. They are not contradictions, for they lie pre-cisely in areas which are not structured because the Azande see no point in thinking them out. It is too extreme to speak of Zande witchcraft as a system of action rather than a theory (Barden 1972:113); but we should certainly not forget the reason for these rules, which may rest in the close link of the concepts to social action. There is, for example, a great emphasis on particularity. The Azande are not so much interested in who is a witch as in who is causing one to be ill at a particular time (Evans-Pritchard 1937:24-5). Hence, while they claim witchcraft to be hereditary, they only punish individuals.

Similar features appear in conceptual systems in other cultures which share a like location with respect to social interests and practical action. For instance, we ourselves speak about being moulded by external cir-cumstances and influences stemming from early childhood, yet our law punishes a culpable individual. To a degree, therefore, our own legal notions operate by not following up certain lines of investigation. As the judge said in Samuel Butler's *Erewhon*, the fault was in the accused in-dividual and he was not there 'to enter upon curious metaphysical ques-tions as to the origin of this or that...questions to which there would be no end were their introduction once tolerated, and which would result in

121

throwing the only guilt on the tissues of the primordial cell'.

Some jurists have even emphasized that their task is a practical rather than a scientific one. A distinction like that between 'cause' and 'conditions' in jurisprudence is clearly related to this practical role. Evans-Pritchard discussing witchcraft beliefs and the practice of divination spoke of a 'socially relevant cause' (1937:73), but essentially the same notion is expressed in Bacon's famous dictum *'in jure, non remota causa, sed proxima spectatur'* (quoted in Cohen 1950:259n27). Since law is closely tied to conceptual structures and moral evaluations, the complexity of notions of causation in this sphere — for instance, attributing an event to 'negligence', 'accident', 'act of God', and so on — is well worth semantic investigation by anthropologists (see Hart & Honoré 1956). *Mens rea*, for example, links culpability to certain conditions of knowledge and intention; in many branches of law a man is punishable only when a 'free' agent. Once the idea of agency in this sense is established, various lines of questioning need not be raised, for the agent is a responsible individual and is punishable as such. Facts which link him causally by chains which are relevant considerations in other contexts, no longer have any interest. To all intents and purposes, each man then becomes an island complete in himself.

Since law is evidently a field for detailed conceptual inquiry, it is unfortunate that the outlook which cast witchcraft studies into a micropolitical form should also have led to an overwhelming stress on social control in the field of law. Of course we have come a good deal further than the taxonomies of social sanctions proposed by Radcliffe-Brown, and we possess some good monographs in the anthropology of law. On the other hand, the general approach has remained that of 'jural sociology', and references to the work of jurists and philosophers of law remain few. Even today some anthropologists (Mair 1972a:210) still almost instinctively separate law from those topics like religion which involve systems of belief as well as systems of action. But to suggest that law does not entail a study of conceptual relations is preposterous. The links between law, morality, and custom may be complex, and what should be included under law is therefore something of a problem. But whatever is included will be intricately related to the cultural systems of notions about statuses, human actions and ethical evaluation. Even if legal terms do not have quite the same sense as the concepts in ordinary language, they nonetheless relate to them. There are consequently areas of law where the rich conceptual structures of ordinary language relating to action — notions of culpability, chance, responsibility, excuses, free will, agency, cause, motive, intention, etc. — make their presence felt. In actual legal proceedings an outcome sometimes depends upon the minutest of distinctions contained in this field of concepts.

Some might argue that this conceptual complexity stems from literacy, or is the result of the existence of a legal profession, but it would be a gross prejudice simply to assume that similar systems could not be detected in primitive societies. Hence, the anthropology of law also needs to be a semantic investigation, and indeed in some cases might quite literally be a linguistic one. The Yakan, for instance, lack our institutions of law; but litigation, as opposed to argument or just ordinary talking is registered as a distinct style of speech (Frake 1969). Clearly, it will not be possible for the more sociologically inclined to turn to jural and political relations as easy alternatives to tackling the more obviously semantic realms of religion or myth, or to profess an interest in law while declaring that language concerns another type of anthropologist. As all human action is of a conceptual order, there can be no adequate approach to any of the topics anthropology tackles which is not a study of meaning.

Legal actions are highly structured rituals involving the definition and redefinition of persons, and it may well be that Austin's idea of 'performative utterances' will be of great value here.[5] When a jury delivers a verdict it does not *state* that a man is guilty, it *makes* him so. 'Guilt' is a public legal status, and consequently a man is guilty when declared so independently of whether he actually committed the offence of which he had been accused. And when found guilty, a man can only escape this category by being part of a second legal performance which annuls the first — the mere discovery of new evidence is not enough. After all, it is not without significance that a jury is asked whether the accused is guilty or not guilty, and not whether he is guilty or innocent. We can therefore construe verdicts as 'performative definitions', so legal proceedings — and we could add the larger field of criminology (Maguire 1974) — are largely concerned with systems of classification.

This kind of idea applies to witchcraft also. Accusations, denials, the findings of divination, change the public definitions of persons. In all these areas where belief and action are closely related, where utterances define situations and reclassify them, the notion of 'doing things with words' may provide fresh insights. Thus, to take a 'phenomenological' religion where ritual is a means of controlling experience (Lienhardt 1961:234,289ff.), among the Dinka a sacrifice may be regarded as creating the situation which it describes (id.1956:327). Just as 'I name this ship the X' actually does confer the name on the ship, so the ritual sacrifice does not state a fact but actually brings a state into being. Hence we may see the ritual of cutting through the genitals of the slain beast as a clarification and redefinition of the articulation of moral space (id.1961:284-5). Kinship ties are severed by the ritual itself, and the new distance created means that action which would have been labelled incest can, in the new space, not be so categorized. The performance (in

123

Austin's terms) is neither true nor false, but either happy or not depending on a highly complex set of conventions.

Because primitive cultures do not have the means of making a public record of events in the way our literate culture does, anthropologists will possibly find the idea of 'speech acts' of wide use. It will require detailed research to establish how fruitful a notion the 'performative' is. However, Austin's work has not gone uncriticized, and he himself thought that the distinction constative/performative would be absorbed into 'more general families of related and overlapping speech acts' (1962:149). Certainly then, even if performative utterances throw valuable light on some problems, they cannot really be expected to solve more than a narrow range of semantic issues. It is clear that our attention is more profitably directed towards the more minute discriminations which compose the more general framework.

Just what contribution 'speech acts' can make to the development of a philosophical semantics is not clear; but anthropologists could at least aid its growth by providing the comparative perspective to what might otherwise easily be a severely culture-bound enterprise by virtue of the small number of societies with which philosophers are normally familiar. Given the total historical experience of humanity, literate industrial cultures are very unrepresentative. It has been an important development in philosophy that the stress should turn to the great diversity of ways in which ordinary language is used. It is a pity that anthropologists were not more interested in language than they have been, for then we might have been able substantially to aid the researches of another discipline. It seems likely that the ceremonial and instrumental uses of speech would be more evident in non-literate societies, so our researches could have put a general theory of speech acts on a firmer empirical basis.

SEMANTIC CHANGES: SCOPE AND EMPIRICISM

The analysis in this chapter has gathered together some ideas from linguistics and linguistic philosophy in order to demonstrate relatively concretely the difference of outlook and style which exists between semantic anthropology and the older sociological tradition in the discipline. Clearly, the discussion does not provide a new theory of witchcraft. It merely gives an outline of a theoretical framework in which a standard topic in structural-functional anthropology could be reformulated. Other topics, like law and politics, were included in the same general schema used to dissolve witchcraft in order to show that the framework possesses sufficient analytical power to help in a more widespread recasting of anthropology. This move was not one from a conceptual problem on to institutional relations, for our notion of human action renders this division nonsensical. By now we are more than prepared to see categories like 'totemism' or 'religion' dispensed with, but it is important to stress that labels like 'politics' may equally seriously impede our comprehension of other cultures.

It was necessary therefore to develop our argument concerning witchcraft by absorbing other topics, for our experience of the last ten years or so in British anthropology might badly mislead us as to the potential scope of the recent semantic trends. Because analytical advances have been so striking in the fields of kinship and symbolic classification, one might be tempted to infer that the discipline is amenable to this type of recasting only in certain limited areas, and that other topics like law and politics must forever remain fixed in the basic form they assumed under the old sociological identity of the subject. Our integrating several traditionally separate topics in the terms of one analysis was meant to demonstrate the fact that the divisions do not fall between different kinds of problems that anthropology studies, but rather that there are deep differences of outlook between different anthropologists over the general nature of the discipline itself. Thus it should not be thought that in our stressing language and meaning we are drawing attention to past deficiencies just in connection with subjects like religion or myth. The whole of anthropology covers a semantic subject matter, and so the kind of analytical interest which lay behind our recasting of witchcraft could radically change other areas, even those seemingly most remote from semantic concerns like ecology and economics. In other words, semantic anthropology is not a sub-department of anthropology; the semantic style covers all the territory which was included in the older functional social anthropology. The new anthropology cannot be an agglutinative discipline — a patchwork of sociological and semantic parts. Gradually, it is hoped, those same sorts of interests which have transformed major topics will inflect the rest. Obviously we shall have to wait to see how semantic anthropology recasts these areas which have so far been virtually untouched by the developments of the last decade. But it is necessary to conclude by pointing out that, because of the broad nature of the aim of the analysis in this chapter, our argument has done little more than provide a suggestive outline framework for application in specific cases. It is vital to stress that semantic anthropology itself is far more detailed analysis than it is the formulating of general schemas. Indeed, we shall only know the value of our proposed recasting of witchcraft when the ideas we employed are applied to detailed bodies of ethnographic data. Because the discipline is in a profound transition, much of the literature that has pointed the way has tended to be polemical and this has somewhat obscured the nature of the work that belongs to the new identity. We should never forget that Evans-Pritchard, who so significantly led the shift from function to meaning, was not a polemicist, and that by far his best work consists of monographs which resulted from his own field-work.

It is important to make this point because many of those who have expressed antipathy towards the recent trends in the discipline have alleged that anthropology is turning from an empirical science into abstract metaphysics. But this is to misperceive the nature of these developments entirely. Any unprejudiced reading of the typical articles which have established the break with the older functional style will see how much they are a matter of close attention to ethnographic facts. Indeed, many spectacular articles have been reworkings of classical functionalist monographs; and the experience has often been that the monographs themselves are shown to be severely deficient in crucial ethnographic information when exposed to modern analytical interests. Semantic anthropology certainly is far more dependent upon detailed ethnography than functionalism ever was.

Of course we can be proud of the fieldwork record of British anthropology during the past half-century. But when, nowadays, we draw attention to the theoretical shortcomings of structural-functionalism yet then praise its representatives for the thoroughness of their field research, we must not forget that the known influence of theoretical interests on research procedure lessens the weight of this compliment considerably. Obviously all theories are selective, and it would be unfair to expect functionalists to have gathered the facts which are relevant to our inquiries when they were not interested in our sorts of questions. This is why a fieldwork tradition must be a part of the newer anthropology: we must clearly gather new data by a process of investigation which is specifically directed by our own concerns.

But this is an issue which has more general implications, for the deficiency in functionalist fieldwork was of a far more fundamental kind than we have so far suggested (Ardener 1971a:450ff.). It is clear from the speciousness which pervades so much functional writing that in a great many cases the functionalists did not even ask those questions which were vital to collecting the information necessary to supporting *their own* contentions. For a discipline which prided itself on its scientific nature and was proud of its fieldwork basis, it is striking how frequently there appeared general statements about the functional relationships between institutions entirely unsupported by any empirical evidence. The failing here was not that of selectivity, but a basic error concerning what scientific investigation of social life involved, and so a mistaken view of what constituted empiricism there. It is therefore doubly important that we emphasize here that our explorations in language have not been part of an effort to convert anthropology into philosophy, but merely an attempt, after a consideration of the character of the subject matter our science deals with, to do anthropology better. We must give attention to the sort of theoretical issues discussed above in order for our empiricism to be more effective. Indeed, unless one acknowledges the conceptual nature of human beings one cannot be scientific in describing their activities at all. It is for that very reason that, as semantic anthropology attempts to rectify some of the theoretical defects of the older style of investigation, it at the same time rectifies its empirical shortcomings too.

7 Understanding Conceptual Structures

The method we followed to show how 'witchcraft' could be analytically dissolved was an illustration of how a semantic approach can rework a traditional anthropological problem by reorganizing the way the materials of the discipline have been customarily arranged. But with these newer interests anthropology is not only reshaped, it is also extended. The present chapter is a contribution to this latter development, and comprises an examination of several systems of collective representations in our own culture. While these conceptual structures are all 'systems of thought', they are also far more than this, although the kinds of relations they have with social life varies considerably.

In order to maximize the value of this extension of interest, the major focus has been on natural science and two conceptual systems related to science — the work of Freud, and alchemy. Clearly any one of these topics could have been the subject for an extensive investigation in its own right. I have instead made several briefer sketches here because, while the aim is to use our ethnography to illuminate the one problem of what it is to know, interpret, understand, and mean, it is better to assemble reminders on this subject piecemeal by exploring a diversity of terrains. By this means we can see a complicated network of similarities, overlaps, and differences, as we pass from one conceptual structure to the next. We can regard the anthropologist's task here as finding ways to read a map in order to understand what Wittgenstein called a 'form of life'. In the explorations below we shall see how in different maps, language can chart, constitute or disguise a landscape.

MAPS, SYSTEMS, AND SEMANTICS

Some clarification of our two central notions of 'map' and 'system' is required before we can begin our investigations. The former is not employed in any technical sense. Thus our cartographic analogy has none of the implications of 'mapping theory', nor of a concept like 'cognitive map'. On the other hand, it is far more than an organizational device, its value here mainly being that something that is itself a representative device can be employed as a means of representation. Having said this, we must remember that there are two broad types of representation which have to be distinguished, and which involve two different conceptions of meaning—a 'mirror' theory, and a 'semantic field' theory. With the former, a map is 'iconic': it is a picture which projects a spatial reality. When dealing with a semantic field, on the other hand, one can speak about finding one's way around a conceptual structure, but the spatial language is now clearly figurative. This second sort of map does not project a spatial reality, and, as we shall see in some of the cases discussed below, the terrain involved is the conceptual structure itself. In other words, some terms have a referential meaning pointing to something existing beyond language; other terms mean by virtue of conceptual relations within a field.

Having stated this distinction abstractly, we can anticipate some of the variations we shall encounter in exploring our conceptual structures by briefly considering the different relations which exist between a terrain and the signs used on an ordnance survey map. To convey accurate information, a road marked on a map, for instance, must duplicate the spatial structure of the real road, but it hardly matters what colour scheme is chosen to differentiate between the various classes of route. One will not observe contour lines in reality, but as an organized system they register data about altitude which someone familiar with carto-graphic symbolism could transform into iconic form. Many signs on a map are arbitrary, but this is unimportant provided there is a key listing the meanings of the signs employed. All that is then needed for the map to convey information is that the sign be in the right location, and that there be a large enough repertoire to allow all the required distinctions between different features to be made. We should also remember that on a map will be information which is not about the landscape at all, but which merely concerns how to read the map. Equally important, no map is a total re-presentation of reality in the sense of charting all its features. All maps are selective because there is a 'point' to their construction which makes only certain kinds of phenomena significant.

Although this chapter explores some of our own conceptual systems, the analyses are linked by the idea of 'system' as set out in Evans-Pritchard's famous study of Zande thought. He was there using ethnography to test views about the nature of primitive modes of thought; but I shall stress the extent to which the systemic features he discovered are in fact properties of all conceptual structures. By this means, there are two gains from our extending anthropology to embrace our culture. We can on the one hand use ethnography to illuminate our own systems of thought, but we also are able to employ this greater understanding of ourselves in the analysis of more orthodox anthropological problems.

Evans-Pritchard showed Zande witchcraft beliefs and the practices of divination and oracular consultation to be interlocking parts of a closed system constructed in a mystical idiom. Within such a structure the Zande reason well, but they have no language in which to be critical of the whole field. The mode of discourse is the very fabric of their thought, and as men are born into conceptual structures in the same way that they are born into a social system, they cannot think that their thought is wrong. Any criticism of the structure must therefore be made in the language of the structure, which as a consequence is actually reinforced. The mystical beliefs hang together; and as the system provides only a limited number and kind of labels for naming events, a problem in one part is necessarily tackled by another mystical notion which is equally a part of the system (Evans-Pritchard 1937: 195, 337-9). No doubt in Zande thought we meet the systemic aspect of conceptual structures in an extreme form. Nonetheless, this feature is characteristic of all maps, and is possibly necessary for something to be a map at all. Whatever differences we note between the landscapes studied below, the notion of system is applicable to all — it certainly does not distinguish 'primitive' from 'civilized' thought.

The implications of the notion of system can be elaborated by viewing a map as a set of answers to a series of questions. A conceptual structure rests upon a metaphysical presupposition which contains the fundamental kind of interrogative with which the map is concerned, and which also determines the nature of the answers. It is vital to recognize this 'correlativity' of questions and answers (Collingwood 1940: 15; cf. Waismann 1965: 405ff.) in the sort of investigations semantic anthropology undertakes. An answer assumes all that the question presupposes. Thus it is necessary to identify the type of question in order to be able to read the map correctly. And indeed, this principle has a further import in our attempts to understand other cultures. An anthropologist is not restricted merely to tracing the links between native concepts; but if he goes beyond, his inquiries must, if they are to be 'to the point', in some sense be a part of the same type of discourse. Thus, Evans-Pritchard received no answer when he asked what the effect would be of giving unaddressed *benge* to a fowl (1937: 314), because the question failed to grasp the nature of *benge* and the place of the oracle in Zande life: the inquiry simply had no sense or relevance for them.

This relation between questions and answers is one example of that 'field dependence' which is implicit in the idea of a map, and which affects many of the characteristics of our knowledge. It means clearly that there will be internal standards which must be grasped in order to understand a map. Thus, we cannot legitimately import the criteria of scientific reliability for judging the correctness of using an oracle to arrive at decisions, since this is wrongly to use one map to construe the 'point' of another (Wittgenstein 1969: para. 609). Similarly, there is little sense in proposing that we view science but not Zande thought as rational, on the grounds that beliefs in the latter case are held uncritically; for there are different standards of criticism and many reasons for being critical. We shall not understand other 'forms of life' unless we appreciate such facts about social semantics. Indeed we risk totally misreading aspects of other cultures. For instance, it would not be pertinent to suggest a genetic examination to test the statement that Zande witchcraft is hereditary, because such beliefs concern the structure of moral space and not biological identities.

'Field dependence' produces both common features in conceptual structures and also a diversity of 'forms of life' to be judged by different criteria and understood in different ways. Anthropologists are concerned with social logic and practical reasoning, and the idea that there is one ideal form of reasoning — in logic this has typically been the deductive schema — is hopeless when dealing with substantive issues. We need rather a historical and comparative inquiry into the diverse principles involved in conceptual structures in different fields (Toulmin 1958: 240, 254-5). Legal reasoning, for instance, is not syllogistic. It does not have the same purpose as an argument in deductive form. Assertion, argument, certainty and criticism have their life in a system (Wittgenstein 1969: para. 105). We need to grasp the nature of the discourse to see whether an argument is good or not. In a diversity of conceptual structures there are different warrants for making inferences, different grounds for rebuttal, different points to argument, and more generally a variety of purposes in using language. The extent of this diversity will appear in our analyses of the conceptual landscapes below.

RELIGIOUS LANGUAGE

That some of the basic features of Zande thought can be replicated in the sphere of religion will occasion no surprise for those who look upon both as irrational. But the nature of the overlap is far more significant than this prejudicial view allows. Religious discourse is a map for which God is the 'integrator' (Ramsey 1961): theology is thus 'God-talk'. From this presuppositional concept may be derived a general idea of the nature of the map, and so insights about how one could best translate landmarks on the map. As the boundary notion, God has a strange status. The nonreligious do not properly use such a map, and for the religious the question of the existence of God does not arise. 'God exists', therefore, is perhaps best treated not as a religious proposition itself, but rather as the presupposition for any religious language.

As the Zande system is a total interpretational structure, so religious language forms a framework which can be applied to the whole of experience. Whether actually mentioned or not, the concept of God is contained in all religious accounts, and underwrites them all. It is a name which can supply labels for all events. In the Zande case, a system of concepts defines events as evidence of personal activity. Someone outside the conceptual structure, however, cannot see the events as of the type they claim them to be. Thus, an anthropologist can see that a granary has fallen, but not accepting the presupposition of the mystical framework, he cannot read any of the events in the same way as the Zande. Likewise, in our culture a religious man may see all of history as testimony to the fact that God works in the world. An unbeliever, on the other hand, unable to employ such a label as 'act of God' cannot see history as evidence in this sense at all. Two observers (one a believer and the other not) can agree on a sequence of facts yet disagree on what they all mean (Wisdom 1944). In some sense, then, since they view from totally different frameworks, the facts were not really the same for both.

The fundamental outlook of the believer has been called a 'blik' in some recent philosophical discussions of religion (Flew & MacIntyre 1963 eds). Bliks are neither true nor false, but as they state the general nature of things they do influence what counts as a fact and an explanation. Because they are fundamental, disagreements cannot be settled by observation. This oddity, however, has nothing specifically to do with religious maps. Similar features mark the edge of any system; the priority of the framework has consequences for the concept of evidence in all spheres. It is thus only one version of a general truth to say that it is not obscurantism which makes the theologian start with God and signs of his activity rather than with raw experience. Belief in the Grace of God, in other words, 'cannot be established by empirical evidence but, once accepted, it can be shown to have empirical application' (Mitchell 1955:174). This clearly is of importance for those who base their claims to religious knowledge on religious experience. The language of 'encounter' is a *petitio,* because it is the use of religious language to label the experience that requires justification (Martin 1952). And this, like all language, exists in the public realm whence it derives its authority. It is shared language which is the source of meaning ; and for many people this public use of religious language may even constitute their religious experience.

Because this subordination of experience and evidence to a discourse structure is general, science too must inevitably be a conceptual system. This does not of course mean that there are not divergences. For instance, science is widely regarded as a search to prove or refute theory. By contrast, some have stressed that as religion is based on faith, evidence must be inadequate. Faith must be a free decision — an 'uncompelled mode of "experiencing as"' (Hick 1967:151). In the Christian religion there are some vital historical events, but Christianity concerns not merely the historicity of these events but their profound significance, and this is quite beyond any notion of empirical evidence.

A characteristic of religious maps which has been commented on by believers and sceptics alike is the oddness of the language employed. Ramsey asserts that 'religious language has to be logically odd to be appropriate currency for such an odd situation as religious people claim to speak about' (1967: 90). It is true that much science is expressed not in ordinary language but in subsidiary systems like mathematics, and that ordinary terms very often receive special definitions; but this does not amount to the peculiarity of the languaging of religious conceptual structures. Christians, for instance, believe in a personal God, but much 'person' language is felt to be inappropriate. One can say that God 'sees' the evil in the world, but it would not be judged a real grasp of the meaning of this statement to inquire whether He had eyes or not. The capitalization in He marks a distinction of logical category of such a kind that some have stated that to ask a question about the reality of God 'is to ask a question about a *kind of reality,* not about the reality of *this or that* being' (Phillips 1967: 67).

Some of these problems are usefully construed as cases where ordinary language operates with critical qualifiers added (Ramsey 1967). Both 'good' and 'cause' are terms employed in ordinary language; but in religious expression one encounters phrases like 'First cause' and 'Infinite good', which clearly mark a profound difference yet also try to say something about it. In the same way that an algebraic expression containing either zero or infinity looks like a fraction yet behaves in a logically different way, so this concept of goodness is not just very extreme, and such a cause is not ordinary but very remote. Such oddities are clearly vital when interpreting religious maps, for some would argue that the fact that we can barely construe 'First cause' is exactly what makes the notion so apposite in a religious context. If one of the assumptions is that one cannot in the ordinary sense 'know' God, then a translator must realize that this may manifest itself in the belief of members of the religious community that religious language is deficient, that all the signs on the religious map signify inadequately. Linguistic shortcoming is thus actually an instance of symbolic appropriateness — a view which is explicit in many religious traditions. The very failure of language reveals something of the subject matter of religion. It draws attention to the significance of silence, for instance. In this way a cumulation of inadequate signs as in the *via negativa* says something positive.

Wittgenstein closed his *Tractatus* by writing that what could be said at all could be said clearly, and that everything else should be passed over in silence. There is a place in religion for silence certainly, as for ritual and the special use of words in hymn and prayer, but the total absence of language is scarcely conceivable. It would be like The Bellman in Lewis Carroll's 'The Hunting of the Snark' who, realizing that the characters on maps were no more than conventional signs, preferred to set out with a blank piece of paper. To abandon language completely would make it difficult to sustain religion as an important human activity (Ferré 1970 : 63). Religious communities may hold their discourse to be inadequate, but they normally hold there are 'rules for significant stuttering' (Ramsey 1966 : 219).

Modern linguistic philosophers have stressed that different language-games have different rules for signification, and that it is better to examine these closely than to try to establish any general distinction between meaning and nonsense. The term 'symbol', of course, implies a relation of 'standing for' rather than one of reproduction. But in calling religious language symbolic one is emphasizing that it conveys meaning in a far more oblique way. Signs on a religious map are accompanied by rules which state their inability to signify adequately. So, whereas unclarity may be a deficiency in scientific discourse, in the religious sphere excessive articulateness may be an error. Indeed, there is a very general difference between the models employed in the two areas (Ramsey 1964). The notion of iconicity is vital in scientific model-making, but in religious discourse there is a predominance of 'disclosure' models which do not picture reality but merely deal in hints. Just as the Nuer statement 'twins are birds' is not a statement of identity, and is intelligible only in terms of the whole system of Nuer religious utterances, so a statement like 'Mary was a virgin mother' contains a disclosive copula. What it discloses requires a grasp of the rest of the symbolic structure of Christian discourse.

Clearly, if anthropologists are to tackle this kind of issue more competently we shall need to cultivate the sort of sensitivities possessed by literary scholars. Indeed, the oddness of religious discourse has been compared to poetic language (Hepburn 1957). This paralled is a useful reminder of a general lesson which creative literature teaches about language and meaning, namely that meaning can often be conveyed in a striking way precisely by breaking the normal linguistic rules. A grammatically well-formed utterance may be quite inappropriate while an ungrammatical one can be semantically 'on form'. Semantic investigations have to cope not only with a diversity of conventions, but also with the semantic power of purposive non-conventionality.

Lastly, we must point out that similarity between Christian religion and Zande moral notions which springs from the close relation to social life which they share. Religion is a 'way of life' attached to personal conduct in a way which is not so of science. Religious events are not facts glanced at by passive observers. There is a discernment revealing a depth to existence which produces a commitment to live one's life in a certain way. Nothing like the scientific 'passion for truth' or the 'striving for objectivity' resemble this. Theology concerns language about God, but religious language, like prayer, is addressed to God in a way which affects one's own life. It is a discourse of 'self-involvement' (Evans 1963), which possibly explains some of the odd features it displays.

This intimacy of religious expression and personal life, combined with the fact that religious language often does not mean what it seems to say, leads to changes in the reading of religious maps over time. Successive generations 'reword' the landscape to make it a better means of expressing its contemporary significance, as is clear from many of the recently proposed translations of theology into philosophical anthropology. Bishop Robinson, for instance, wishing to make God as real for our modern secular scientific world as He was for the ages of faith, was profoundly unsure what in Christian thought he should defend. To make a religion meaningful for our society seemed to require a very radical recasting of the traditional categories (1963). In a similar vein, Bultmann has said that the phraseology of the New Testament is no longer significant for us and so must be 'demythologized' by being converted into existentialist terms (Buren 1963). Tillich reflects a like outlook when he defines religion as that which is of 'ultimate concern', and declares that 'God' means the depth of human being.

The difficult semantic problem here is whether such a reading is not so unorthodox as to destroy the religiousness of the discourse. Karl Barth, for instance, has strongly protested that theology is about God and not about man. MacIntyre has claimed that those theologians who entertain the possibility of translating religion into other terms are atheists: the modern situation is like a culture having the words of a language-game but not knowing what to play with them (1963: 23). No one could possibly deny the close link between religion and social life; but the conative view (Brathwaite 1955) that religious beliefs are mere backings for moral action — one extreme form which the 'anthropological' rewriting of theology can take — is quite unacceptable. The ethical aspect of religious beliefs is undeniable, but it does not constitute religion. Religious assertions lie somewhere between between ethics and science. They are 'too factual to be called specifically moral, and yet too closely bound up with our conduct to be called in the ordinary sense factual' (Hare 1957: 189). There is an essentially cognitive dimension to a religious map (Macquarrie 1967: 110), so to be a Christian requires assent to certain 'beliefs that'. To acknowledge the human and social dimension of such a map does not allow us to eliminate this element by a reductive translation.

Just as we may stress the role of Zande beliefs in their ordinary life, but not interpret them as mere backings for social existence — enshrining values which maintain the social structure, and so on — so we cannot exclude the presuppositions of religious discourse without so altering it as to destroy the nature of the map.

SCIENCE AND SEMANTICS

Many of those features of Zande thought which we have stressed are evident in the conceptual structure of natural science (Polanyi 1962: 287ff.), and it is unfortunate that such parallels have so rarely been followed up. No doubt this is partly owing to the prestige that science enjoys in our society. It is so set apart from other maps that the idea that it is in one perspective a linguistic structure seems absurd. Positivism destroyed epistemology and so allowed science a scientistic self-understanding. Only methodological problems were tackled, so science was quite unreasonably protected from genuine philosophical scrutiny. Knowledge was defined by the existence and achievements of science (Habermas 1972: 67).

But one need only reflect on the discrepancies between logical positivism, inductivism, Popperism, and the view of science associated with Kuhn, to realize that even in science notions like 'fact' and 'evidence' are extremely problematic. That there are features of scientific maps which overlap with those of others clearly makes science, too, an appropriate subject for semantic investigation: science also is a conceptual system which belongs to a certain community. Moreover, science — like all knowledge — is in language, even if in this case we are dealing with a mode of discourse which is most carefully constructed. The neo-Kantians have valuably emphasized that science is one morphology of significance among others: one symbolic form manifesting man's semantic capacity. Even in natural science, therefore, man is 'constantly conversing with himself' (Cassirer 1965: 25). Quite apart from the fact that anthropology still suffers from Radcliffe-Brown's ill-based image of a 'natural science of society', this is a good reason why we cannot afford to remain ignorant of the real nature of science. If we are to extend the subject to include the civilization in which science is so important, ignorance here will be a crippling illiteracy. To begin with, it is vital to realize how profoundly the prominence of scientific discourse in our experience may affect our translational predispositions when interpreting other cultures.

To stress the semantic side of science necessarily involves the problem of the relation between the map and the map maker. Despite modern developments in theoretical physics which have prompted reflection regarding the link between the 'knower' and the 'object', the scientific community generally subscribes to the view that its maps describe and explain the external world. Of course, we know that human beings are not passive recorders: our perception is selective and organizational, which clearly must affect science (N.R. Hanson 1958). But the human mind also plays an imaginative and creative role in theoretical construction. The scientific map may be realist (Harré 1970), but it is still a humanly created conceptual structure.

This difficulty has to be somewhat re-expressed when one realizes that science is not a self-supporting system. Its practices are the result of epistemological choices, and its presuppositions rest it on a metaphysical framework. It is not just in our century that science has become philosophical — it has never been free of philosophy. A science cannot be built independently, for some metaphysical system will always find expression through the constraints that are felt in the choice of basic concepts.

This larger theoretical structure has been termed a 'general conceptual system' (Harré 1964). There is an 'idea of nature' which at any time determines the basic features of science, but which cannot be explained by the science built upon it. There is a presupposition in a scientific system which, because it constitutes the limits of explanation, cannot be regarded as either true or false (Collingwood 1940: 31-3). In other words, scientific knowledge and all our critical powers exist inside a basically fiduciary framework (Polanyi 1962: 297, 266-7). Most of our beliefs have foundations, but ultimately there are beliefs which lack grounds and which we simply trust (Wittgenstein 1969: para. 253). These basic foundations, however, determine 'the direction in which the analysis of phenomena should proceed and the content which must be included to make an explanation acceptable' (Harré 1964:105). The presuppositions, in other words, produce a language and determine what will be regarded as acceptable scientific method. Theory, in this way, determines 'the kinds of things, properties and processes we are prepared to admit (ibid.: 50). Newtonian mechanistic corpuscularianism, for instance, required discrimination between the 'primary' and 'secondary' qualities of Lockean philosophy. A different outlook like Berkeley's *esse est percipi* would have produced another kind of conceptual structure. Sciences exist within a larger 'epistemological space', so their histories are only surface effects of an 'archaeology' which forms the unconscious of all knowledge, which decides how it shall be arranged and approached, and what shall not be formulated at all (Foucault 1970: xi, 280). Different scientific paradigms therefore do not really refute one another. They chart different landscapes; so rather than think of theoretical clashes here it is perhaps more useful to see the situation as that of a community dispensing with one language and acquiring another.

As with the Zande case, the semantic priority of the system means that a theoretical framework in science supplies a limited type of label for the events charted by the map. The language of scientific questions thus influences the kind of answers that are appropriate. It is because a whole conceptual structure supplies events with their significance that inductivism is untenable. One cannot proceed from an accumulation of separate facts to generalizations, because facts only become significant as landmarks on a map. Neither single facts nor raw experience are basic in science: it is the whole theoretical construct which is primary.

This view conflicts with many widely accepted accounts of the nature of scientific thought and activity, but these familiar self-images have recently been severely challenged as science has been described in new terms. Most notable here is the work of Kuhn (1970), with its employment of disturbing notions like 'paradigm' and 'scientific revolution'. Although Popper's 'conjectures and refutations' view (1963) rightly challenged the inductivist myth, it now forms a conventional wisdom. The recent redescriptions of the scientific 'forms of life' can thus usefully be understood by pointing out the inadequacies of his philosophy of science.

We may say that those who share a certain 'form of life' constitute an epistemic community. Such a community constructs maps upon the basis of shared assumptions about the world. The sociology of various communities will naturally reveal significant differences. For example, we might expect a hierarchical and authoritarian ethos in a religious community where some members are accorded a special authority which destroys the equivalence of observers. For Popper, the essence of the scientific community is the competitive and critical spirit born in Greece. Science is egalitarian and antagonistic to tradition. The rationality of science is constituted by a 'free competition of thought'.

Although Popper well captures in these terms some characteristics of science, there are other important features which he either omits or misdescribes — and they often involve exactly those features which the scientific map shares with others. For instance, Popper contends that the most basic property of a scientific assertion is its openness to falsification. So he requires a radical demarcation between the metaphyical and the empirical. But, as we have seen, science is built up on a metaphysical framework. Secondly, scientific language forms a heterogeneous system just like the discourse of other maps.[1] Some terms are labels for real objects; some are theoretical fictions; yet others serve a logical function. It makes no sense to propose a single distinguishing characteristic for the scientific map — whether it be falsifiability, verifiability, or any other.

Popper is quite correct to point out that, besides the critical aspect of science, there is a creative process. But his notion of 'conjecture' disguises the extent to which the structure of this formative phase is under control. Certainly it is not inductive, and cannot be handled adequately by Aristotelian logic. But the semantic principles involved are describable, and it soon becomes clear that although concepts like 'falsifiability' and 'corroboration' are part of the life of science, to describe its semantic structure more fully we need to resort to other principles like 'simplicity' and 'elegance'. Analogical thinking for example, which plays a very important part in religious discourse, is also prominent in the model construction which constitutes so much of the growth of science (Hesse 1966). Theorizing in science is often by a conscious 'displacement of concepts' (Schon 1963) from a familiar context to one that is less understood, although here it is vital to stress a basic difference between the sort of models in religious discourse and those in science where iconic charting is essential. In the former, the link constructed by language may itself be sufficient (Emmet 1966: 87). In science, on the other hand, a projective model establishes a field for empirical investigation in order to see which analogies are positive and which negative — that is, such a model is a spur to determining how much of the original situation is duplicated by the new.

Lastly, as theoretical revision — especially on a large scale — is comparatively rare in science, Popper's critical ethos actually describes untypical phases in the life of the scientific community. For Kuhn, science is 'a succession of tradition-bound periods puncuated by non-cumulative breaks' (1970:208), so that a theory of scientific development must describe a value system and an institutional structure through which it is enforced and transmitted (1972a: 21). 'Normal' science is not critical. It is governed by a paradigm which dictates the problems and limits the conceptual resources for dealing with them, In normal periods a traditional framework is accepted, and most research is mere puzzle-solving within its terms. This structure defines the puzzles by its very language. Moreover, since paradigms embody a general 'idea of nature', paradigm shifts cannot be cumulative. The history of scientific thought is not a succession of solutions to eternal problems since the problems alter as the framework changes. This is why scientific choice here is of a conceptual —even translational—nature (Kuhn 1972:267ff.): there cannot be any completely neutral evidence to decide factually between rival paradigms.

Since Kuhn's 'paradigm' is a kind of closed system, we can see the way in which a scientific conceptual structure must resemble Zande thought — a system which for Popper is essentially unscientific. It has been said that one of the defining characteristics of primitive thought is its ability to escape wholesale refutation by absorbing all events into its terms, or at least by marking off those which cannot be accommodated as anomalous. But the paradigm nature of science means there is only a difference of degree in this respect. Because it is only occasionally that problems lead to large-scale theoretical revision, most of the time science lives with its anomalies and seeks for solutions in traditional terms. Of scientists too, therefore, it could be said that they reason well within a system: 'secondary elaboration' is found in scientific just as in primitive thought. Because science is an intricate conceptual structure, it is never obvious where difficulties should be located — perhaps the framework must be changed; perhaps an orthodox solution will be found; perhaps the experimental evidence will be discounted. A scientific system is conceptually stratified, so we can investigate one level only by accepting what lies beneath it. Unless we do this we have no language to frame our problem. The underlying levels supply the meaning of the terms we use in constructing our scepticism (Toulmin 1953: 80-2), so there can be no total doubt (Wittgenstein 1969: para. 115). Thus, just as the Zande cannot escape their mystical idiom, so at any time a certain language constitutes the fabric of scientific thought.

If this is a characteristic which science shares with other maps, one fact must not be overlooked. Anomaly may be a permanent feature of systems of classification in primitive societies, but it is part of the scientific 'form of life' to regard problems as theoretical challenges which demand some answer. We know nothing of the historical development of Zande ideas, but the stability of primitive models is probably a well grounded facet of societies which tend to exclude history from their self-definition. If science is not that continual critical process of the Popperite view, nonetheless the scientific map is one which does evolve, and which sometimes goes through radical restructurings.

Behind such a difference many kinds of factors will be at work. But the problem cannot be posed satisfactorily as the question why primitives do not evaluate and revise their beliefs in the light of contrary empirical evidence (F. A. Hanson 1970: 61). Neither the Zande nor scientists have brute empirical evidence. Our evidence here is what our culture's system of beliefs say the facts are. Likewise, the difficulty is not solved by saying that the Zande have only a single language available and so are not able to reject their one map, for the paradigm nature of science also restricts the available discourse. A paradigm is rejected not when something is seen to be wrong with it but when a second language is formed (Kuhn 1970: 77). But in normal science no second map is ready to hand. It is the way it is formed, where its elements come from, and how it grows into a paradigm, that is puzzling.

One obvious difference between the maps of science and those commonly found in primitive societies is that they are languaged in very different terms. Pre-literate societies have a strong preference for constructing 'anthropomorphic' models, that is, models in the idiom of social relations. This might be a factor in differential stability, but it also raises the problem of what influences the choice of language for the various maps made in different kinds of society. Lévi-Strauss suggests that our civilization places its emphasis on culture (the relationship of society to the environment), which leads to our technological advance but which also produces our social dislocations (in Charbonnier 1970 ed.: 40-2). Primitive cultures, by contrast, place a higher value on the social, thus attaining a degree of harmony our society lacks. Possibly their preference for maps in a personal idiom is one manifestation of this outlook. And primitive society itself, because stable, can make a very good source for models (Horton 1964: 99), although not of course for dynamic ones. Perhaps, therefore, more than a contingent relationship was involved when scientific and technical progress in the West was accompanied by the stripping away of the anthropomorphic qualities from major areas of culture.

Certainly many of our conceptual systems were reworked in mechanistic language, thereby producing a different sort of map. In some areas of our thinking this process has gone too far. It seems strange to us, in a scientific culture, that there should be others who use anthroposocial maps in such a widespread way. On the other hand, it is no less intriguing that our own social sciences have borrowed concepts and methods from the physical sciences to construct maps which actually are about human action. Unfortunately we know little about the intricacies of these processes of conceptual influence. Historians of science, for instance, while not all writing in normative tones, nonetheless have tended to offer very general models of the development of science — whether it be in terms of accumulation, catastrophism, rejectionism, or a populational schema. It would be much more valuable — as is now being recognized (Toulmin 1969; N. R. Hanson 1969) — if generality were abandoned in favour of seeing the history of science as a field for detailed inquiry into particular processes of conceptual change.

It would be a pity if semantic anthropology had nothing to offer here. In particular, that complex construct known as common sense could be an object of our study. It is incorrect to think that common sense forms an unchanging map, unaffected by the evolving nature of the constructs of the scientific community. But the linkage between the two is complex. Science clearly grows out of ordinary experience, problems and language, although once a theoretical system is crystallized the map tends increasingly to be constructed in a mathematical language and to refer to events which are not a part of daily experience. There is also the reverse process whereby elements of scientific maps, after a time-lag, are displaced and filter back into common parlance. A Freudian rhetoric is now spoken by those who have never read the works of Freud, and it is no wonder that some of the concepts have been radically changed in transmission. Likewise, one age would have found Newtonian science strange, whereas today — since our common sense is by now Newtonian — it is relativity theory which seems to tamper with obvious categories.

THE FREUDIAN MAP

The historical relationships of influence between different maps can show us why so many disciplines concerned with human thought and action have taken the form they have. This process can be illustrated by the Freudian conceptual system itself. The status of natural science in our culture makes it a privileged source for constructing other maps. Thus, there is no doubt that the succession of associationism by gestalt psychology was influenced by the growth of field physics in the late nineteenth century. But this same prestige also gives science the potential to infect other maps and to cause us to misread them. Freudian discourse is a victim of this kind of contamination. It suffers from a carto-graphic interference which could justly be called a 'disease of language', and so is mythology in Müller's sense. The Freudian landscape is languaged with scientific metaphors which have become so familiar that the subject matter dealt with by psychological maps is disguised. Mythology, one should realize, need not be anthropomorphic (Toulmin 1957), and in our type of society it is not really suprising that an increasing amount is being supplied by science. But it may not always be recognized as such, precisely because it does have a scientific background. Psychology has sought for what it thought to be a genuinely scientific identity; but, like the other social studies, the price it has paid has been too high. For, when a map is concerned with human action, it is not only misleading but also unscientific to base it upon the sort of scientific images which the social sciences have found so attractive.

So many different criteria for defining science have been proposed that the decision to include or exclude any system involves controversy as to the legitimacy of various competing definitions.[2] The issue is the less important (on this general level) in this case, since Freud's thought was complex, ever growing, and finally did not really form one integrated system. The discussion here is therefore concerned with only one leading tendency of Freudian rhetoric. The scientific shortcomings of psychoanalysis have frequently been decried; many have emphasized the odd relationship which exists there between data and theory, for instance. I shall stress the fact that what constitutes science must depend on the nature of the

143

phenomenon being investigated. In this view, psychology is, on the contrary, already harmfully scientistic and ought to look far less like physics than it already does. As philosophers have pointed out (Toulmin 1948: 134: Wittgenstein 1966: 28-9, 42), scientific analogies here have become dangerously misleading.

Psychoanalytic theory grew out of a practice of therapy which consisted largely of a process of communication between patient and analyst. At this level, Freud was aware that he was dealing with motives and meanings, and that he was investigating semantic phenomena like the principles of disguise and transformation in human semiotics. (The writings of Lacan are a valuable reminder of this aspect of his work.) That this is the subject matter of psychology is in part revealed by the very oddity of the relation between therapy and explanation: therapy largely is the giving of an explanation (Wollheim 1971: 150-1).However, when Freud expresses his thought in general theoretical terms, he speaks of psychology as if it were concerned with a deterministic-physical system. Freud's achievements in revealing unsuspected complexities in human semantics are undeniable; but he also presents us with a map constructed out of technological and hydraulic images — a mental topography thus resembling a Newtonian dynamic system, a model which was already out of date when Freud was writing. Freud's map now refers not to human communication but to an energistic structure. Aspects of a sign system are transmuted into entities: the unconscious is a causal realm and not a name for what we do not ordinarily communicate to ourselves or others.

To understand this strange mixture, we should recall that Freud himself was trained in physiology by ardent anti-vitalists, and was an heir to the nineteenth-century materialistic-reductionist view of science. In such a scheme, psychology would one day be coordinated with physiology. Much of Freud's language becomes intelligible when we see how his system grew in the shadow cast by the success of the natural sciences. At the end of the nineteenth century — especially with the establishment of evolutionism — our culture was prepared to accept a map offering naturalistic explanation in the mental sphere. When the mind is construed as a hydraulic system, we naturally begin to devise activities which enable people to 'let off steam'. The status of science here has allowed and validated a linguistic projection. Normally our metaphors do not mislead us, but when our images are backed by scientific credentials we may be led astray by them. There are bound to be strange results when attempts are made to build such a 'physical science' of human action. Maps of human semantics and those concerned with physiology are not just worded differently; they are different kinds of map, because of the profound conceptual gulf in our language which separates 'cause' and 'meaning'. To forget this gulf—as when man the meaning-maker is forced into a theoretical construction like those of the physical sciences—does not grant to the psychological map the scientific status it was hoped, but quite the reverse.

Many of the troubles of a map like this can be stated by employing the distinction made above between the nature of theorizing in the natural sciences and in human studies. Instead of taking human meanings as largely constituting the phenomena to be explained, and then seeing the task of science as building on this structure to find its deeper form, Freud adopts the method of theory construction in natural science. He constructs a map in a new language which obliterates this pre-existing semantic system. This leads not to a rewording of a conceptual structure with which we are all familiar, but to a new discourse formation, an autonomous structure with a new theoretical potential which makes it independent of the conceptual landscape it should realistically chart. The new map disguises some features, destroys others, and generates new ones. Such a map cannot be iconic since so much of the terrain of the map is the Freudian conceptual system itself. But we tend to view it as a picture of a projected reality just because it is cast in the language of science.

This viewpoint helps us to see why the efforts to integrate psychology into the social sciences or anthropology have been so unsatisfactory. It is not simply that psychology is culture-bound, but because it and the social sciences are themselves specialist conceptual structures which fracture that semantic field relating to human thought and action which exists in ordinary language. Psychology and sociology do not refer to different subject matters — the individual versus the collective, for instance — they are both concerned with communication, shared rules, and meanings. Yet one cannot synthesize the two disciplines, because they are not two differently worded descriptions of the same landscape, but two systems, the languages of which have partially created their own terrains. Clearly two different terrains cannot be coordinated.

That there is something radically wrong with the psychological map has been recently alleged by several critics who have argued that the discourse has been totally misconstrued. The 'medical model' of psychology and psychiatry is, they claim, quite inappropriate (Szasz 1962; Goffman 1971). Psycho-analysis is concerned not with illness but with the complex use people make of signs (Szasz 1962: 129; Laing 1971b: 89ff.); and one of the chief tasks of therapy is the translation of non-discursive symbols into ordinary language. Hysteria, for instance, should be recognized as a language; it is not an identifiable illness. The nature of the distinction here can be made clear by saying that illnesses like smallpox exist and are merely labelled by medical science. On the other hand, terms like 'insanity' and 'schizophrenia' do not refer to natural facts in the same way, but rather create the identities that they name. They are segments of a moral space, just in the way that 'witch' is an identity in the person category system of other cultures. We should not allow a seemingly scientific terminology to prevent our seeing our own taxonomy as an instrument of oppression. After all, it was not any advance in natural science which brought unreason and illness together. What we call psychiatric practice is a 'moral tactic contemporary with the end of the eighteenth century, preserved in the rites of asylum life, and overlaid by the myths of positivism' (Foucault 1967: 276). This one example contains a vital message for all disciplines concerned with human action: an authentic science of persons can only come into being once the general climate of thought has exposed the harmful consequences which can so easily follow when physical science dominates our modes of thought (Laing 1971a: 23-4).

TWO VERSIONS OF ALCHEMY

Freudian discourse shows how easy it is for science to interfere with maps in a culture where natural science is esteemed. In the case of alchemy we can see how, depending on the way one views its relation to science, wholly different interpretations of the conceptual structure can be given. There are two different readings, where the map is translated by two entirely different types of discourse. There is a 'symbolic' interpretation which views the system as intelligible quite apart from science. There is also the 'literalist' view that alchemy was a proto-science which was refuted and superseded by Boyle's chemistry.

The reason for alchemy being read as a proto-chemical map is fairly obvious. Many of the labels were names of chemical substances, and alchemical practice did in fact increase our knowledge of the properties of matter. On the other hand, as Jung suggested, the signs may seem metallurgical but the language is inherently ethical and symbolic (1963: 4,172). The alchemists, in his view, had a profound grasp of the nature of religious symbolism and were attempting to state in their own terms the doctrine of the Assumption (ibid.: 467, 541-2). Alchemy, thus, was a ritual not a chemical experiment; whatever the source of the signs, they worded a landscape which was not scientific. The literalist view of alchemy as an erroneous science strongly resembles the way in which nineteenth-century ethnologists interpreted primitive magic as something mistaken by its practitioners as efficacious. Like them, those who fail to see alchemy as symbolic statement presume that it is a technique. But once we see both magic and alchemy as 'languages', it is clear that neither need be viewed as instances of childish and misguided science. One theory can compete with another only if they both deal with the same sort of landscape. On the symbolist interpretation, no chemical theory could possibly refute alchemy because the maps are of entirely different kinds.

In the literalist reading of alchemy we have something like that confusion between sign and message which lay behind Victorian theories of totemism. As Lévi-Strauss points out, animal signs can be formed into a concrete code for making sociological statements. Similarly, the terms of alchemy constitute a 'logique métallurgique' for making assertions about a very different subject matter. Alchemy uses concrete symbols from chemistry to form propositions about states of the soul. After the Fall, man was in a chaotic condition, and the alchemical transmutation of base metal into gold symbolized the attainment of that spiritual purity by which man is again able to reflect the *Logos* (Burckhardt 1967: 72). Alchemy was a complex of the objective and the subjective — chemical signs were part of the expression of an abstract mystery. The alchemist symbolizes with his experience of the world of objects. His ritual is a memento of his intimate meditations (Bachelard 1970: 46-8). In other words, chemical substances are valuable carriers for conceptual projections (Jung 1963: 250). They constituted a good code; but the message is in no way chemical.[3]

We should recall that broad intellectual context in which alchemy was set — neo-Platonism, and doctrines of microcosm and macrocosm. The latter particularly lends itself to the use of one language to speak about another subject matter. So in alchemy we find a great number of concordant systems of symbolism, from the realms of astronomy, colour, metallurgy, and so on. There are correspondences between them: the leading oppositions of male/female and active/passive appear in the astronomical system as *Sol* and *Luna*; *Luna* mediates heaven and earth, just as *Mercurius* is the mediator of the metallurgical realm. Clearly if each substance has a whole host of 'synonyms' in this way, the valency of the signs is transformed. *Sol* is not an astronomical body but a generative and transmuting power. The sign for gold in alchemy is not 'Au', since it does not refer to chemical gold, but rather 'purity'. The signs on an alchemical map have a weight which scientific symbols do not possess, and which fits them to state articulately propositions about religious matters: they have a symbolic not an atomic weight.

This symbolic load carried by alchemical signs derives from several classificatory planes. Although the alchemical map projects the form of some natural structures — the realms of metals and astronomy — one can only grasp the point of alchemy by seeing that these terrains are combined into a multi-dimensional semantic field which is not concerned with any one of them. The alchemical transmutation is a concrete image for a fundamental change in the human soul. Alchemical practice is no more a mistaken chemical experiment than the Hell rings in Dante's

Divine Comedy are an erroneous version of the stratification of a geological map. Similarly, no one would suggest that a chemical test were relevant to the truth of the statement 'the wine is the blood of Christ'. Transubstantiation does not assert that the wine is chemically blood, only that it is 'substantially' blood. The 'is' in this context does not say that the wine is made of corpuscles and haemoglobin — these are two entirely different systems.

This study of alchemy is a forcible reminder that 'literalism' is not the only principle of interpretation. Anthropologists, whose thinking must inevitably be influenced by their roots in the sort of culture where science is so prominent, must nonetheless endeavour to appreciate the validity of other sorts of maps that human beings construct. Alchemy is not a scientific map, but it is built on definite semantic principles. Metaphors can generate systems of symbolism no less coherent than those we call scientific. In alchemy we have seen how the language of a map may mislead us as to its meaning. This danger should not be underestimated, since interpretation is systematic like the map itself. It is not just a question of misconstruing some of the signs, for once the general nature of the discourse is decided, all the individual labels on the map will be read in the light of that decision. To adopt one view instead of another thereby creates or annuls a whole range of features. For instance, those who see alchemy as proto-science commonly omit to mention the *coniunctio* which for others is the very essence of the alchemical art. All the same, it is not clear what we could mean by the 'true' interpretation when we are dealing with systems of human meaning. Jung, for example, claimed that while the alchemists did not possess his psychological understanding of their activity, they said the best they could (ibid.: 172). Yet, if psychology could throw some light on alchemy, the secrets of the secrets would still remain. So, suggested Jung, there might come a time when his view would seem no less inadequate than that of the alchemists themselves (ibid.: 173).

SEMANTICS AND DIVERSITIES

In the last chapter I shall argue that this lack of finality in the interpretation of conceptual structures arises from the very nature of translation. But it is important to conclude by noting an unresolved tension which has existed throughout our explorations of various 'forms of life'. Attention has been drawn both to properties which seem essential to all maps, and to semantic characteristics which distinguish one map from another. The resulting tension between diversity and invariance is clearly locatable in our two central notions of system and map — the one with its implications of closure, and the other involving limited presuppositions.

The analytical problem is that the diversity which they enable us to explore seems to lead us into a form of extreme relativism, a semantic solipsism which, amounting to a thesis of untranslatability, would render anthropology impossible. Thus it is important to be reminded that religious discourse is a language with certain peculiarities that may be absent from other maps. But if one suggests that the only criteria for grasping and criticizing a language-game are internal, then one ends with the attitude of Karl Barth — that there is no point in conversing with an unbeliever, since he cannot understand the language of belief in the first place. If a fideist grasp alone is to qualify as understanding, there could be no semantic anthropology. As much as the recognition of different language-games may be useful, it loses its value for us when interpreted in such an extreme way. For in this analysis the boundaries of each 'form of life' become barriers across which communication would be impossible (Nielson 1967), which seems an untenable thesis. After all, despite all the heterogeneity of natural languages, we do actually speak a language and not just a heap of language-games.

Although these problems are real, they are extremely difficult to formulate. While acknowledging their existence, my explorations have not shrunk from emphasizing diversity because it seems more important for anthropologists to avoid an opposite error which is far more easily stated. There is a constant temptation to privilege one 'form of life' and judge all conceptual structures by its standards. But it is clearly unacceptable to regard a diversity of maps as, for example, more or less deficient instances of the scientific type. Since one of the labels we can attach to semantic anthropology is 'post-positivistic', there is an added reason for stressing this. Positivism, which has had such an extremely harmful influence on all the social sciences, is profoundly unanthropological. It is a philosophy acting in the service of natural science, and moreover of a science which has been equated with human knowledge. The effort to raise certain criteria like 'verifiability' into universal standards of judgment naturally led to the declaration that whole areas of human discourse were meaningless. Even when one sees how badly positivism misunderstood science itself, and how scientific language is considerably more complex than has often been made out, we still need not think of scientific discourse as in any sense the correct or basic use of language. In fact, so important is the principle of iconicity here that science often operates with several of the semantic conventions of other maps not in operation. In view of its being only one map among many, there might even be wisdom in stressing that, in some respects, scientific language is impoverished rather than that all the others are too elaborate. At least it is important to remember that logical positivism sought to limit knowledge in its function as a scientistic defence of a threatened civilization, and that it is not inaccurately described as a 'collection of prohibitions'

(Kolakowski 1972: 18, 203).

The term science itself has had its current meaning for a little over a century, in what is historically a rather atypical culture. So the elevation of this map as a general standard of interpretation can only result in the most grotesque sociocentrism. A sociologist has, for example, recently declared that if a doctrine 'conflicts with the acceptance of the superiority of scientific industrial society over others then it really is out' (Gellner 1968b: 71). An anthropologist is obviously more familiar with some conceptual systems than with others, since he — like the discipline of anthropology itself — grew in, and belongs to, a particular culture. But it is an indisputable fact that man as a meaning-maker creates a vast diversity of conceptual structures, and we have no grounds to accord a priority to any one. We have seen what a diversity of features maps can display in the relationship between language and terrain. This means that language has ontological implications in different ways. In some, representation is iconic; in others, no sign system can portray adequately; in yet others — and here the very field of human action is an instance — language can constitute the reality being mapped. It is for exactly this reason that so much attention has been paid to the ideas of Wittgenstein here. In his later work he showed by concrete investigations of conceptual landscapes how human discourse can mean in many different ways. In these writings, philosophy is no longer an activity tied to the needs of science. Indeed, we capture its spirit if we see it as giving expression to a fear that the dominance of science in our lives would distort our view of the nature and powers of the human mind (Pears 1971: 103).

When we refuse to privilege one map we are not losing our grip on reality, for the diversity itself is patently real. The different 'forms of life' are just given. As Wittgenstein remarked when pondering on the beliefs and customs of other cultures, this is simply how human beings are (1967a: 30). It is in a diversity of modes of discourse that human beings think and act. Yet we can perhaps do more than merely register this fact. We would not think nowadays of describing all languages in our familiar grammatical categories, but equally we are not content with the assumption that all languages are unique. Through comparison, we would hope to locate deeper common structures, and perhaps finally be able to state those powers of the human mind that make us a language-possessing species. Similarly, in the face of cultural diversities we would hope to discover features which at least overlapped between them. Finally, however, we should have to transcend 'forms of life' to locate the invariants in constructive semantic powers themselves. But to go beyond the conventional framework of diversities and invariants is fraught with difficulties. The recent history of linguistics and the problem of universals is sufficient evidence of this. Moreover, assaults on universals only seem feasible when the conventional barriers between disciplines are broken down, and this creates yet more problems. And finally, in any case, the basic tension between unity and difference is inescapable because all our knowledge has a historical character. Throughout history, human beings have given a succession of formulations of what the invariants of human nature are: anthropology as itself a creation of the human mind is inevitably located in this flux too.

8   The Translation of Cultures

In the previous chapter, attention was concentrated on our own conceptual structures because part of that consciousness which lies behind our shift to a newer type of anthropology is a realization that our discipline cannot exclude from its terms of reference the civilization in which it grew. We have a wider basis than other disciplines, but the advantage that accrues from this is sacrificed if we do not expend the same kind of attention on ourselves as we do on other cultures. For as long as 'we' remains an unexamined term of comparison, what we say about 'the other' will be of that much less value. One could even go so far as to assert that if we are unable to relate our work to ourselves there is little point in beginning it at all. No doubt other disciplines which study the social life of human beings need to be reminded that the true dimensions of human facts cannot be realized until other cultures are included in their scope; but, it is necessary for anthropologists to see that an equivalent deficiency is involved while the opposite exclusion exists in their discipline.

A more particular reason for this stress here is that, even if anthropology is defined as the study of pre-literate peoples, it inevitably shares the autobiographical nature of all human knowledge. The 'we', therefore, has always had an implicit presence in anthropological writings, as is clear from the history of the subject. The Victorian ethnologists clearly reflected the larger intellectual concerns of their age. The colonial context of much twentieth-century anthropology has unquestionably left its mark also. Semantic anthropology requires this 'presence' to be made explicit. This is not because the discipline now finds itself in a political context which makes its traditional research habits difficult, but because a discipline with the title 'anthropology' cannot reasonably adopt any other position. An insufficient comprehension of the conceptual structures of one's own society, and an inadequate familiarity with the complex resources of one's own language, can easily be a source of mistranslation and so cause misunderstanding of another culture.

153

Clearly then, self-knowledge is highly relevant to the more orthodox tasks of anthropology — namely the interpretation of alien systems of thought and action. Given the desirability of the expansion of anthropology advocated here, it might be felt that the discipline is still essentially concerned with 'the other'. This is correct; but, unless we already understand ourselves sufficiently, 'we' *are* 'other' from a scientific point of view. Moreover, since we share a common humanity, 'the other' and 'we' cannot be absolutely opposed to one another. In the analysis below, we move from the diversity of 'forms of life' in our culture to explore the differences between our culture and other societies, by tackling a series of interpretational problems. In this way we shift back to the customary terrain of anthropology. These studies of the symbolic systems of alien cultures also form a path by which we reach the general topic of translation — the experience and process which not only constitutes the link between the diversity of cultures but also provides the most fundamental bond between anthropology and language.

Having seen the different ways in which language charts, constitutes and disguises reality in different conceptual systems, we can now appreciate why semantic anthropology must be based not only on broad but also on diverse links between anthropology and language. So it becomes clear how limited must be the value of those uses of linguistic models which we have studied in the works of Lévi-Strauss and the American linguistic anthropologists. As we approach the topic of translation, the degree of these deficiencies will become even more clear. Interestingly, it was as an Orientalist familiar with the hazards of translation that Müller felt himself more able to interpret other cultures than the Victorian ethnologists, who evidently 'thought their task was much easier than it really is' (1897: 193,205). Since translation is indeed the very basis of semantic anthropology, it is of considerable import that the American linguistic anthropologists should have failed to discuss the process at length, and that in Lévi-Strauss' system this highly autobiographical type of interpretation should appear as an impersonal channel of conversion. It is no wonder that they have not provided us with the kind of insights we needed for our semantic analyses.

SOME RECENT SEMANTIC DISPUTES IN BRITISH ANTHROPOLOGY
Several recent publications on ritual, the nature of magic, and the analysis of symbolic statement have brought to the fore in British anthropology that general division between 'literalist' and 'symbolist' styles of interpretation which separated Müller and the Victorian ethnologists on so many issues. In the previous chapter we saw how a strong positive valuation placed upon the achievements of the physical sciences, and a sense that scientific discourse was somehow more correct

154

than others, could interfere harmfully with the construction and reading of our own symbolic structures. Now we shall see how this privilege accorded to scientific discourse can affect the way anthropologists interpret the semantic systems of other societies. The approach of the modern literalist intellectualists is deficient in the same way as was the work of the nineteenth-century ethnologists: thus they are appropriately labelled 'neo-Tyloreans' (Ardener 1965:57). But the controversy which their work has aroused is important, since it has led to the raising of the central anthropological issue: which part of the discourse of our culture is the best available translational instrument for construing the different systems of thought and action of an alien society?

The modern literalists, like their forebears, favour the assimilation of a wide range of conceptual structures to the scientific domain. For Tylor, primitive religion was an explanatory metaphysics. For Frazer, magic was proto-science being based on a causal hypothesis, and not a matter of symbolic statement — this is why he described his *Golden Bough* as a 'melancholy record of human error and folly' (1963:930). Much of the ideological infrastructure of Victorian ethnology has vanished from current anthropology; but this same unreasonable enticement by supposed scientific parallels survives in the modern literalist writings. The intellectualists of both periods seem not to understand, and so they translate literally — just like translation machines bereft of human empathy. As Wittgenstein said (reflecting on the *Golden Bough*), Frazer only made an ass of himself in adopting the attitude and approach that he did. It was he who was the savage, unable to sense the deep mystery of being human because of the spiritual impoverishment of his own life (1967a:28).

As we pointed out above, language is used in different ways in different kinds of map. It is as if the intellectualists either could not accept the legitimacy of non-scientific discourse, or else could not grant preliterate peoples the symbolic use of symbols. The literalist thus is in something like the position of a highly prejudiced man, from a culture where the game of draughts is very popular, having to observe and report on a game of chess. Some of the moves look familiar, but he cannot avoid the sense that the pieces are badly shaped. Moreover, there are features of the behaviour of the pieces which from his own experience seem completely odd. So he begins — as the Victorians did, aided by associationist psychology — to guess what errors of reasoning lie, for instance, behind finishing the game while the opponent still has pieces on the board. A mistake of this sort is like someone using a geological map to motor through the streets of a town: it is bound to be inefficient when used for the wrong purpose, since the whole point of the map has been missed. In the same way, an activity which looks pointless or based on a confusion of ideas may not seem so when one grasps that one is witnessing a ritual and not an experiment. Such an understanding requires one to accept that human beings are capable of creating a diversity of types of conceptual systems — it also involves detailed semantic investigation. It is not possible to assume, as Tylor did, that the meaning of ethnographic evidence is obvious. To presume that certain practices show a blind belief in processes wholly irrelevant to their supposed results, as was common in Victorian accounts of primitive magic, begs the question of what in this particular circumstance were the processes involved, what 'relevance' means here, and what type of results are expected (Phillips 1970:42ff.).

Wittgenstein's major shift, from his early concern with the limits of language to the examination of its complex inner structure, gives us the general framework in which we can see the nature of the semantic deficiencies of the literalists. When he spoke of how analogies between expressions in different domains of language can make us forget its internal boundaries (1953:para.91), he was concerned with a source of philosophical errors. But this illuminates the difficulties of anthropological investigation too. Thus, he claimed that when we do philosophy we are 'like savages who hearing the expressions of civilised men, put a strange interpretation on them and then draw the queerest conclusions' (1953:194). Intellectualism, we may say, is a case of civilized men hearing the expressions of savages, misinterpreting, and so being led to ask the strangest questions. Neo-Tyloreans, in other words, mislocate the discourse and so necessarily misconstrue the point of the map. And because discourse is systematic, once the misidentification has taken place, all the statements are liable to be misunderstood and a whole host of impertinent questions raised.

The recent 'virgin birth' debate in anthropology is clearly a controversy based on problems of discourse location. The issue began as a matter of interpreting the meaning of several pieces of classical ethnography. There are people like the Trobriand Islanders of whom we have reports about beliefs in 'spirit conception' (Malinowski 1916:215ff.). Spiro (1968) has argued that these beliefs should be taken 'at their face value'. That is, they are efforts at scientific explanation and should be put in the realm of biological statements. As such, clearly they are false, and so expose a vast native deficiency in knowledge of scientific causation. Leach (1966b), on the other hand, has maintained that these beliefs are not evidence of any ignorance because they are not biological assertions at all. Rather, they embody a cultural dogma. They are a set of theologico-social statements — perhaps somewhat like 'legal fictions' (Derrett 1971) — expressing the fact that the father is an affine. They are not erroneous versions of casual relationships, because their point is to state connections between important social categories. This whole debate has been closely argued in connection with the Trobriand ethnography, and the symbolist solution of 'cultural ideology' may be eminently suited to this case. It might therefore seem that recent evidence that the patrilineal Bellonese claimed themselves to be ignorant of physiological paternity prior to European contact (Monberg 1975) reintroduces the general issue of the possibility that there are primitive peoples without this item of biological knowledge. But perhaps this is not the case; for, after all, Leach's contention about a cultural dogma did not actually settle the Trobriand instance in terms of the knowledge/ignorance dichotomy, though it might appear to have done so. The very concept of ideology itself blurs these categories; and, as it will be suggested that the stark literalist/symbolist divide in general leads to misleading semantic problems, so it seems reasonable to contend that knowledge and ignorance are not in an absolute opposition. There is, after all, the daily experience of not knowing what knowing is and finding out that not knowing is a form of knowledge.

Another basic conflict between symbolic and non-symbolic interpretation similar to that over 'virgin birth' has been visible in modern disagreements over the nature of magic and ritual. Literalists have contended that magic is purposive, like technical action, and that ritual is a response to purely intellectual problems (Jarvie & Agassi 1967; Jarvie 1964:167). Beattie has rightly challenged this type of approach. He has argued that there is such a rich symbolic and expressive element in both religion and ritual that they are far better likened to art than to science and technology (1966:60;1970). Certainly this symbolist counterargument is valuable, but we shall see below that the terms in which the position is stated are far from being semantically adequate.

The most general statement of the issue whether the conceptual structures of pre-literate cultures can be likened to Western science has been provided by Horton in his contention that 'ritual man' is but a subspecies of 'theory-building' man (1964;1967). In this view, primitive religions are like scientific models, being comprised of explanatory theoretical terms which reduce a diversity of phenomena to a unified scheme. Now Horton may well be right to suggest that one reason for the general reluctance to parallel primitive religion and science is the widespread positivistic image of science which certainly is unlike primitive thought (1967:299). However, granted this, it does not follow that we can adequately treat the difference between elementary particles and spiritual beings as one of mere idiom. We have argued (in discussing the nature of human action) that there are some striking differences between description and explanation in the social as opposed to the physical sciences, so we should beware of thinking that primitive conceptual structures built in an anthroposocial language can be readily assimilated to the explanatory schemes of physical science. Again, Horton has a point when he remarks on the odd history of the Christian religion's relationship with science. After centuries of sometimes extreme hostility, our religion no longer gives explanations to rival those of science (1964: 96, 103). But it does not follow that if we cannot too closely liken primitive religions to our own the best translational discourse we have left is science. There are other options open to us, so that even with cultures of a strong pragmatic bent (like the Kalabari, among whom Horton did fieldwork) we need not construe expressions as explanatory in the way scientific statements are. Nor, even were we to grant that religious discourse had an overall model structure, would we be forced to concede the literalist case. Both religion and science may be highly articulate conceptual structures, but they are normally construed as being about entirely different types of landscape. Religion and science do not give competing answers, because they ask different sorts of question — a fact which may have been obscured for the Victorian intellectualists by the clash between a fundamentalist interpretation of some dogmas of the Church, and that aspect of contemporary science — evolutionism — on which ethnological theory itself was based.

The issue of the similarity of primitive thought to Western science, like the more particular debates over ritual and magic, have brought out some very basic disagreements as regards the relation of our culture and other cultures. That being so, it is hardly surprising that they should have heightened our awareness that anthropology, as the product of a culture, is itself part of a larger ideological formation. The literalists have been accused of socio-centrism and gross prejudice, for example, with the result that 'neo-Tylorean' now has derogatory overtones (Horton 1968 : Ross 1970). To regard savage thought as science, after all, exposes societies with systems of belief which are wholly false. Some of the intellectualists, moreover, are not hesitant to expound the view that social science has a duty to evaluate. Jarvie, for one, looks forward to the spread of developed standards of rationalism along with industrialization (1970 : 245-7). On the other hand, literalists have suggested that those living in a troubled complex civilization may find some satisfaction in imagining traditional cultures as warmly organic and emotional. The symbolists therefore are no less guilty of prejudice. So obvious is the cognitive superiority of the West, argue the literalists, that primitive beliefs must be interpreted as symbolic simply in order to avoid passing adverse judgments on cultures which could not then fulfil the requirements of the symbolist's image (Horton 1973 : 94).

That such ideological issues are involved is undeniable. Anthropology is not free of those influences which not only mark but in some cases appreciably constitute our social knowledge. However, in this context such a general problem would divert us from our immediate concern of how semantic anthropology can concretely confront the difficulty raised by the existence of very different types of interpretation of any ethnographic data. Clearly, in the first place, we may get some clues to help solve this problem of diversity if we obtain more detailed bodies of ethnography and if we try to analyse in a more painstaking fashion. Thus, for the Mandari it would be quite wrong to stress 'expressiveness', because participants in ritual activities emphasize instrumentality (Buxton 1973:259nl,358). At the same time, Mandari 'instrumentality' is not the same as empirical action. It is a multi-dimensional category in which are combined aspects from several levels, synthesized into a meaningful whole so that neither 'religion' nor 'science' are terms adequate to indicate the full qualities of the thought involved. Here then is one good empirical case which reveals not only that one misinterprets if one chooses wrongly between likening a set of statements to religion or to science, but that one misunderstands if one thinks of the choice in these terms at all. Thus it has the general value of reminding us that some of the terms we have used to frame our analytical discussions have been highly culture-bound. 'Religion' itself must certainly be included among these. Other cultures (even Hindu and Islamic) do not have concepts at all equivalent to our term 'religion', so it is extremely doubtful that using a general opposition science/religion will be of any great use.[1]

We can generalize this feeling, for it may well be that ethnography will not decide between the literalist/symbolist rivals but rather will suggest that the very oppositions of technique/art, explanation/expressiveness, and so on, must be dispensed with. Notwithstanding the value of these recent disputes, a semantic anthropology must go beyond these terms and the whole dualistic framework in which the discussion has been couched. If these notions point to real aspects of conceptual structures, they nonetheless harmfully abstract from them and oppose them, in ways which generate false problems and mislead when one is trying to give an adequate account of the structure of discourse. For instance, the rigid distinction between the metaphorical and the literal may belong not to ordinary thought but rather to thought about thought. Thus, Dinka assertions according to Lienhardt tend to fall somewhere in between (1954:106,99). And similarly, when one inquires into the question of whether religious discourse is fraudulent or not, the most striking fraud of all soon emerges as the use of those dualisms like cognitive and emotive which are normally proposed to solve the issue (Ferré 1959). Our language is not bundled into a cognitive area and an amorphous area of 'expressiveness'. Most of what is most important to us is spoken about in discourse which mixes inextricably the analytical oppositions which logical positivism offered. Most of our assertions combine both cognitive and emotive aspects, yet there are still recognizable standards of appropriateness in the conceptual systems we build. Perhaps it is worth remembering that a linguist is more likely to offer an erroneous grammatical model than is a speaker to utter something devoid of meaning.

Linguistic philosophy has gone beyond the kind of 'bifocalism' of which we have complained, and semantic anthropology will have to follow this example. Human discourse forms a very delicately patterned system of overlapping styles of meaning.[2] To see that speaking is related in a diversity of ways to social action will be one way of searching for the form of this complexity. And attention to notions like 'speech acts' might further break down the misleading oppositions which have encumbered our thinking (Searle 1965:63). Consequently, important as it is to point out to the intellectualists that religious language in primitive cultures has a richly symbolic dimension, it is not sufficient to employ terms like 'expressiveness'. In any case, mention of 'symbolic qualities' is less a solving of the ethnographic problem than the starting point for a complicated task of discovering what are the semantic conventions in the 'forms of life' found in other societies.

But if semantic anthropology must involve itself in more detailed investigations, we cannot envisage this as a path to any final solutions to the disputes we have looked at. The essential 'indeterminacy' of translation makes the idea of finality impossible in this context. We simply cannot produce totally independent evidence to decide the issue between rival translations, because for something to be evidence it must already be part of a map. Whatever reality is 'in itself', it is significant for us only if it is part of our meanings. Thus we cannot escape from the realm of meaning to decide semantic questions. Nor, as Evans-Pritchard well pointed out (1936:197), can one hope to translate and leave the problem of interpretation till later — the translation is the interpretation. In more general terms, language is not a mere vehicle for a meaning which exists independently of it. There is no non-symbolic realm of neutral transportable semantic entities (Haas 1962), and in this sense the very term *trans*lation is somewhat misleading.[3] If we must dispense with the image of meanings being conveyed between languages, so we must also do away with the idea that rival types of translation are simply additive. Competing translations are not like several perspectives of a mountain which can be integrated so as to give a fuller picture. These facets of translation do not make the position for a semantic anthropology as unhappy as might appear to be the case. Clearly, by the style of translation chosen one can make alien peoples seem as peculiar as one likes. But if one reminds the translator of the autobiographical nature of his activity, one can see that there must be a point at which his misunderstanding is more likely than native stupidity. One can also remind those like the intellectualists that their style of interpretation is not inevitable, and that they have made a definite choice in locating alien beliefs in the domain of science. They are therefore responsible for the consequences generated by this framework, for in exercising a choice they have excluded other types of reading. More than this, semantic investigations because of their minuteness can show anthropologists that there are many more alternatives available than they appear to think. We can expect some of our 'forms of life' to match those in other cultures, but as Wittgenstein himself said, one need not find exactly the same language-games in different cultures (1967b: 370). There is the one error of too closely likening primitive thought to Western science, but there may be some primitive conceptual systems for whose leading characteristics we can find no readily available analogy in our culture at all. Hence, to refuse the scientific parallel and propose that primitive thought be likened to our religion instead would also achieve so partial a calibration as to be a mistranslation. This difficulty forces anthropological thought to be creative: we have to envisage new maps with which we are not familiar. This is why in interpreting other cultures we translate by exploring the 'further potentialities of our own thought and language' (Lienhardt 1954:97).

OURSELVES AND OTHERS

We have seen illustrations of how semantic anthropology tackles the problem of understanding conceptual systems in both our own and other cultures, so we can now turn to the 'ourselves'/'others' opposition itself. We stressed in exploring our own systems of collective representations that we could not regard different 'forms of life' as totally idiosyncratic. In dealing with translation between cultures we have to emphasize how logically we need a link across diversity. We have seen some of the unacceptable consequences of our using familiar modes of discourse like that of science to provide the required conceptual continuity. So here I shall suggest as a valuable means of constructing a bridge between 'we' and 'them' those characteristics which Lévy-Bruhl thought definitive of the primitive mentality, particularly as the systemic aspects of Zande thought proved useful as a means of connecting a series of our 'forms of life'.

It is something of an understatement to say that the work of Lévy-Bruhl has been widely misunderstood. His early views are still often interpreted in a fashion which makes them add up to a quite untenable picture of human thought. But we should remember that he deliberately exaggerated the contrasts between the 'primitive' and

161

'civilized' mentalities since the English ethnologists, in his opinion, had already made the similarities sufficiently clear (1952:119). But they had also taken it as axiomatic that what they regarded as the laws of thought would be found universally. Their investigations, thus, could not extend our knowledge of the human mind, whereas an inquiry deliberately seeking for possible variations in the principles of collective thought would surely do so (id.1912:7). It was not good enough to regard primitive thought as merely an inferior childish version of our own. If there were other factors or laws at work it was vital to give a positive definition of them (id.1923:32-3, 59). Lévy-Bruhl in this way showed a far greater sensitivity to conceptual issues than his English colleagues. He recognized how the very semantic structure of our language would violate primitive thought, for in employing our notions like 'soul' or 'property' we should severely disfigure their categories (ibid.:433-4).

We must not underestimate the importance of this advocacy of research into our 'natural logic'. Even today our views as to what are the unvarying properties of the human mind are not founded on sufficient comparative evidence. When Lévy-Bruhl made his plea he had in mind the fact that those who investigated other cultures should not forget that there was a strong solidarity between thought, language, and social ambience (1912:70),[4] which could well affect the principles by which categories were related to one another. This general emphasis on 'solidarity' is strikingly reminiscent of Wittgenstein's notion of a 'form of life'; and indeed the other leading ideas for which Lévy-Bruhl has been criticized bear a strong resemblance to stresses in modern linguistic philosophy. For instance, he suggested that the ideas of primitive peoples tend to 'participate' in one another in ways which defy Aristotelian logic. Similarly, linguistic philosophers have shown that the ordinary concepts in natural languages have no very definite boundaries and so considerably overlap one another. Again, Lévy-Bruhl's concept of prelogicality — that primitives do not go out of their way to avoid contradictions (ibid.:79) — obviously captures some vital aspects of our own 'practical' thinking.

But this very parallelism exposes what from our viewpoint is the great deficiency in Lévy-Bruhl's writings — the fact that he introduced these valuable notions alongside the civilized/primitive contrast. Ironically, the very clear correspondences between ordinary thought in all cultures which his concepts highlight so outweigh the differences, that the opposition of 'us'/'them' is transcended by them. It is true that he recognized the existence of primitive elements in our own collective representations, especially in the spheres of religion and morality (ibid.:452-3), but he failed to see how very much farther the features of the 'primitive' mentality reach in our culture. Clearly, to explain this failure we cannot resort to the standard excuse that the quality of the ethnographic data on which he worked left much to be desired. Rather, the major deficiency in his work stems directly from the fact that he never made a detailed study of the collective representations of his own culture (Evans-Pritchard 1970:43-4). Using 'civilized mentality' simply as a term of contrast, assuming that psychologists, philosophers and logicians have already adequately sketched its main features, is not a stance an anthropologist can regard as acceptable. Pareto, after all, came to the same conclusions about our own thought as Lévy-Bruhl did about primitive thought (id.1974:1). And the comic situation is possible where, for example, Bergson (the most influential philosopher at the time Lévy-Bruhl wrote) thought — according to Lévi-Strauss — like a savage (1969b:170-2).

The shortcoming is severe, but as we stressed in the previous chapter, it is very common. The case of Lévy-Bruhl is but one more illustration of the chronic deficiency in anthropology which stems from the fact that the discipline is not turned back on itself. It is difficult to see how one can expect valid knowledge of the 'other' so long as the acquisition of 'self'-knowledge is avoided. Lévi-Strauss, for instance, has spoken of an unspecialized type of thought common to all humanity, but he has never written at any length on *la pensée sauvage* as it manifests itself in civilized society. It might be valuable to do exactly this in order to sketch out a possible link between 'us' and 'them'. Alternatively, since the prelogicality and participation of ideas which characterize the primitive mentality do not separate it from our own, perhaps they are good candidates for universals of the human mind and so a better way of bringing 'us' into anthropology than the concepts of Lévi-Strauss. Certainly it will be more useful for anthropologists to explore our own conceptual structures with notions which are thought to constitute another kind of mentality, than to force primitive thought into the stereotype we hold of our own.

Whatever the value of this suggestion, the need for overlapping features of some sort is a logical necessity, since no translation could take place were we dealing with absolute differences. This is why it is important to realize that Lévy-Bruhl did not really challenge the idea of the psychic unity of mankind. He did not argue that his findings showed that primitives had an entirely different system of logic (1912:68). Indeed, he specifically stated that, apart from collective ideas, sentiments, and the social institutions affecting thought, the savage would think and infer exactly as we do (ibid.:77). What Lévy-Bruhl was doing was not suggesting a fundamental difference in mentalities but rather exploring the consequences of the solidarity of social facts upon the collective representations of societies very different from our own. To use the cartographic

163

analogy again, he was surveying maps with which our culture was not very familiar, stressing the fact that we could adapt our minds to interpret such strange terrains only with great difficulty (1923:442). Anthropologists could not just hope to guess the nature and point of these maps, as the Victorians in effect did by using associationist psychology to explain all manner of belief systems in primitive cultures.

Clearly then Lévy-Bruhl was examining diversities within an assumed unity. The more extreme thesis that there are basic differences of logic between cultures cannot be contended seriously by anthropologists. For one thing, the very title of their discipline presupposes a fundamental human unity. But besides this, the thesis would fall foul of the general fact that extreme relativism cannot be cogently expressed. A totally different mind would just be unintelligible to us, so we could not have any warrants for recognizing it as a mind. Likewise, if an alien language did not manifest what we take to be the basic principles of logic, we could not recognize it as a language (Lukes 1973). Unless we assume some common ground — a bridgehead, in Hollis' terms (1967) — the process of translation could never begin. To conclude that there are differences requires some understanding, and this would not be possible if the differences were fundamental. The very possibility of translation depends on assuming there are overlaps between cultures, otherwise we should not have any 'entering wedge' into another language. Given this way in, we then have to go on from our premises interpreting alien utterances even though lacking independent evidence for our constructions (Quine 1960:70,72). Since these premises are necessary for translation, the fact that we translate neither proves nor disproves that our assumptions are warranted (ibid.:77;1951:61-2). It is simply that these are the only premises open to us. And this means that we cannot settle the issue of whether or not there are people with radically different ways of thinking, since the very act of producing a translation places alien utterances into our own mould. Completely different standards of reasoning simply could never show up — we either translate according to our principles, or we leave untranslated.

Anthropology is an art of translation and must for logical reasons accept as axiomatic the maxim of Terence '*nihil humani a me alienum puto*'. Vico also stated the basic principle for anthropological investigation when he remarked that, however strange another culture might appear, it rested upon principles which are but modifications of those of our own minds (1968:para.331). But this necessarily means that any inquiry into other cultures extends our understanding of our own, that any study of 'primitive' mentality has to advance comprehension of our own. This is one recognition of the fact that when we speak of the 'psychic unity' of man we are not dealing with a simple empirical notion.

This expression is rather the metaphysical foundation of the anthropological conceptual system. It is the presupposition for anthropological discourse—the fundamental unifier of a semantic structure which explores the diversity of 'ourselves' and 'others'. The pair is thus subsumed, and so the meanings of both terms are interdependent. A change in the value of the 'self' inevitably alters the image of the 'other', and vice versa; and either change alters the nature of the difference which they constitute, and by which they are constituted. Different cultures characterize the diversities and the unifying features differently, and over time the images of what is universal and what separates one culture from another change. An anthropological statement of this situation can only result in yet another announcement of the invariants and diversities, so there can be no final definition of the relation between 'ourselves' and 'others'. The real meaning of the relation is thus all its versions.

INTIMATIONS OF AN IDENTITY

Our semantic explorations have led to conclusions which many anthropologists may find somewhat disturbing. But a shift from a prime interest in social functions to a concern with meaning erases more than the surface characteristics of the old identity of the discipline. The semantic powers of humankind make it a self-constituting species, and anthropology as a manifestation of these powers must itself be regarded as a conceptual system. Anthropological thinking belongs to a 'form of life' and builds yet another map of human significance. There is no freedom even for our discipline from man's semantic abilities — all anthropology can do is construct more maps.

If this picture necessarily involves the abandonment of one view of scientific objectivity, at the same time it reveals what the identity of a semantic study is and, indeed, must be. Since there is an irremovable indeterminacy in translation, the lack of finality in semantic investigations should not be surprising. But we can express this situation in more helpful and positive terms by seeing that translation is a form of commentary. Thus, in translating a text we create another. To use the cartographic imagery again, giving the meaning of a map is a complex process, which involves both loss and creation of features of a landscape, and which in effect produces a second map to place beside the first. Our increase in understanding can thus be regarded as the ability to refract one structure through a second.

We could see the process of interpretation which leads to the existence of an anthropological text as one which constitutes it as a sign in a complex semantic system of relations between relations. Evans-Pritchard's *Nuer Religion*, for instance, is the long-term consequence of a profound personal experience of wrestling with the utterances and actions of human beings in an alien culture. But to understand the inner form of the monograph we must bear in mind several dimensions of the hermeneutic space in which it took shape. There are the author's writings on other aspects of Nuer society; his other essays on primitive religion; the work of fellow anthropologists on primitive thought. Moreover, there are more personal factors, such as Evans-Pritchard's own attitude towards religion. And we cannot forget that each text has a certain place in the theoretical history of the discipline to which it belongs. Here *Nuer Religion* is an important sign in the general shift from function to meaning.[5] There is no upper limit to the dimensions we can list in construing a text; but the general principle is clear that anthropological writings, like any others, derive their 'value' (in the Saussurian sense) from their place in a semantic field.

The legitimacy of anthropological thinking also derives from the same source as that from which all 'forms of life' gain theirs — 'forms of life' are simply there. In other words, human beings are naturally anthropological. But perhaps we can say that a conceptual structure which specifically seeks to understand other systems cannot be regarded as just one map among others. Of course, all maps, including those of anthropology, are culture-bound; but if we build maps about maps we can at least strive to avoid employing the maximally specific discourse of some 'forms of life'. This is the vital significance of our realization that the analytical notions of French sociological thought — 'polarity', 'opposition', 'exchange', 'totality', 'liminality', and so on — are the real theoretical capital of social anthropology (Evans-Pritchard, in Hertz 1960:24). They are richly paradigmatic, and sufficiently empty to express the deep structure of cultural facts without violating their surface form (Ardener 1971a:466; Needham, in Durkheim & Mauss 1963:xlii). This gives them the formal properties which make for the best framework for the establishing of equivalences, although their translational value has seldom been explicitly mentioned (Hallpike 1971:135). Understanding social facts requires our respecting the associations and discriminations made by others. But this does not rule out the possibility of comparison — it merely obliges us to find categories of the right analytical kind.

Even so, this search cannot of itself cancel the fact that the discipline of anthropology is the product of a particular type of culture. Indeed, anthropology like other conceptual systems also has personal as well as cultural roots (Pocock 1973). The ideological facets of our interest in the past clearly make history 'history-for', but since translation is commentary anthropology cannot avoid being 'translation-for'. The discipline is still largely one of the results of Western civilization using other cultures.

There has been a virtual monologue in which the only definitions of 'us' and 'them' have been given by us. If understanding lies with the creation of more maps, obviously the more cultures engaged in this commentating activity the better. Some of the structure of inter-cultural relations which lay behind the original framework of our anthropological tradition has now disappeared, so perhaps it is not rash to hope that other cultures will take their place in that communicational exchange upon which human understanding rests. And we should hope not only that those cultures which have been the objects of our inquiries will develop anthropological traditions of their own — scrutinizing themselves in ways which are not just a pale reflection of our interests in them — but also that they will make us the object of their speculation.

This image of an expanding 'translational space' has the advantage of allowing us to see the relationship between 'ourselves' and the 'other' in its changing historical reality. Some means of increasing the dimensions of the communication system seem feasible now. Anthropology can be turned back on itself by the sort of semantic investigations of the conceptual structures of one's own society that were carried out in the previous chapter. Other possible ways of increasing the dimensions of our maps seem at this time somewhat remote. But at least this manner of presenting the anthropological situation enables us to see why we need not pose the question whether understanding is in 'their' terms or 'ours'. If 'their terms' entails a fideistic grasp or an understanding in no way influenced by the fact that we ourselves belong to a conceptual structure, then anthropology cannot envisage attaining it. The notion that interpretation could be determined solely by the object of study and not at all by the fact that the investigator is a member of a culture (Peel 1969:69) is absurd because it denies the conditions required for understanding of any sort. One cannot, in translating alien conceptual systems, leave oneself out. In human studies objectivity is a type of disciplined inter-subjectivity. To deny this can only lead to less objectivity and not more.

The trouble with the stark 'our'/'their' dichotomy is that it leaves out the mutual benefits to be derived from the exchange of meaning. This is why an anthropological understanding is not just in 'our' terms. To study another culture seriously — like knowing another individual human being intimately — is to extend one's own life. We do not simply force one 'form of life' into the framework of another, we may have to realign our own categories (Winch 1964:33). If the indeterminacy and interminability which characterize these moves in semantic explorations veto the word 'truth', our search will at least have added a greater richness to our maps. I.A. Richards once suggested that interpreting alien utterances was like 'an adventure among the possibilities of thought and feeling rather than an encounter with facts' (1964:1). One has to avoid violating the thought of others in the process of interpretation, and this is possible if the act of understanding involves a genuine broadening of oneself. Translation in this way contributes to the process of human growth, since through it we learn to comprehend what comprehending is (id.1953:247).

These final reflections on translation remind us what human understanding is, and so make it clear that although British anthropology has recently made an explicit shift from function to meaning, all anthropology is a semantic investigation whether this is expressly recognized or not. And if the scene of human self-understanding as a process with no end shocks somewhat, it is an important piece of self-knowledge to see that this growth could not be other than interminable. For positivist social scientists to deny this and strive for some scientistic objectivity only reveals a false consciousness which is the worse because the result of a search for misidentified scientific credentials. We cannot distinguish radically between facts and values: facts are theory-laden, and theoretical choice is value-laden. Nor can we seriously speak about making all our interests and value judgments explicit. Out of such a pretence can flow only yet more methodological tracts which overlook the profound internal semantic bonds linking our knowledge to our sociohistorical being. We cannot leap out of ourselves to observe from the outside, for this would be to sever those ties with our humane roots which are the conditions for any meaning at all. If it is our particular position which separates 'us' from 'others', it is also the only relationship we have with the whole of human experience. There is a gap; but as we are a part of that total experience, 'we' will ultimately find ourselves in the 'other', as the 'other' will find themselves in 'us'.

Historians no longer believe, as Acton did at the end of the nineteenth century, that increasing knowledge will lead to 'ultimate' history. And a modern philosopher has remarked that 'if inquiry starts from the institution of language, as it has existed in all the variety of its forms, no finality can be claimed for any system of distinctions. The nature of the human mind has to be investigated in the history of the successive forms of its social expression' (Hampshire 1970:234). In the corresponding terms of anthropological discourse, there is no absolute definition of the relation 'self'/'other', for the truth about man is the accumulation of his self-definitions. Many great thinkers have expressed this point: man makes himself in history; man creates a past which comments on its author; man has no nature but his history. Change is of the essence of this human universal, since one expression of a self-defining capacity is the process of redefinition.

This undeniable fact profoundly affects one's vision of the nature of anthropological investigation because the search which it represents into human understanding is a part of its own subject matter. Anthropology yields one system of meaning which relates to all the others, and so our inquiry is bound up with them in an endless development. The bond between anthropology and human nature is thus simultaneously both metaphorical and metonymical. Anthropology speaks about such a nature, yet is also a partial expression of it. Semantic anthropology concerns the powers of human beings to construct meanings, and is itself one manifestation of this capacity. Humanity is a self-announcing species and anthropology is one of its declarations.

The subject of translation has not brought us to an end; for, by confronting us with some fundamental elements of the semantic identity for which this book has been a search, it has shown us that the identity is the search itself. Such a volume cannot have a conclusion; but we should reflect here that semantic anthropology is rather more than metaphor and metonym because it is a conceptual system which can absorb all others, a language which can speak of all the others. Certainly 'semantic anthropology' is only one announcement of human meaning, made at a certain point in time. But all that humanity utters is a statement about itself, so our label includes all systems. Even those who are most hostile to the spirit which animates semantic anthropology can disagree with it only by using their semantic powers to construct an opposed system. In so doing they are embraced by its scope and interests.

Notes

2   The Philological Anthropology of Friedrich Max Müller

1 Müller insisted that the 'inseparability' of language and thought was true only if language was broadly defined. Under language should thus be included other symbolic systems such as gesture, algebra, ideographic signs, and all other embodiments of conceptual thought (1871:356).

2 Ardener's suggested parallel between *bricolage*, folk etymology and the mythopoeic faculty (1971c:226,237n14).

3 For surveys of nineteenth-century ethnology and language, see Hymes 1963; Lounsbury 1968; Henson 1974:5-20.

4 However, we should not forget that Lang in fact later adopted a theory about the origin of religion which was, as he himself realized, very close to that which Müller had always held (1900:790).

5 Müller (1885) used the complexity of savage languages as evidence that savages had decayed from a higher state. It is worth remembering in this context that the image of 'decay' was very prominent in accounts of linguistic change during the nineteenth century. Lang regarded the 'decay of language' as one of the most serious threats to the evolutionist view (in Tylor 1907:2).

6 There are many aspects of Müller's approach to myth, including the 'degeneration of language', which Vico had anticipated (Bidney 1969:266ff.).

7 There are some historical links involved in these parallels. Mauthner was familiar with Müller's work, and Wittgenstein took the idea of a mythology being embedded in the language from the nineteenth-century German philologist Grimm (Rhees, in Wittgenstein 1967a:18n).

8 Since Müller's eclipse is so often regarded as a victory for Tyloreanism, we should remember Tylor's caution in the field of myth as elsewhere. He accepted that different myths had different kinds of origin. He even granted validity to the idea of a 'disease of language', though only in advanced civilizations (1871:270ff.).

3   The Structuralism of Claude Lévi-Strauss

1 Although quick to see the importance of such developments for the social sciences, Lévi-Strauss' epistemology has oddly remained that of the closed system of classical physics, so he has not exploited those teleonomic-

171

morphogenetic models which would seem more suitable for human facts (Wilden 1974:279).

2 The notion of 'structure' is not included here. There are disciplines like mathematics where the notion is clear, but this is not so in Lévi-Strauss' writings. For instance, it is debatable whether the 'structures' in his kinship work are similar to those in his myth analyses. It is even worth reflecting that 'structure' may be a secondary term generated by those elements of the conceptual infra-structure discussed below.

3 For instance the idea that history is a privileged form of consciousness. Lévi-Strauss has never denied that all societies are in historical flux, but the use of history as a means of self-definition is confined to a limited number of cultures (1966:256,263).

4 cf. Foucault's view that 'man' was fabricated in the eighteenth century and will be obliterated in a new configuration of knowledge (1970:308,387). Foucault is not a structuralist; but his view that anthropomorphism is a threat to knowledge, and his attempt to cleanse history of transcendental narcissism by analysing 'discourse formations' in terms of anonymous rules (1972:203,210), achieves a 'decentering' similar to structuralism.

5 Lévi-Strauss generally accords a secondary place to affectivity, arguing that what is refractory to explanation cannot be satisfactorily used in explanation (1969b:140-42,177). No doubt the lack of caution shown by his predecessors in the French sociological tradition has had an influence here.

6 Some of these concepts used in the first volume do not reappear in subsequent ones; some survive, but with a different sign.

7 Barthes suggests that the very duplicity of myth means that its signs cannot possibly be arbitrary (1973:126).

8 The terms 'metaphor' and 'metonym' (which he uses in very diverse ways) derive not from literary theory but, via Jakobson, from the Frazerian distinction between homeopathic and contagious magic.

4 A Critique of Some Recent Developments in American Linguistic Anthropology

1 American anthropology is far from being a large enough context in which to locate this tradition. Sapir, who taught Whorf, had himself been trained by Boas, who had been an intimate friend of Steinthal who had edited the works of Wilhelm von Humboldt. In Germany, the tradition continued in the work of the 'semantic field' theorists who were contemporaries of Sapir and Whorf.

2 The work of Bernstein (1970) is valuable for its stress on speech style as a function of social matrix, which reverses the earlier tendency to see language as the independent variable.

3 In view of recent stress in linguistics on just how much knowledge a native speaker does possess about his language, Hale has expressed general doubts about the adequacy of any tradition of anthropological linguistics (1972:368).

4 Symbolic analyses are normally performed by anthropologists under circumstances of considerable linguistic disadvantage, and the desired level of

contextualization may well be beyond their powers (Beidelman 1973:155n). For the difference advanced linguistic skills can make to symbolic analysis, see Fox 1974.

5 Metaphor continues to perplex philosophers also. For some, it is an abuse of language since it lessens its clarity; for others, it is merely an example of ornate expression which can be satisfactorily re-expressed in simpler terms; for yet others, it is a conceptual interaction which constitutes a kind of meaning which cannot be put in literal terms.

6 It is now recognized that there was never any clear notion of what that scientific rigour was which was so highly prized in post-Bloomfieldian linguistics (Hockett 1968:27).

7 This is the importance of ethnomethodological inquiries into 'practical theorising' (Garfinkel 1967; R. Turner 1974 ed.). In exploring everyday shared understanding, and the vast common background against which ordinary communication takes place, it locates those features of human action which make both social life and sociological inquiry possible.

5 Ordinary Language and Human Action

1 Kant denied the possibility of a 'Newtonian' psychology, because such a framework could not handle the fundamental fact of human agency. In this way he may be regarded as an ancestor of the 'ethogenic' approach (Mischel 1967).

2 On the importance of the concept of 'powers' in the realist philosophy of science, see Harré & Secord (1972:78-82). It is worth recalling in this context the similar way Chomsky has granted scientific import to speakers' knowledge.

3 In fact, the notion of 'behaviour' — seemingly such an easily identifiable and universal phenomenon — was picked up by the infant social sciences from chemistry, where its history is still little more than a century long (Ardener 1973b).

4 It does not follow from this viewpoint that a scientific account is concerned only with noting the forms of events which ordinary language traces. One has also to account for the nature of these forms; and to express their deep structures it will often be necessary to go beyond the resources of ordinary concepts, even to systems like non-metrical mathematics, for instance.

5 The term 'paradigmatic' is taken from Saussure, but as the notion of paradigm now has such a diversity of uses — particularly after the work of Kuhn — to free his terminology from these associations, Ardener now prefers to talk simply of p- and s-structures.

6 The *verstehen* literature is often very confusing, since it sometimes makes the act of understanding another human being seem like an unverifiable and intuitive fathoming, rather than that exchange of meanings with which people are perfectly familiar.

7 Of course, while rules and meanings are public, we are all ultimately individuals with unique histories and with very different experiences of our language. But if we therefore all speak slightly differing tongues, these ideolects are nonetheless not private languages. There is an inevitable

interpretative act which is quite rightly regarded as translation (Steiner 1975:45,47), even for communication in one language. And, as with interlingual translation, the negotiation over semantic issues lacks finality in that interpretations are always further negotiable. But disagreements are possible only because people can understand each other: if other minds were inaccessible there could be no negotiation at all.

8 For those who find notions like 'sacred space', 'moral space', and so on, abstruse, it has to be stressed that it is the flat descriptions of human action found in the supposedly scientific disciplines that are metaphysical. It is precisely our semantic powers which create those multi-dimensional realities in which we live, move and have our being. And we should not forget the fact that what we call 'real' space is itself defined by a conceptual structure — that of Western science (Ardener 1975).

9 This framework may be capable of expressing the dualisms used elsewhere in this chapter — paradigmatic/syntagmatic, deep structure/surface structure, and so on.

10 A human kinship system, for instance, cannot be construed simply as a combination of elements found in primate behaviour — as has been suggested (R. Fox 1975:12-13) — because, among other things, the rules involved here are not mere labels for activities which would occur independently of them.

11 It is for this reason that biological concepts cannot be an 'ideal language' for plotting kinship systems (Gellner 1957). A kinship system, being a structure of semantic categories, is a system of an entirely different kind. In Ardener's terms, we could regard kinship as a paradigmatic structure, and biological events like birth and death as a syntagmatic sequence. In the latter we are dealing with organic individuals; in the former with person categories. And because of the logical relations between p- and s-structures, the elements of a syntagmatic discourse cannot provide the terms for a paradigmatic structure.

6 Recasting Witchcraft

1 The idea employed below of a conceptual field may be of value for their work, since this perspective allows a structural approach to be followed in the diachronic dimension. Historians thus might be able to plot the changing dimensions and articulation of the historical field of which witchcraft was a part over a time span in a certain culture.

2 The French sociological tradition of analysing systems of 'collective representations' has provided valuable comparative material on different cultural concepts of the person (see *La Notion de Personne en Afrique Noire*. Editions du Centre National de la Recherche Scientifique. Paris 1973).

3 A debt to the work of Strawson must be acknowledged here (1958; 1964), although my interest is not in the philosophical 'primitiveness' of the notion of a person. Also, by virtue of its slender linguistic base, there must be a worry that Strawson's studies of the relations between supposed invariant categories may be a mere *a priori* anthropology.

4 This is an absolutely minimal set of the most institutionalized person categories which will suffice here for giving our outline framework.

Naturally, when analysing a particular body of ethnographic data we should set out the person field using the native categories themselves, and this would involve considering the less formal 'dramaturgical' roles as well.

5 Finnegan has suggested that the notion may illuminate the fields of religion and ritual in general (1969b:550); Tambiah has applied the concept to magic (1973).

7 Understanding Conceptual Structures

1 The 'language of science' of the positivist philosophical tradition was less a refinement of its actual language than an invention. And, like many logical systematizations, it has been scarcely relevant to the real life of the scientific community (Toulmin 1972:63).

2 Disagreements here have been partly responsible for the long series of schisms in the history of psychology and psychoanalysis since Jung's split from Freud.

3 This interpretation does not deny the existence of the sort of people, satirized in medieval literature, who actually did intend to make gold by alchemical means.

8 The Translation of Cultures

1 Possibly the term 'religion' now has such a wide comparative usage that it cannot be dispensed with. Even so, the discipline 'comparative religion' is a product of Western thought, so we should be wary in case it has created its own objects of study.

2 The great energy expended on the 'rationality problem' seems largely wasted, because several legitimate semantic issues have been fused into one unreal difficulty. Given that there is a diversity of games with different rules of procedure, the concept of rationality is used either as an abbreviation for the rules of one game we arbitrarily privilege, or else as the rules for a super-game which does not exist. Recent discussions have been the less fruitful for their employment of the dualisms we have shown to be semantically coarse.

3 Despite the fact that the art of translation is as old as the human species, it is a process which is governed by surprisingly meagre theoretical equipment. Not only has the history of theories of translation produced very few original ideas, it has seen general models far more off the mark than actual pieces of translating carried out in terms of them. Steiner has suggested that translation may be a phenomenon for which it would be a mistake to look for a general theory (1975:273).

4 Under social ambience one would naturally include affectivity, and here the almost panchrestonic role which Lévi-Bruhl (like the *Année sociologique* writers) assigned to emotions in accounting for the form of collective representations certainly is unacceptable.

5 Evans-Pritchard uses the notion of 'refraction', for instance, to indicate how Nuer religious concepts bear the impress of the social structure, while at the same time arguing forcibly that the Nuer concept of God can neither be reduced to nor explained by Nuer society (1956:320).

Bibliography

ACHINSTEIN, P. A. and BARKER, S. F. 1969 (eds). *The Legacy of Logical Positivism: Studies in the Philosophy of Science*. Johns Hopkins Press, Baltimore.

ALBERT, E. 1972. Culture Patterning of Special Behavior in Burundi. *In* Gumperz and Hymes 1972 (eds): 72-106.

ARDENER, E. W. 1965. Review of Jarvie 1964. *Man* 65:57.

— 1970. Witchcraft, Economics, and the Continuity of Belief. *In* M. Douglas 1970 (ed.): 141-60.

— 1971a. The new anthropology and its critics. *Man* (n.s.) 6:449-67.

— 1971b. Introductory Essay. *In* 1971 (ed.): ix-cii.

— 1971c. Social anthropology and the Historicity of Historical Linguistics. *In* 1971 (ed.): 209-41.

— 1971 (ed.). *Social Anthropology and Language*. Tavistock, London.

— 1972. Belief and the Problem of Women. *In* La Fontaine 1972 (ed.): 135-58.

— 1973a. Some Outstanding Problems in the Analysis of Events. A.S.A. Conference Paper.

— 1973b. Behaviour: A social anthropological criticism. *Journal of the Anthropological Society of Oxford* 4:152-4.

— 1974. Social Anthropology and Population. *In* Parry 1974 (ed.): 25-50.

— 1975. The Voice of Prophecy: Further Problems in the Analysis of Events. Munro Lecture, Edinburgh

ARDENER, E. W. and ARDENER, S. G. 1965. A Directory Study of Social Anthropologists. *British Journal of Sociology* 16:295-314.

AUSTIN, J. L. 1956. A Plea for Excuses. *In* Chappell 1964 (ed.): 41-63.

— 1962. *How To Do Things With Words*. Clarendon Press, Oxford.

BACHELARD, G. 1970. *La Formation de l'esprit scientifique*. Vrin, Paris.

BARDEN, G. 1972. Method and Meaning. *In* Singer and Street 1972 (eds): 104-29.

BARTH, F. 1965. *Political Leadership among Swat Pathans*. Athlone Press, London.

BARTHES, R. 1967. *Elements of Semiology*. Jonathan Cape, London.

— 1973. *Mythologies*. Paladin, St. Albans.

BATESON, G. 1964. The logical categories of learning and communication. *In* 1973: 250-79.

— 1973. *Steps to an Ecology of Mind*. Paladin, St. Albans.

177

Bibliography

BEATTIE, J. H. M. 1955. Contemporary Trends in British Social Anthropology. *Sociologus* 5:1-14.

— 1966. Ritual and Social Change. *Man* (n.s.) 1:60-74.

— 1970. On Understanding Ritual. *In* Wilson 1970 (ed.): 240-68.

BEIDELMAN, T. O. 1970. Towards more open Theoretical Interpretations. *In* M. Douglas 1970 (ed.): 351-6.

— 1971. Nuer Priests and Prophets. Charisma, Authority, and Power among the Nuer. *In* 1971 (ed.): 375-415.

— 1971 (ed.). *The Translation of Culture*. Tavistock, London.

— 1973. Kaguru Symbolic Classification. *In* Needham 1973 (ed.): 128-66.

BENNETT, J. 1971. *Rationality*. Routledge and Kegan Paul, London.

BERLIN, B., BREEDLOVE, D. E. and RAVEN, P. H. 1968. Covert Categories and Folk Taxonomies. *American Anthropologist* 70:290-9.

BERLIN, B. and KAY, P. 1969. *Basic Color Terms. Their Universality and Evolution*. University of California Press, Berkeley.

BERNSTEIN, B. 1970. A Socio-linguistic Approach to Socialization with special reference to educability. *Human World* 2:1-9,233-47.

BERREMAN, G. D. 1966. Anemic and Emetic Analyses in Social Anthropology. *American Anthropologist* 68:346-54.

BIDNEY, D. 1969. Vico's New Science of Myth. *In* Tagliacozzo 1969 (ed.): 259-77.

BLACK, M. 1968. *The Labyrinth of Language*. Pall Mall Press, London.

BORGER, R. and CIOFFI, F. 1970 (eds). *Explanation in the Behavioural Sciences*. Cambridge University Press.

BRAITHWAITE, R. B. 1955. An Empiricist's View of the Nature of Religious Belief. *In* Santoni 1968 (ed.): 333-47.

BREW, J. O. 1968 (ed.). *One Hundred Years of Anthropology*. Harvard University Press, Cambridge, Mass.

BRIGHT, W. 1966 (ed.). *Sociolinguistics*. Mouton & Co., The Hague.

BROWER, R. A. 1959 (ed.). *On Translation*. Harvard University Press, Cambridge, Mass.

BULMER, R. 1967. Why is the Cassowary not a Bird? A Problem of Zoological taxonomy among the Karam of the New Guinea Highlands. *Man* (n.s.) 2:5-25.

BURCKHARDT, T. 1967. *Alchemy. Science of the Cosmos, Science of the Soul*. Stuart & Watkins, London.

BUREN, P. van 1963. *The Secular Meaning of the Gospels based on an analysis of its language*. S.C.M. Press, London.

BURLING, R. 1964. Cognition and Componential Analysis: God's Truth or Hocus-Pocus? *In* Tyler 1969 (ed.): 419-28.

— 1965. Burmese Kinship Terminology. *In* Hammel 1965 (ed.): 106-17.

— 1969. Linguistics and Ethnographic Description. *American Anthropologist* 71:817-27.

BUXTON, J. 1963. Mandari Witchcraft. *In* Middleton and Winter 1963 (eds): 99-121.

— 1973. *Religion and Healing in Mandari*. Clarendon Press, Oxford.

CALLAN, H. 1970. *Ethology and Society. Towards an Anthropological View*. Clarendon Press, Oxford.

CASAGRANDE, J. B. 1963. Language Universals in Anthropological Perspective. *In* Greenberg 1966 (ed.): 279-98.

CASSIRER, E. 1965. *An Essay on Man*. Yale University Press, New Haven.

CHAPPELL, V. C. 1962 (ed.). *The Philosophy of Mind*. Prentice-Hall Inc., Englewood Cliffs.

— 1964 (ed.). *Ordinary Language*. Prentice-Hall Inc., Englewood Cliffs.

CHARBONNIER, G. 1970 (ed.). *Conversations with Claude Lévi-Strauss*. Jonathan Cape, London.

CHOMSKY, N. 1957. *Syntactic Structures*. Mouton, The Hague.

— 1959. Review of Skinner 1957. *In* Fodor and Katz 1964 (eds): 547-78.

— 1965. *Aspects of the Theory of Syntax*. M.I.T. Press, Cambridge, Mass.

— 1968. *Language and Mind*. Harcourt, Brace & World Inc., New York.

CICOUREL, A. V. 1973. *Cognitive Sociology, Language and Meaning in Social Interaction*. Penguin, Harmondsworth.

COHEN, F. S. 1950. Field Theory and Judicial Logic. *Yale Law Journal* 59: 238-72.

COLBY, B. N. 1966. Ethnographic Semantics: A Preliminary Survey. *Current Anthropology* 7: 3-32.

COLLINGWOOD, R. G. 1940. *An Essay on Metaphysics*. Clarendon Press, Oxford.

— 1944. *An Autobiography*. Penguin, Harmondsworth.

CONKLIN, H. C. 1955. Hanunóo Color Categories. *Southwestern Journal of Anthropology* 11: 339-44.

— 1962. Lexicographical Treatment of Folk Taxonomies. *In* Fishman 1968 (ed.): 414-33.

COOMARASWAMY, A. K. 1942. *Spiritual Authority and Temporal Power in the Indian Theory of Government*. American Oriental Society, New Haven.

DAVIDSON, D. and HARMAN, G. 1972 (eds). *Semantics of Natural Languages*. Reidel, Dordrecht.

DERRETT, J. D. M. 1971. Virgin Birth in the Gospels. *Man* (n.s.) 6: 289-93.

DIAMOND, S. 1974. The Myth of Structuralism. *In* Rossi 1974 (ed.): 292-335.

DORSON, R. M. 1968. *The British Folklorists*. Routledge & & Kegan Paul, London.

DOUGLAS, J. 1971 (ed.). *Understanding Everyday Life. Towards the Reconstruction of Sociological Knowledge*. Routledge & Kegan Paul, London.

DOUGLAS, M. 1966. *Purity and Danger. An Analysis of Concepts of Pollution and Taboo*. Routledge & Kegan Paul, London.

— 1967. Witch Beliefs in Central Africa. *Africa* 37: 72-80.

— 1970a. *Natural Symbols. Explorations in Cosmology*. Cresset, London.

— 1970b. The Healing Rite. *Man* (n.s.) 5: 302-8.

— 1970 (ed.). *Witchcraft Confessions and Accusations*. Tavistock, London.

— 1973 (ed.). *Rules and Meanings. The Anthropology of Everyday Knowledge*. Penguin, Harmondsworth.

DUMONT, L. 1961. Caste, Racism and 'Stratification'. Reflections of a Social Anthropologist. *Contributions to Indian Sociology* 5: 20-43.

— 1972. *Homo Hierarchicus. The Caste System and its Implications*. Paladin, St. Albans.

DURBIN, M. 1966. The Goals of Ethnoscience. *Anthropological Linguistics* 8: 22-41.

179

Bibliography

DURKHEIM. E. 1906. The Determination of Moral Facts. *In* 1953:1-34.

— 1912. *Les Formes Elémentaires de la Vie Religieuse*. Alcan, Paris.

— 1953. *Sociology and Philosophy*. Cohen & West Ltd., London.

DURKHEIM. E. and MAUSS. M. 1963. *Primitive Classification*. Routledge & Kegan Paul, London. (1903).

EMMET. D. 1966. *The Nature of Metaphysical Thinking*. Macmillan, London.

EMMET. D. and MACINTYRE. A. 1970 (eds). *Sociological Theory and Philosophical Analysis*. Macmillan, London.

EVANS. D. 1963. *The Logic of Self-Involvement. A Philosophical Study of Everyday Language with Special Reference to the Christian Use of Language about God as Creator*. S.C.M. Press Ltd., London.

EVANS-PRITCHARD. E. E. 1929. The Morphology and Function of Magic: A Comparative Study of Trobriand and Zande Ritual and Spells. *In* Middleton 1967a (ed.):1-22.

— 1936. Zande Theology. *In* 1969:162-203.

— 1937. *Witchcraft, Oracles and Magic among the Azande*. Clarendon Press, Oxford.

— 1950. Social Anthropology: Past and Present. *Man* 50:118-24.

— 1956. *Nuer Religion*. Clarendon Press, Oxford.

— 1965. *Theories of Primitive Religion*. Clarendon Press, Oxford.

— 1969. *Essays in Social Anthropology*. Faber & Faber, London.

— 1970. Lévy-Bruhl's Theory of Primitive Mentality. *Journal of the Anthropological Society of Oxford* 1:39-60.

— 1973. The Intellectualist (British) Interpretation of Magic. *Journal of the Anthropological Society of Oxford* 4:123-42.

— 1974. Science and Sentiment: an Exposition and Criticism of the Writings of Pareto. *Journal of the Anthropological Society of Oxford* 5:1-21.

FERRÉ. F. 1959. Is Language about God Fraudulent? *Scottish Journal of Theology* 12:337-60.

— 1970. *Language, Logic, and God*. Fontana, London.

FINNEGAN. R. 1969a. Attitudes to Speech and Language among the Limba of Sierra Leone. *Odu* (n.s.) 2:61-77.

— 1969b. How to do things with Words: performative utterances among the Limba of Sierra Leone. *Man* (n.s.) 4:537-52.

— 1973. Literacy versus Non-literacy: The Great Divide? Some Comments on the Significance of 'literature' in Non-literate Cultures. *In* Horton and Finnegan 1973 (eds):112-44.

FIRTH. J. R. 1957. Ethnographic analysis and language with reference to Malinowski's views. *In* 1968:137-67.

— 1968. *Selected Papers of J.R. Firth 1952-9* (ed. F.R. Palmer). Longmans, Green and Co., London.

FIRTH. R. 1951. Contemporary British Social Anthropology. *American Anthropologist* 53:474-89.

— 1973. *Symbols, Public and Private*. George Allen & Unwin Ltd., London.

FISHMAN. J. A. 1968 (ed.). *Readings in the Sociology of Language*. Mouton, The Hague.

FLEW, A. 1951 (ed.). *Logic and Language* (First Series). Blackwell, Oxford.

FLEW, A. and MACINTYRE, A. 1963 (eds). *New Essays in Philosophical Theology*. S.C.M. Press, London.

FODOR, J. A. and GARRETT, M. 1966. Some Reflections on Competence and Performance. *In* Lyons and Wales 1966 (eds): 135-54.

FODOR, J. A. and KATZ, J. J. 1964 (eds). *The Structure of Language. Readings in the Philosophy of Language*. Prentice-Hall Inc., Englewood Cliffs.

FORTES, M. 1953. *Social Anthropology at Cambridge since 1900*. Cambridge University Press.

— 1959. *Oedipus and Job in West African Religion*. Cambridge University Press.

FORTES, M. and DIETERLEN, G. 1966 (eds). *African Systems of Thought*. Oxford University Press, London.

FOUCAULT, M. 1967. *Madness and Civilization. A Study of Insanity in the Age of Reason*. Tavistock, London.

— 1970. *The Order of Things. An Archaeology of the Human Sciences*. Tavistock, London.

— 1972. *The Archaeology of Knowledge*. Tavistock, London.

FOX, J. J. 1971. Sister's Child as Plant. Metaphors in an Idiom of Consanguinity. *In* Needham 1971 (ed.): 219-52.

— 1975. On Binary Categories and Primary Symbols. Some Rotinese Perspectives. *In* Willis 1975 (ed.): 99-132.

FOX, R. 1975. Primate Kin and Human Kinship. *In* Fox 1975 (ed.): 9-35.

— 1975 (ed.). *Biosocial Anthropology*. Malaby Press, London.

FRAKE, C. O. 1961. The Diagnosis of Disease among the Subanun of Mindanao. *American Anthropologist* 63 : 113-32.

— 1964. Notes on Queries in Ethnography. *In* Romney and D'Andrade 1964 (eds): 132-45.

— 1969. Struck by Speech: the Yakan Concept of Litigation. *In* Gumperz and Hymes 1972 (eds): 106-29.

FRAZER, J. G. 1908. The Scope of Social Anthropology. *In* 1913: 159-76.

— 1913. *Psyche's Task. A Discourse Concerning the Influence of Superstition on the Growth of Institutions*. Macmillan, London.

— 1926. *The Worship of Nature*. Macmillan, London.

— 1927. *The Gorgon's Head and Other Literary Pieces*. Macmillan, London.

— 1963. *The Golden Bough. A Study in Magic and Religion*. Macmillan, London. (1922).

FREEMAN, D. 1966. Social Anthropology and the Scientific Study of Human Behaviour. *Man* (n.s.) 1 : 330-42.

GARFINKEL, H. 1967. *Studies in Ethnomethodology*. Prentice-Hall Inc., Englewood Cliffs.

GEERTZ, C. 1960. Linguistic Etiquette. *In* Fishman 1968 (ed.): 282-95.

— 1966. *Person, Time, and Conduct in Bali. An Essay in Cultural Analysis*. Yale South East Asia Studies Cultural Report Series No. 14.

GELLNER, E. 1957. Ideal Languages and Kinship Structure. *Philosophy of Science* 24 : 235-42.

— 1968a. *Words and Things*. Penguin, Harmondsworth.

Bibliography

— 1968b. The new idealism — cause and meaning in the social sciences. *In* 1973:50-77.

— 1973. *Cause and Meaning in the Social Sciences* (eds Jarvie & Agassi). Routledge & Kegan Paul, London.

GLUCKMAN, M. G. 1944. Review of Evans-Pritchard 1937. *Human Problems in British Central Africa* 1:61-71.

— 1964 (ed.). *Closed Systems and Open Minds*. Oliver & Boyd, Edinburgh.

— 1972 (ed.). *The Allocation of Responsibility*. Manchester University Press.

GOFFMAN, E. 1959. *The Presentation of Self in Everyday Life*. Doubleday Anchor Books, New York.

— 1967. *Interaction Ritual. Essays in Face-to-Face Behavior*. Doubleday Anchor Books, New York.

— 1971. *Asylums. Essays in the Social Situation of Mental Patients and Other Inmates*. Penguin, Harmondsworth.

GOODENOUGH, W. H. 1956. Componential Analysis and the Study of Meaning. *Language* 32:195-216.

— 1965. Yankee Kinship Terminology: A Problem in Componential Analysis. *In* Hammel 1965 (ed.):259-87.

GOODY, E. 1970. Legitimate and Illegitimate Aggression in a West African State. *In* M. Douglas 1970 (ed.):207-44.

GOODY, J. 1958 (ed.). *The Developmental Cycle in Domestic Groups*. Cambridge University Press.

— 1968 (ed.). *Literacy in Traditional Societies*. Cambridge University Press.

GOODY, J. and WATT, I. 1963. The Consequences of Literacy. *In* J. Goody 1968 (ed.):27-68.

GOSSEN, G. H. 1974. *Chamulas in the World of the Sun. Time and Space in a Maya Oral Tradition*. Harvard University Press, Cambridge, Mass.

GREENBERG, J. H. 1966 (ed.). *Universals of Language*. M.I.T. Press, Cambridge, Mass.

GUMPERZ, J. and HYMES, D. H. 1972 (eds). *Directions in Sociolinguistics. The Ethnography of Communication*. Holt, Rinehart & Winston Inc., New York.

GURVITCH, G. 1947 (ed.). *La Sociologie aux XXe Siècle*. Presses Universitaires de France, Paris.

HAAS, W. 1962. The Theory of Translation. *In* Parkinson 1970 (ed.):86-108.

HABERMAS, J. 1972. *Knowledge and Human Interests*. Heinemann, London.

HALE, K. 1972. Some Questions about Anthropological Linguistics: The Role of Native Knowledge. *In* Hymes 1974 (ed.):382-97.

HALLPIKE, C. 1971. Some Problems in Cross-Cultural Comparison. *In* Beidelman 1971 (ed.):123-40.

HAMMEL, E. A. 1965 (ed.). Formal Semantic Analysis. *American Anthropologist* 67 No.5, part 2 (Special Publication).

HAMPSHIRE, S. 1970. *Thought and Action*. Chatto & Windus, London.

HANSON, F. A. 1970. Understanding in Philosophical Anthropology. *Journal of the Anthropological Society of Oxford* 1:61-70.

HANSON, N. R. 1958. *Patterns of Discovery. An Inquiry into the Conceptual Foundations of Science*. Cambridge University Press.

— 1969. Logical Positivism and the Interpretation of Scientific Theories. *In* Achinstein and Barker 1969 (eds): 57-84.

HARE, R. M. 1957. Religion and Morals. *In* Mitchell 1957 (ed.): 176-93.

HARRÉ, R. H. 1964. *Matter and Method*. Macmillan, London.

— 1970. *The Principles of Scientific Thinking*. Macmillan, London.

— 1974. Some Remarks on 'Rule' as a Scientific Concept. *In* Mischel 1974 (ed.): 143-84.

HARRÉ, R. H. and SECORD, P. 1972. *The Explanation of Social Behaviour*. Blackwell, Oxford.

HARRIS, M. 1968. *The Rise of Anthropological Theory. A History of Theories of Culture*. Routledge & Kegan Paul, London.

HART, H. L. A. 1961. *The Concept of Law*. Clarendon Press, Oxford.

HART, H. L. A. and HONORE, A. M. 1956. Causation in the Law. *Law Quarterly Review* 72: 58-90, 260-81, 398-417.

HARWOOD, A. 1970. *Witchcraft, Sorcery and Social Categories among the Safwa*. Oxford University Press, London.

HENSON, H. 1974. *British Social Anthropologists and Language. A History of Separate Development*. Clarendon Press, Oxford.

HEPBURN, R.W. 1957. Poetry and Religious Belief. In *Metaphysical Beliefs*, S.C.M. Press 1970: 75-156.

HERTZ, R. 1960. *Death and the Right Hand*. Cohen & West, London. (1907/9).

HESSE, M. 1966. *Models and Analogies in Science*. University of Notre Dame Press, Indiana.

HICK, J. 1966 (ed.). *Faith and the Philosophers*. Macmillan, London.

— 1967. *Faith and Knowledge*. Macmillan, London.

HOCART, A. M. 1970. *Kings and Councillors. An Essay in the Comparative Anatomy of Human Society* (ed. Needham). Chicago University Press. (1936).

HOCKETT, C. F. 1963. The Problem of Universals in Linguistics. *In* Greenberg 1966 (ed.): 1-29.

— 1968. *The State of the Art*. Mouton, The Hague.

HOCKETT, C. F. and ALTMANN, S. A. 1968. A Note on Design Features. *In* Sebeok 1968 (ed.): 61-72.

HODGEN, M. 1936. *The Doctrine of Survivals. A Chapter in the History of the Scientific Method in the Study of Man*. Allenson & Co. Ltd., London.

HOENIGSWALD, H. M. 1966. A Proposal for the Study of Folk-linguistics. *In* Bright 1966 (ed.): 16-20.

HOIJER, H. 1954 (ed.). *Language in Culture*. American Anthropological Association Memoir 79. University of Chicago Press.

HOLLIS, M. 1967. The Limits of Irrationality. *In* Wilson 1970 (ed.): 214-20.

HOOK, S. 1969 (ed.). *Language and Philosophy*. New York University Press.

HORTON, R. 1964. Ritual Man in Africa. *Africa* 34: 85-104.

— 1967. African Traditional Thought and Western Science. *Africa* 37: 50-71, 155-87.

— 1968. Neo-Tyloreanism: sound sense or sinister prejudice. *Man* (n.s.) 3: 625-34.

Bibliography

— 1973. Lévy-Bruhl, Durkheim and the Scientific Revolution. *In* Horton and Finnegan 1973 (eds): 249-305.

HORTON, R. and FINNEGAN, R. 1973 (eds). *Modes of Thought. Essays on Thinking in Western and Non-Western Societies.* Faber & Faber, London.

HUMPHREY, C. 1971. Some ideas of Saussure's applied to Buryat Magical Drawings. *In* Ardener 1971 (ed.): 271-90.

HYMES, D. H. 1962. The Ethnography of Speaking. *In* Fishman 1968 (ed.): 99-138.

— 1963. Notes Towards a History of Anthropological Linguistics. *Anthropological Linguistics* 5:59-103.

— 1964. Directions in (Ethno-) linguistic Theory. *In* Romney and D'Andrade 1964 (eds): 6-56.

— 1964 (ed.). *Language in Culture and Society. A Reader in Linguistics and Anthropology.* Harper & Row, New York.

— 1966. Two Types of Linguistic Relativity (With Examples from Amerindian Ethnography). *In* Bright 1966 (ed.): 114-58.

— 1971a. Sociolinguistics and the Ethnography of Speaking. *In* Ardener 1971 (ed.): 47-93.

— 1971b. On Communicative Competence. *In* Pride and Holmes 1972 (eds): 269-93.

— 1971. (ed.). *Pidginization and Creolization of Languages.* Cambridge University Press.

— 1972a. Models of the Interaction of Language and Social Life. *In* Gumperz and Hymes 1972 (eds): 35-71.

— 1972b. Editorial Introduction. *Language and Society* 1:1-14.

— 1974 (ed.). *Reinventing Anthropology.* Vintage Books, Random House, New York.

JAKOBSON, R. 1959. On Linguistic Aspects of Translation. *In* Brower 1959 (ed.): 232-9.

— 1967. Linguistics in Relation to Other Sciences. *In* 1971: 655-91.

— 1971. *Selected Writings* (Vol.2). Mouton, The Hague.

JARVIE, I. C. 1964. *The Revolution in Anthropology.* Routledge & Kegan Paul, London.

— 1970. Understanding and Explanation in Sociology and Social Anthropology. *In* Borger and Cioffi 1970 (eds): 231-48.

JARVIE, I. C. and AGASSI, J. 1967. The Problem of the Rationality of Magic. *In* Wilson 1970 (ed.): 172-93.

JUNG, C. G. 1963. *Mysterium Coniunctionis. An Inquiry into the Separation and Synthesis of Psychic Opposites in Alchemy.* Routledge & Kegan Paul, London.

KAY, P. 1969. Some Theoretical Implications of Ethnographic Semantics. Working Paper No.24, Language-Behavior Laboratory, Berkeley.

KEESING, R. M. 1972. Paradigms Lost: The New Ethnography and the New Linguistics. *Southwestern Journal of Anthropology* 28:299-332.

KEYNES, R. H. 1972. Witchcraft in Sixteenth and Seventeenth Century England. *Journal of the Anthropological Society of Oxford* 3:149-57.

184

KOLAKOWSKI, L. 1972. *Positivist Philosophy. From Hume to the Vienna Circle.* Penguin, Harmondsworth.

KORN, F. and NEEDHAM, R. 1970. Permutation Models and Prescriptive Systems. *Man* (n.s.) 5:393-420.

KUHN, T. S. 1970. *The Structure of Scientific Revolutions.* University of Chicago Press.

— 1972a. Logic of Discovery or Psychology of Research. *In* Lakatos and Musgrave 1972 (eds):1-23.

— 1972b. Reflections on my Critics. *In* Lakatos and Musgrave 1972 (eds):231-78.

LA FONTAINE, J. S. 1972 (ed.). *The Interpretation of Ritual.* Tavistock, London.

LAING, R. 1971a. *The Divided Self.* Penguin, Harmondsworth.

— 1971b. *The Politics of the Family and Other Essays.* Tavistock, London.

LAKATOS, I. and MUSGRAVE, A. 1972 (eds). *Criticism and the Growth of Knowledge.* Cambridge University Press.

LAKOFF, G. 1972. Linguistics and natural logic. *In* Davidson and Harman 1972 (eds):545-665.

LANG, A. 1884a. *Custom and Myth.* Longmans, London.

— 1884b. Mythology. *Encyclopedia Britannica* (9th edition).

— 1897. *Modern Mythology.* Longmans, London.

— 1900. Max Müller. *Contemporary Review* 78:784-93.

— 1901. *Myth, Ritual and Religion.* Longmans, London.

LEACH, E. R. 1958. Concerning Trobriand Clans and the Kinship Category Tabu. *In* J. Goody 1958 (ed.):120-45.

— 1961. Rethinking Anthropology. *In* 1968:1-27.

— 1964. Telstar and the Aborigines or La Pensée Sauvage. *In* Emmet and MacIntyre 1970 (eds):183-203.

— 1966a. Ritualisation in Man in Relation to Conceptual and Social Development. *In* Lessa and Vogt 1972 (eds):333-7.

— 1966b. Virgin Birth. *In* 1969:85-112.

— 1968. *Rethinking Anthropology.* Athlone Press, London.

— 1969. *Genesis as Myth and Other Essays.* Jonathan Cape, London.

— 1970. *Lévi-Strauss.* Fontana/Collins, London.

LENNEBERG, E. H. 1964. A Biological Perspective of Language. *In* 1964 (ed.):65-88.

— 1964 (ed.). *New Directions in the Study of Language.* M.I.T. Press, Cambridge, Mass.

— 1968. Language in the Light of Evolution. *In* Sebeok 1968 (ed.):592-613.

— 1969. *Problems in the Systematization of Communicative Behaviour. In* Sebeok and Ramsay 1969 (eds):131-7.

LESSA, W. A. and VOGT, E. Z. 1972 (eds). *Reader in Comparative Religion. An Anthropological Approach* (3rd edition). Harper & Row, New York.

LÉVI-STRAUSS, C. 1945. Structural Analysis in Linguistics and in Anthropology. *In* 1968b:31-54.

— 1947. La Sociologie Française. *In* Gurvitch 1947 (ed.):513-45.

— 1949. History and Anthropology. *In* 1968b:1-27.

— 1950. Introduction à l'Oeuvre de Marcel Mauss. *In* Mauss 1950:ix-lii.

Bibliography

— 1951. Language and the Analysis of Social Laws. *In* 1968b:55-66.
— 1953a. Linguistics and Anthropology. *In* 1968b:67-80.
— 1953b. Social Structure. *In* 1968b:277-323.
— 1954a. The Mathematics of Man. *International Social Science Bulletin* 6, No.4:581-90.
— 1954b. The Place of Anthropology in the Social Sciences and Problems raised in teaching it. *In* 1968b:346-81.
— 1955. The Structural Study of Mythology. *In* 1968b:206-31.
— 1956. Do Dual Organisations Exist? *In* 1968b:132-63.
— 1958a. Postscript (chapter 5). *In* 1968b:81-97.
— 1958b. La Geste D'Asdiwal. In *The Structural Study of Myth and Totemism* (ed. Leach). 1968. Tavistock, London. 1-47.
— 1960a. L'Analyse Morphologique des Contes Russes. *International Journal of Slavic Linguistics and Poetics* 3:122-49.
— 1960b. On Manipulated Sociological Models. *Bijdragen* 116:45-54.
— 1961. *World on the Wane*. Hutchinson & Co. Ltd., London.
— 1962. Jean Jacques Rousseau: Fondateur Des Sciences De l'Homme. *In* 1973b:45-56.
— 1964. Criteria of Science in the social and human disciplines. *International Social Science Journal* 16:534-52.
— 1966. *The Savage Mind*. Weidenfeld & Nicolson, London.
— 1968a. *The Scope of Anthropology*. Jonathan Cape, London.
— 1968b. *Structural Anthropology*. Allen Lane/Penguin, London.
— 1968c. *L'Origine des Manières de Table*. Plon, Paris.
— 1968d. *Race and History*. UNESCO, Paris.
— 1969a. *The Elementary Structures of Kinship* (ed. Needham). Eyre & Spottiswoode, London.
— 1969b. *Totemism*. Penguin, Harmondsworth.
— 1970a. A Confrontation. *New Left Review* 62:57-74.
— 1970b. *The Raw and the Cooked. Introduction to a Science of Mythology*. Harper & Row, New York.
— 1971. *L'Homme Nu*. Plon, Paris.
— 1973a. *From Honey to Ashes. Introduction to a Science of Mythology*. Jonathan Cape, London.
— 1973b. *Anthropolgie Structurale Deux*. Plon, Paris.
LEVY-BRUHL, L. 1912. *Les Fonctions Mentales dans les Sociétés Inférieures*. Alcan, Paris.
— 1923. *Primitive Mentality*. George Allen & Unwin, London.
— 1952. Letter to Evans-Pritchard. *British Journal of Sociology* 3:117-23.
LEWIS, I. M. 1970. A Structural Approach to Witchcraft and Spirit Possession. *In* M. Douglas 1970 (ed.):293-309.
— 1971. *Ecstatic Religion. An Anthropological Study of Spirit Possession and Shamanism*. Penguin, Harmondsworth.
LIENHARDT. R. G. 1951. Some Notions of Witchcraft among the Dinka. *Africa* 21:308-18.
— 1954. Modes of Thought. In *The Institutions of Primitive Society*. Blackwell, Oxford. 95-107.

— 1956. Religion. *In* Shapiro 1956 (ed.): 310-29.

— 1961. *Divinity and Experience. The Religion of the Dinka.* Clarendon Press, Oxford.

LLOYD, B. 1972. *Perception and Cognition. A Cross-Cultural Perspective.* Penguin, Harmondsworth.

LOUCH, A. R. 1966. *Explanation and Human Action.* Blackwell, Oxford.

LOUNSBURY, F. L. 1962. The Structural Analysis of Kinship Semantics. *Proceedings of the 9th International Congress of Linguistics* (ed. Lunt): 1073-93. Mouton, The Hague.

— 1964. A Formal Account of the Crow- and Omaha-Type Kinship Terminology. *In* Tyler 1969 (ed.): 212-55.

— 1965. Another View of Trobriand Kinship Categories. *In* Hammel 1965 (ed.): 142-85.

— 1968. One Hundred Years of Anthropological Linguistics. *In* Brew 1968 (ed.): 153-264.

— 1969. Language and Culture. *In* Hook 1969 (ed.): 3-29.

LUKES, S. 1973. On the Social Determination of Truth. *In* Horton and Finnegan 1973 (eds): 230-48.

LYMAN, S. M. and SCOTT, M. B. 1970. *A Sociology of the Absurd.* Appleton-Century-Crofts, New York.

LYONS, J. 1969. *Structural Semantics. An Introduction to Part of the Vocabulary of Plato.* Blackwell, Oxford.

— 1970. *Chomsky.* Fontana/Collins, London.

LYONS, J. and WALES, R. J. 1966 (eds). *Psycholinguistic Papers.* Edinburgh University Press.

MACDONALD, M. 1954 (ed.). *Philosophy and Analysis.* Blackwell, Oxford.

MACFARLANE, A. 1970. *Witchcraft in Tudor and Stuart England. A Regional and Comparative Study.* Routledge & Kegan Paul, London.

MACINTYRE, A. C. 1963. God and the Theologians. *In* 1971a: 12-26.

— 1964. Is Understanding Compatible with Believing? *In* Hick 1966 (ed.): 115-33.

— 1966. The Antecedents of Action. *In* 1971a: 191-210.

— 1971a. *Against the Self-Images of the Age. Essays on Ideology and Philosophy.* Duckworth, London.

— 1971b. Philosophy and Sociology. *In* Magee 1973 (ed.): 236-48.

— 1971c. *A Short History of Ethics.* Routledge & Kegan Paul, London.

MACQUARRIE, J. 1967. *God-Talk. An Examination of the Language and Logic of Theology.* S.C.M. Press, London.

MAGEE, B. 1973. *Modern British Philosophy.* Paladin, St. Albans.

MAGUIRE, M. 1974. Criminology and Social Anthropology. *Journal of the Anthropological Society of Oxford* 5: 109-17.

MAIR, L. P. 1969. *Witchcraft.* Weidenfeld & Nicolson, London.

— 1972a. *Introduction to Social Anthropology.* Clarendon Press, Oxford.

— 1972b. Some Recent Writings on Witchcraft. *Journal of the Anthropological Society of Oxford* 3: 33-41.

MALINOWSKI, B. K. 1916. Baloma: the Spirits of the Dead in the Trobriand Islands. *In* 1954: 149-274.

187

Bibliography

— 1923. The Problem of Meaning in Primitive Languages. *In* Ogden and Richards 1946:296-336.
— 1925. Myth in Primitive Psychology. In *The Frazer Lectures 1922-32* (ed. Dawson). Macmillan, London. 66-119.
— 1937. The dilemma of Contemporary Linguistics. *In* Hymes 1964 (ed.):63-5.
— 1944. *A Scientific Theory of Culture and Other Essays*. University of North Carolina Press, Chapel Hill.
— 1954. *Magic, Science and Religion and other Essays*. Doubleday Anchor Books, New York.
— 1966. *Coral Gardens and their Magic*. (Vol. 2. The Language of Magic and Gardening). George Allen & Unwin Ltd, London. (1935).
MARETT, R. R. 1936. *Tylor*. Chapman & Hall, London.
— 1941. *A Jerseyman at Oxford*. Oxford University Press, London.
MARTIN, C. B. 1952. A Religious way of Knowing. *In* Flew and MacIntyre 1963 (eds):76-95.
MARWICK, M. G. 1966. Some Problems in the Sociology of Sorcery and Witchcraft. *In* Fortes and Dieterlen 1966 (eds):171-91.
— 1970 (ed.). *Witchcraft and Sorcery. A Reader*. Penguin, Harmondsworth.
— 1972. Anthropologists' Declining Productivity in the Sociology of Witchcraft. *American Anthropologist* 74.378-85.
MAUSS, M. 1923. On Language and Primitive Forms of Classification. *In* Hymes 1964 (ed.):125-7.
— 1936. Les Techniques du Corps. *In* 1950:365-86.
— 1938. Une Categorie de l'esprit humain. La Notion de Personne, Celle de 'Moi'. *Journal of the Royal Anthropological Institute* 68:263-81.
— 1950. *Anthropologie et Sociologie*. Presses Universitaires de France, Paris.
— 1969. *The Gift*. Cohen & West, London. (1925).
MIDDLETON, J. 1960. *Lugbara Religion. Ritual and Authority among an East African People*. Oxford University Press, London.
— 1963. Witchcraft and Sorcery in Lugbara. *In* Middleton and Winter 1963 (eds):257-75.
— 1967a (ed.). *Magic, Witchcraft, and Curing*. Natural History Press, New York.
— 1967b. *Myth and Cosmos. Readings in Mythology and Symbolism*. Natural History Press, New York.
MIDDLETON, J. and WINTER, E. 1963 (eds). *Witchcraft and Sorcery in East Africa*. Routledge & Kegan Paul, London.
MILLER, G. A., GALANTER, E. and PRIBRAM, K. H. 1967. *Plans and the Structure of Behavior*. Holt, Reinhart & Winston Inc., New York.
MISCHEL, T. 1967. Kant and the Possibility of a Science of Psychology. *The Monist* 51:599-622.
— 1974 (ed.). *Understanding Other Persons*. Blackwell, Oxford.
MITCHELL, B. 1955. The Grace of God. *In* 1957 (ed.):149-75.
— 1957 (ed.). *Faith and Logic*. George Allen & Unwin Ltd, London.
MONBERG, T. 1975. Fathers were not Genitors. *Man* (n.s.) 10:34-40.
MORRIS, C. 1955. *Signs, Language and Behavior*. Geo. Braziller Inc., New York.
MORRIS, D. 1969. *The Naked Ape*. Corgi Books, London.

MOUNIN, G. 1970. Lévi-Strauss' Use of Linguistics. *In* Rossi 1974 (ed.): 31-52.

MÜLLER, F. M. 1851. Comparative Philology. *Edinburgh Review* 94: 297-339.

— 1853a. On Indian Logic. *In* Thomson 1853: 367-89.

— 1853b. Letter on the Turanian Languages. *In* C. Bunsen *Christianity and Mankind*. 1854. Vol.3: 263-521. Longmans, London.

— 1855. *The Languages of the Seat of War in the East*. Williams & Norgate, London.

— 1856. Comparative Philology. In *Oxford Essays*. Vol.1.1-87. Parker & Son, London.

— 1860. Semitic Monotheism. *In* 1867: 341-79.

— 1861. *Lectures on the Science of Language*. 1st Series. Longmans, London.

— 1864. *Lectures on the Science of Language*. 2nd Series. Longmans, London.

— 1867. *Chips from a German Workshop*. Vol.1. Essays on the Science of Religion. Longmans, London.

— 1870. On false analogies in Comparative Theology. *In* 1873a: 283-334.

— 1871. On the Philosophy of Mythology. *In* 1873a: 335-403.

— 1873a. *Introduction to the Science of Religion*. Longmans, London.

— 1873b. Lectures on Mr. Darwin's Philosophy of Language. *Fraser's Magazine* 7: 525-41, 659-78; 8: 1-24.

— 1876. The Original Intention of Collective and Abstract Terms. *Mind* 1: 345-51.

— 1878a. *Lectures on the Origin and Growth of Religion, as Illustrated by the Religions of India*. Longmans, London.

— 1878b. On the Origin of Reason. *Contemporary Review* 31: 465-93.

— 1881. Translator's Preface in Kant's Critique of Pure Reason: xxvii-lxxix. 1896 edn. Macmillan Company, New York.

— 1882a. Mythology among the Hottentots. *In* 1882b: 273-97.

— 1882b. *Introduction to the Science of Religions*. Longmans, London.

— 1884. Introduction to Réville's *Prolegomena of the History of Religions*. Williams & Norgate, London. vii-x.

— 1885. The Savage. *In* 1901b: 139-82.

— 1886. Metaphor as a Mode of Abstraction. *Fortnightly Review* (n.s.) 40: 617-32.

— 1887. *The Science of Thought*. Longmans, London.

— 1888a. *Three Introductory Lectures on the Science of Thought*. Longmans, London.

— 1888b. *Biographies of Words and the Home of the Aryas*. Longmans, London.

— 1889. Can We Think without Words? *In* 1901b: 63-84.

— 1891a. *Physical Religion*. Longmans, London.

— 1891b. On the Classification of Mankind by Language or by Blood. *In* 1894: 217-63.

— 1892a. *Anthropological Religion*. Longmans, London.

— 1892b. *Natural Religion*. Longmans, London.

— 1893. *Theosophy or Psychological Religion*. Longmans, London.

— 1894. *Chips from a German Workshop*. Vol.1. Recent Essays and Addresses. Longmans, London.

189

Bibliography

— 1895. *Chips from a German Workshop*. Vol.4. Essays on Mythology and Folklore. Longmans, London.
— 1897. *Contributions to the Science of Mythology*. Longmans, London.
— 1899. Language and Mind. *In* 1903: 105-52.
— 1901a. *My Autobiography. A Fragment*. Longmans, London.
— 1901b. *Last Essays* (1st Series). Essays on Language, Folklore, and other subjects. Longmans, London.
— 1902. *The Life and Letters of the Rt. Hon. F.Max Müller* (ed. G.A. Max-Müller). Longmans, London.
— 1903. *The Silesian Horseherd. Questions of the Hour Answered* by F. Max *Müller*. Longmans, London.
MURDOCK. G. P. 1951. British Social Anthropology. *American Anthropologist* 53: 465-73.
NEEDHAM, R. 1960a. The Left Hand of the Mugwe: An analytical note on the Structure of Meru Symbolism. *In* 1973 (ed.): 109-27.
— 1960b. A Structural Analysis of Aimol Society. *Bijdragen* 116: 81-108.
— 1967. Right and Left in Nyoro Symbolic Classification. *In* 1973 (ed.): 299-346.
— 1970. The Future of Social Anthropology: Disintegration or Metamorphosis? In *Anniversary Contributions to Anthropology*: 34-46. Brill, Leiden.
— 1971a. Introduction. *In* 1971 (ed.): xiii-cxvii.
— 1971b. Remarks on the Analysis of Kinship and Marriage. *In* 1971 (ed.): 1-34.
— 1971 (ed.). *Rethinking Kinship and Marriage*. Tavistock, London.
— 1972. *Belief, Language and Experience*. Blackwell, Oxford.
— 1973. Introduction. *In* 1973 (ed.): xi-xxxix.
— 1973 (ed.). *Right and Left. Essays on Dual Symbolic Classification*. University of Chicago Press.
NEURATH. O. 1966. *Foundations of the Social Sciences*. University of Chicago Press.
NIELSON, K. 1967. Wittgensteinian Fideism. *Philosophy* 42: 191-209.
OGDEN, C. K. and RICHARDS, I. A. 1946. *The Meaning of Meaning. A Study of the Influence of Language upon Thought and of the Science of Symbolism*. Kegan Paul, Trench, Trubner & Co. Ltd., London.
PARKINSON. G. 1970 (ed.). *The Theory of Meaning*. Oxford University Press, London.
PARRY, H. B. 1974 (ed.). *Population and its Problems*. Clarendon Press, Oxford.
PEARS, D. 1971. *Wittgenstein*. Fontana/Collins, London.
PEEL, J. D. Y. 1969. Understanding alien belief-systems. *British Journal of Sociology* 20: 69-84.
PERCIVAL, K. 1968. A Reconsideration of Whorf's Hypothesis. *Anthropological Linguistics* 8: 12.
PHILLIPS, D. Z. 1967. Faith, Scepticism and Religious Understanding. *In* 1967 (ed.): 63-79.
— 1967 (ed.). *Religion and Understanding*. Blackwell, Oxford.
— 1970. Religious Beliefs and Language-Games. *Ratio* 12: 26-46.

190

PIKE, K. 1956. Towards a Theory of the Structure of Human Behavior. *In* Hymes 1964 (ed.): 54-61.

POCOCK, D. F. 1971. *Social Anthropology*. Sheed & Ward, London.

— 1973. The Idea of a Personal Anthropology. A.S.A. Conference Paper.

POLANYI, M. 1962. *Personal Knowledge. Towards a Post-Critical Philosophy.* Routledge & Kegan Paul, London.

POPPER, K. 1963. *Conjectures and Refutations. The Growth of Scientific Knowledge.* Routledge & Kegan Paul, London.

PRIDE, J. B. and HOLMES, J. 1972 (eds). *Sociolinguistics*. Penguin, Harmondsworth.

QUINE, W. van O. 1951. The Problem of Meaning in Linguistics. *In* 1961: 47-64.

— 1960. Translation and Meaning. *In* 1964: 26-79.

— 1961. *From a Logical Point of View. Logico-Philosophical Essays.* Harvard University Press, Cambridge, Mass.

— 1964. *Word and Object.* M.I.T. Press, Cambridge, Mass.

RADCLIFFE-BROWN, A. R. 1945. Religion and Society. *In* 1952: 153-77.

— 1952. *Structure and Function in Primitive Societies.* Cohen & West Ltd, London.

— 1957. *A Natural Science of Society.* The Free Press, Glencoe, Illinois.

— 1964. *The Andaman Islanders.* The Free Press of Glencoe, New York. (1922).

RADIN, P. 1953. *The World of Primitive Man.* Henry Schuman, New York.

RAMSEY, I. T. 1961. On the Possibility and Purpose of a Metaphysical Theology. *In* 1961 (ed.): 153-77.

— 1961 (ed.). *Prospect for Metaphysics. Essays in Metaphysical Exploration.* George Allen & Unwin Ltd, London.

— 1964. *Models and Mystery.* Oxford University Press, London.

— 1966. Talking about God. *In* 1971 (ed.): 202-23.

— 1967. *Religious Language. An Empirical Placing of Theological Phrases.* S.C.M. Press, London.

— 1971 (ed.). *Words about God. The Philosophy of Religion.* S.C.M. Press, London.

READ, K. E. 1955. Morality and the Concept of the Person among the Gahuku-Gama. *In* Middleton 1967b (ed.): 185-230.

REGNIER, A. 1968. De la Théorie des Groupes à la pensée sauvage. *In* Richard and Jaulin 1971 (eds): 271-98.

REYNOLDS, V. 1973. Ethnology and Anthropology. *Man* (n.s.) 8: 384-92.

RICHARD, P. and JAULIN, R. 1971 (eds). *Anthropologie et Calcul.* Union Générale d'Editions, Paris.

RICHARDS, I. A. 1953. Towards a Theory of Translating. *American Anthropological Association Memoir* 75, Vol.55, no.5, part 2 (Studies in Chinese Thought, ed. A.F. Wright).

— 1964. *Mencius on the Mind. Experiments in Multiple Definition.* Routledge & Kegan Paul, London.

RICOEUR, P. 1963. Structure et Herméneutique. *Esprit* 31, Nov.: 596-627.

RIVIÈRE, P. G. 1971a. The Political Structure of the Trio Indians as manifested in a system of Ceremonial Dialogue. *In* Beidelman 1971 (ed.): 293-312.

— 1971b. Marriage: A Reassessment. *In* Needham 1971 (ed.): 57-74.

Bibliography

ROBINSON, J. A. T. 1963. *Honest to God*. S.C.M. Press, London.

ROMNEY, A. K. and D'ANDRADE, R. G. 1964 (eds). Transcultural Studies in Cognition. *American Anthropologist* 66, No.3, part 2. (Special Publication).

ROSALDO, M. Z. 1972. Metaphors and Folk Classification. *Southwestern Journal of Anthropology* 28:83-99.

ROSS, G. 1970. Neo-Tyloreanism: A Reassessment. *Man* (n.s.) 6:105-16.

ROSSI, I. 1973. The Unconscious in the Anthropology of Claude Lévi-Strauss. *American Anthropologist* 75:20-48.

— 1974 (ed.). *The Unconscious in Culture. The Structuralism of Claude Lévi-Strauss in Perspective*. E.P. Dutton & Co. Inc., New York.

RYLE, G. 1932. Systematically Misleading Expressions. *In* Flew 1951 (ed.):11-36.

— 1966. *The Concept of Mind*. Hutchinson & Co., London.

SANTONI, R. 1968 (ed.). *Religious Language and the Problem of Religious Knowledge*. Indiana University Press, Bloomington.

SAPIR, E. 1929. The Status of Linguistics as a Science. *In* 1949:160-6.

— 1949. *Selected Writings of Edward Sapir in Language, Culture and Personality* (ed. D.G. Mandelbaum). University of California Press, Berkeley.

SAUSSURE, F. de, 1949. *Cours de Linguistique Générale* (eds C. Bally and A. Sechehaye). Payot, Paris.

SCHEFFLER, H. W. and LOUNSBURY, F. L. 1971. *A Study in Structural Semantics. The Sirionó Kinship System*. Prentice-Hall Inc., Englewood Cliffs.

SCHOLTE, B. 1966. Epistemic Paradigms: Some Problems in Cross-Cultural Research on Social Anthropological History and Theory. *American Anthropologist* 68:1192-1201.

— 1972. Towards a Reflexive and Critical Anthropology. *In* Hymes 1974 (ed.):430-57.

SCHON, D. 1963. *The Displacement of Concepts*. Tavistock, London.

SEARLE, J. 1965. What is a Speech Act? *In* 1971 (ed.):39-53.

— 1971 (ed.). *The Philosophy of Language*. Oxford University Press, London.

SEBEOK, T. A. 1968 (ed.). *Animal Communication. Techniques of Study and Results of Research*. Indiana University Press, Bloomington.

— 1973. Between animal and animal. *Times Literary Supplement* 5th Oct.:1187-9.

SEBEOK, T. A. and RAMSAY, A. 1969 (eds). *Approaches to Animal Communication*. Mouton, The Hague.

SHAPIRO, H. 1956 (ed.). *Man, Culture and Society*. Oxford University Press, London.

SHWAYDER, D. S. 1965. *The Stratification of Behavior*. Routledge & Kegan Paul, London.

SIMONIS, Y. 1968. *Claude Lévi-Strauss ou le 'Passion de l'inceste': Introduction au Structuralisme*. Aubier Montaigne, Paris.

SINGER, A. and STREET, B. V. 1972 (eds). *Zande Themes. Essays presented to Sir Edward Evans-Pritchard*. Blackwell, Oxford.

SKINNER, B. F. 1957. *Verbal Behavior*. Appleton-Century-Crofts, New York.

SPENCER, H. 1876. *The Principles of Sociology*. Williams & Norgate, London.

SPIRO. M. E. 1968. Virgin birth, parthenogenesis and physiological paternity: an essay in cultural interpretation. *Man* (n.s.) 3:242-61.

STANDEFER. R. 1970. African Witchcraft Beliefs: The Definitional Problem. *Journal of the Anthropological Society of Oxford* 1:11-7.

STEINER. G. 1966. Conversations with C. Lévi-Strauss. *Encounter* 26th Apr.: 32-8.

— 1975. *After Babel. Aspects of Language and Translation.* Oxford University Press, London.

STRAWSON, P. F. 1958. Persons. *In* Chappell 1962 (ed.): 127-46.

— 1964. *Individuals: An Essay in Descriptive Metaphysics.* Methuen & Co. Ltd, London.

STURTEVANT, W. C. 1964. Studies in Ethnoscience. *In* Romney & D'Andrade 1964 (eds): 99-131.

SZASZ, T. 1962. *The Myth of Mental Illness.* Secker & Warburg, London.

TAGLIACOZZO, G. 1969 (ed.). *Giambattista Vico.* Johns Hopkins Press, Baltimore.

TAMBIAH, S. J. 1968. The Magical Power of Words. *Man* (n.s.) 3:175-208.

— 1969. Animals are Good to Think and Good to Prohibit. *Ethnology* 8:423-59.

— 1973. Form and Meaning of Magical Acts: A Point of View. *In* Horton and Finnegan 1973 (eds): 199-229.

THOMAS, K. 1970. The Relevance of Social Anthropology to the Historical Study of English Witchcraft. *In* M. Douglas 1970 (ed.): 47-79.

— 1971. *Religion and the Decline of Magic. Studies in Popular Beliefs in Sixteenth and Seventeenth Century England.* Weidenfeld & Nicolson, London.

THOMSON, W. 1853. *An Outline of the Necessary Laws of Thought.* Pickering, London. (3rd edition).

TIGER, L. and FOX, R. 1966. The zoological perspective in social science. *Man* (n.s.) 1:75-81.

— 1972. *The Imperial Animal.* Secker & Warburg, London.

TONKIN, J. E. A. 1971a. The Use of Ethnography. *Journal of the Anthropological Society of Oxford* 2:134-6.

— 1971b. Some Coastal Pidgins of West Africa. *In* Ardener 1971 (ed.): 129-55.

TOULMIN, S. 1948. The Logical Status of Psychoanalysis. *In* Macdonald 1954 (ed.): 132-9.

— 1953. *The Philosophy of Science.* Hutchinson & Co. Ltd, London.

— 1957. Contemporary Scientific Mythology. In *Metaphysical Beliefs.* S.C.M. Press, London: 3-71.

— 1958. *The Uses of Argument.* Cambridge University Press.

— 1969. From Logical Analysis to Conceptual History. *In* Achinstein and Barker 1969 (eds): 25-53.

— 1972. *Human Understanding* (Vol.1: The Collective Use and Evolution of Concepts). Clarendon Press, Oxford.

TURNER, R. 1974 (ed.). *Ethnomethodology.* Penguin, Harmondsworth.

TURNER, V. W. 1964a. Witchcraft and Sorcery. Taxonomy versus Dynamics. *Africa* 34:314-24.

— 1964b. Lunda Medicine and the Treatment of Disease. *In* 1967: 299-358.

Bibliography

— 1967. *The Forest of Symbols. Aspects of Ndembu Ritual.* Cornell University Press, Ithaca.

TYLER, S. A. 1969. The Myth of P: Epistemology and Formal Analysis. *American Anthropologist* 71:71-9.

— 1969 (ed.). *Cognitive Anthropology.* Holt, Rinehart & Winston Inc., New York.

TYLOR, E. B. 1865. *Researches into the Early History of Mankind and the Development of Civilisation.* John Murray, London.

— 1871. *Primitive Culture.* John Murray, London.

— 1907. *Anthropological Essays Presented to E.B. Tylor.* Clarendon Press, Oxford.

ULLMANN, S. 1958. Semantics at the Cross-roads. *In* 1966:3-16.

— 1966. *Language and Style.* Blackwell, Oxford.

— 1972. Semantics. *Current Trends in Linguistics* (Vol.9, ed.Sebeok): 343-94. Mouton, The Hague.

URBAN, W. M. 1939. *Language and Reality. The Principles of Language and the Principles of Symbolism.* Allen & Unwin, London.

VAN DER PITTE, F. 1971. *Kant as Philosophical Anthropologist.* Nijhoff, The Hague.

VICO, G. 1968. *The New Science Concerning The Common Nature of the Nations.* Cornell University Press, Ithaca. (1744).

WAISMANN, F. 1965. *The Principles of Linguistic Philosophy* (ed. Harré). Macmillan, London.

— 1968. *How I See Philosophy* (ed. Harré). Macmillan, London.

WALLACE, A. F. C. 1965. The Problem of the Psychological Validity of Componential Analysis. *In* Hammel 1965 (ed.): 229-48.

WEBBER, J. 1973. Language Use and Social Change. *Journal of the Anthropological Society of Oxford* 4:32-41.

WEINREICH, U. 1963. On the Semantic Structure of Language. *In* Greenberg 1966 (ed.): 142-216.

WERNER, O. 1969. The Basic Assumptions of Ethnoscience. *Semiotica* 1:329-38.

WHITELEY, W. H. 1971. A Note on Multilingualism. *In* Ardener 1971 (ed.): 121-7.

— 1973. Colour Words and Colour-Values: The Evidence for Gusii. *In* Horton and Finnegan 1973 (eds): 145-61.

WHORF, B. L. 1956. *Language, Thought and Reality* (ed. J.B. Carroll). M.I.T. Press, Cambridge, Mass.

WILDEN, A. 1972. *System and Structure. Essays on Communication and Exchange.* Tavistock, London.

— 1974. Structuralism as Epistemology of Closed Systems. *In* Rossi 1974 (ed.): 273-90.

WILLIAMS, D. 1974. Deep Structures of the Dance. *Unpublished typescript.*

WILLIAMS, G. E. 1968. Linguistic Reflections of Cultural Systems. *Anthropological Linguistics* 8:13-21.

WILLIS, R. G. 1975 (ed.). *The Interpretation of Symbolism.* Malaby Press, London.

WILSON, B. 1970 (ed.). *Rationality.* Blackwell, Oxford.

WINCH, P. 1958. *The Idea of a Social Science and its relations to Philosophy.* Routledge & Kegan Paul, London.

— 1960. Nature and Convention. *Proceedings of the Aristotelian Society* (n.s.) 60: 231-52.

— 1964. Understanding a Primitive Society. *In* 1972: 8-49.

— 1972. *Ethics and Action.* Routledge & Kegan Paul, London.

WISDOM, J. O. 1944. Gods. *In* Santoni 1968 (ed.): 295-314.

WITTGENSTEIN, L. 1953. *Philosophical Investigations.* Blackwell, Oxford.

— 1966. *Lectures and Conversations on Aesthetics, Psychology and Religious Belief.* Blackwell, Oxford.

— 1967a. Remarks on Frazer's *Golden Bough. Human World* 1, no. 3: 18-41. (1971).

— 1967b. *Zettel.* Blackwell, Oxford.

— 1969. *On Certainty.* Blackwell, Oxford.

— 1972. *The Blue and Brown Books.* Blackwell, Oxford.

WOLLHEIM, R. 1971. *Freud.* Fontana/Collins, London.

Index

197

201